MUSLIMS AND INDIA

MUSLIMS AND INDIA

By

DR. ASGHAR ALI ENGINEER

GYAN

ISBN : 978-81-212-0882-6

Published, 2018

Published by

Gyan Publishing House
5, Ansari Road
Daryaganj, New Delhi-110002
Phone: 011-47034999, 9811692060
www.gyanbooks.com
E-mail: books@gyanbooks.com

Printed at: G. Print Process, Delhi.

Contents

Preface

The Minority Question in India

The minority question has been quite controversial in India. The secular forces and parties of course not only acknowledge minority question but also want to treat them fairly and give them equal status in matters of social, cultural, political and economic rights. The freedom fighters and national leaders like Mahatma Gandhi, Jawaharlal Nehru and others duly recognised existence of minorities and championed their cause. It was because of their efforts that the constitution makers gave equal political rights to them and also recognised their distinct social, cultural, religious and economic status. The Constitution of India protected their religious and cultural rights under Articles 25 to 30.

However, those who espouse communal ideology are even today refusing to recognise the minority status and their distinct socio-cultural status. The RSS, VHP and BJP leaders continue to question status of religious minorities like Christians and Muslims. Sometimes they accuse secular parties of 'appeasement of minorities' and sometimes they question their loyalty to the country and sometimes they are described as ones who came from outside and hence alien to India and Indian culture.

The Sangh Parivar and votaries of Hindutva have always described Muslims as 'Babar *ki aulad*' (i.e., children of Babar) and used to raise slogans "Babar *ki aulad, jao Pakistan ya qabrastan*" (i.e., children of Babar go to Pakistan or to cemetery). Christians were also dubbed as loyal to Vatican (even forgetting that Protestant Christians have nothing to do with Vatican) and described them too as alien to India and Indian culture, if not by BJP, by its more extremist outfits like RSS and VHP.

Now the RSS leaders, in the Pratinidhi Sabha session in Mangalore, have taken 180 degree turn and maintained that the Christians and Muslims cannot be construed as minorities because people of both the communities have *not come from outside* and hence their minority status should be done away with. The general secretary of RSS Mohanrao Bhagwat said in his speech in the Mangalore session that 99.9 per cent Muslims and Christians have not come from outside and hence they cannot be called minorities. He said that their ancestors were Hindus some years ago and in their veins also same blood is running as in those of Hindu veins.

Mark the words of Mohanrao Bhagwat, particularly those italicised. Were they not aware of the fact all these years that same blood is flowing in the veins of Christians and Muslims? Why were Christians and Muslims being described as outsiders or Babar *ki aulad?* Why now this fact has dawned on them suddenly. It is not very difficult to understand. All these years they dubbed Christians and Muslims as foreigners so that they could be deprived of their political rights. They attacked Sonia Gandhi too as foreigner and hence a danger for the security of India.

But years of dubbing them (Christians and Muslims) as foreigners did not result in depriving them of political rights, now they have changed their strategy and have begun to say that since they have not come from outside and same blood flows in their veins as that of Hindus why give them minority status. The Indian secular democracy is well established and no one can be deprived of his or her political rights on the basis of religion and hence the RSS leaders want to settle for lesser bargain, i.e., delegitimising Christians and Muslims of their minority status, if not of their political rights altogether.

Can such demand have any political sense? Of course, it is as senseless as making minorities outsiders and depriving them of their political rights. The RSS leaders in their blind hatred of Christians and Muslims have even forgotten distinction between ethnic and religious minorities. Christians and Muslims are hundred per cent Indians and will remain Indians. But that does not mean they will cease to be religious minorities. Here the example of Jains is also quite apt. The Sangh Parivar has never doubted their Indianness. But Jains do not consider themselves as Hindus but instead they fought for their minority status. Why then the Sangh Parivar does not question their minority status? Why this duplicity in their demand? Thus, Christians, Muslims and Jains will remain religious minorities as much as they are of Indian ethnic stock.

Let us also not forget that all Christians and Muslims are not of same ethnic stock in India. The Kashmiri Muslims claim separate ethnic identity from rest of Indian Muslims. The Muslims of Kerala and Tamil Nadu too are of Dravidian stock and so are Muslims of Karnataka and Andhra Pradesh. The Christians of North East do not share same ethnic identity with Christians of North or South India. Thus, in Kashmir Muslims are double minority religious as well as ethnic and Christians of North East are, similarly, double minority religious as well as ethnic.

The Muslims of north India in states like U.P., Bihar or M.P. share same ethnicity as that of Hindus but are minority in religious sense. The Christians and Muslims of Kerala and Tamil Nadu share same ethnic identity with rest of Hindus there yet they are religious minority. This is as clear as crystal even to common person but the RSS ideologues, clouded as they are by their rightwing ideology, cannot understand this simple truth.

In fact the Sangh Parivar's goal is to deprive religious minorities, particularly Christians and Muslims of their minority status but now they have been caught in the web of their own ideology. All these years they described Islam and Christianity as alien religions and Sikhism and Buddhism though minority religions but of Indian origin. They have no objection in accepting Sikhs and Buddhists as 'religious minorities' as they are of Indian origin and now that RSS leaders themselves are saying that Christians and Muslims are also of Indian origin and same blood is flowing in their veins why are they demanding that Christians and Muslims be deprived of their minority status. Is it not obvious contradiction?

It clearly means that they are hostile to Christians and Muslims for ideological reasons, not for being Indian or non-Indian. They are opposed to Article 30 of the Constitution also as it gives Christians and Muslims right to set up their own institutions to preserve their religion and culture. But they forget that among Hindus too there are cultural and linguistic minorities. Will those ethnic, cultural and linguistic minorities agree to the Article 30 being abolished from the Constitution?

Mr. Lal Krishna Advani is a Sindhi and a migrant from Sindh in 1947. Do Sindhis claim status of cultural and linguistic minority or not? If Lal Krishna Advani's party or RSS (Mr. Advani is supposedly hardcore RSS man) demands abolition of Article 30 how Mr. Advani will reconcile this demand with the status of his own community? Will he be able to carry his own community with him?

Even Ramkrishna Mission petitioned Calcutta High Court to declare them as religious minority as they too wanted to benefit from the provisions of Article 30. Why the RSS leaders did not launch any vigorous movement to oppose this demand of the Ramkrishna Mission? Obviously because they are neither Christian nor Muslim. RSS has problem with these two communities only because of their religion, not because of their ethnic stock. The RSS espouses a political ideology, which rejects religious pluralism.

Thus, real problem is with the RSS ideology, not with Christians or Muslims or Jains or Sikhs or with status of religious minorityness. And the real strength of secular democracy is inclusivity, not exclusivity. No secular democracy can ever succeed without acceptance of pluralism. For a pluralist society like India, it is not only democracy but secular democracy, which is important. In secular democracy a 'religious other' does not become a 'political other'. But an exclusivist ideology like that of RSS, religious other becomes a political other and hence to be rejected.

The globalised world's very *raison d'etre* is religious pluralism and India has a unique distinction of being religiously plural for centuries, not since globalisation. The RSS came into existence in 1925 by rejecting this pluralism. All those who reject religious pluralism support political separatism. The Mus League by espousing Muslim exclusivism brought about physic partition of India. But RSS espouses on one hand, the ideolog of *akhand Bharat* (India which can never be divided) could not support physical partition but unashamedly supports invisible and psychological partition, which is any time worse than physical and visible partition.

One has to fight against both visible as well as invisible partitioning of minds. The RSS refuses to reconcile with religious pluralism though reluctantly it has accepted political pluralism. Its ideology of cultural nationalism is not only simplistic but also harmful for the country of India's diversity. For RSS diversity is weakness, for democracy it is its very basis in the modern pluralist world. No one can succeed in creating uniformity in a democracy. Democracy's very life-blood is diversity. But RSS has no love lost for democracy. It believes in authoritarianism and discipline of submission to authority.

A true democrat, on the other hand, never believes in submitting but in the right to be differ and right to be different. A democrat would never compromise on the right to differ and would never surrender his/her freedom to criticise. In secular democracy the other sterling quality is respect for 'otherness'. A true democrat will concede right to other to be 'other'. On the other hand, RSS wants other to be mirror image of majority community. Such an ideology can only succeed by destroying democracy and democratic values.

Introduction

Indian Muslims—Myth and Reality

Indian Muslims have been at the centre of controversy ever since the beginning of the British rule either because of their own behaviour or because of the policy of divide and rule pursued by the British or because of communal forces in both the communities. Even long after partition and independence of India the controversies do not die down; they are being intensified in the present situation.

Whenever I have the occasion to speak on Indian Muslims or communalism or secularism I am asked certain questions invariably, whatever the nature of gathering, i.e., of intellectuals, of social activists or teachers or police officers. Certain myths about Indian Muslims are being propagated today especially by communal forces. It is, therefore, necessary to discuss some of these controversies and throw light on reality. Those who spread such myths are serious obstacles to the process of nation building and are bent upon destroying not only secular character of this country but also peace and harmony. However, this article is not addressed to these forces as they do so not out of lack of information but out of their own political agenda. This essay is addressed to those who become victims of this propaganda.

Before we throw light on these controversies it is necessary to throw some light on the concept of majority and minority. Some people keep on arguing that one should do away with this concept as all citizens have equal rights in Indian Constitution irrespective of religion, caste and creed. There is no place for the concept of 'religious minority' and 'religious majority' in Indian democracy. All citizens of India have right to profess, practice their own religion and also propagate it. Even otherwise many well-meaning people also argue on these lines.

Well this is highly desirable in an ideal democracy where there is absolutely no discrimination on the basis of religion or caste and people of all religions enjoy their constitutional rights without letup or hindrance. In such a society there will be complete absence of communalism in open or subtle forms, much less repeated outbursts of communal violence.

There are not only strong prejudices against minorities–whatever the reasons–but these prejudices are getting stronger and stronger day by day thanks to intense propaganda by communal forces. Moreover, in no democracy in the world be it democracy in western countries, they have been able to do away with this category of racial or religious minority and majority. These categories exist in all western democracies too. In our case it is also our historical legacy further strengthened by partition of our country. Partition still rankles in our minds.

The framers of our Constitution were also quite aware of this problem and hence they made special provisions for minority rights in the Constitution specially in Articles 25 to 30. Also, since this problem is universal the UNO has also drafted declaration of minority rights. And it is not religious minorities only who insist on their minority status the majority itself has not been able to liberate itself from this category.

One usual question asked is why Muslims refuse to become part of Indian mainstream? It is thought that Muslims in India live in their own shell and refuse to be integrated in Indian mainstream. This is not true by and large. There may be few isolated cases but overwhelming majority of Muslims is very much part of Indian mainstream. Perhaps following their religion, i.e., Islam itself is thought to be the cause of isolation. One is not required to renounce ones religion to become part of Indian mainstream.

The important question is who defines what Indian mainstream is? Is Indian mainstream constituted by upper caste Brahminical Hinduism? Certainly not. Then only a small percentage of Indians, probably not more than 20 per cent people can qualify for that. A vast number of Hindus themselves will be left out from this concept of mainstream.

Our mainstream is basically constituted by our composite culture and Muslims have richly contributed to this composite culture. There have been great musicians among Muslims throughout history and continue to be even today. Bismillah Khan, Zakir Ali Khan, Vilayat Ali Khan, Fayyaz Ali Khan and several others are shining stars of Indian music. Bismillah Khan was also honoured with 'Bharat Ratna' few years ago. In other fields of fine arts like painting, poetry and fiction writing there have been some of the greatest name of minority communities, particularly Muslims. Their contribution in these fields is recognised by India as well as the world.

In sports too religious minorities have made significant contribution be it cricket, hockey or any other sports. Some of the greatest names of cricket world come from amongst Muslims. In film world who can deny the contribution of Muslims? Be they directors, actors actresses and music directors and background singers, there have been great Muslim names. They are so well known that there is no need to mention them here. Dilip Kumar, Mehboob Khan, Naushad, Meena Kumari are some of the legends from the film world. Among new generation Shabana Azmi, Shahrukh Khan, A.R. Rehman are great names. And if literature, music, fine arts, sports, films etc. do not constitute national mainstream what else does? And if it does where Muslims are lacking?

It is also not true that Muslims do not speak regional languages and insist on speaking Urdu. This is utterly mischievous propaganda. In Tamil Nadu they speak Tamil, in Kerala they speak Malayalam, in Gujarat they speak Gujrati, in interior Maharashtra they speak Marathi or variant of Marathi, in West Bengal they speak Bengali, in Assam, Assamese and so on. In these regions which I visit frequently I need services of interpreters to speak to Muslims in their regional language. Now even in the Hindi heartland Muslims speak chaste Hindi and the new generation of Muslims do not know Urdu at all. In this respect Urdu has hardly any future in India. It will soon become like Persian or Arabic learnt by some specialists.

Another myth is that all Muslim children go to madrasas and avoid modern secular education. This too, like other myths about Muslims, is far from true. It is children of the poor who mostly go to madrasas because of their locations, convenient timings and lack of means to send them to secular schools though poor also have ambition to give good education to their children. No one from middle class families among Muslims sends their children to madrasas. They send their children to modern schools, and if possible to English medium school. Middle class families among Muslims are now sending their daughters also for higher education and this trend is on increase and Muslim girls are greater achievers in modern education than boys. All available data shows this clearly. Thus the myth that Muslims do not send their daughters to schools also needs to be demystified.

Another myth is that Muslims do not practice family planning. The Sangh Parivar publishes pamphlets saying Muslims believe in '*ham panch hamare pacchis*' (We five, our twenty-five). Needless to say that this is highly mischievous propaganda. There are two parts of this popular myth: firstly, Muslims marry four wives as per their *shari'ah* and that they beget highest number of children.

Both these myths need to be exposed. It is true Islamic *shari'ah* permits (does not make obligatory) to take four wives. But this does not mean all Muslim males take four wives. Even if they want sheer male/female ratio will not permit them to do so. In India according to 2001 census there are 935 female for every 1000 male. Among Muslims this ratio is even more adverse, i.e., there are about 930 females for every thousand male. Even an males cannot get one wife according to this census figure let alone one Muslim male marrying four wives.

Such propaganda is motivated by sheer animosity or prejudice. Fact is that highest number of bigamous marriages take place among tribals (about 14 per cent) and Muslims are at the bottom with 5.6 per cent bigamous marriages and upper caste Hindus have 5.8 per cent bigamous marriages (according to the Government of India survey of 1974, the only all India survey ever conducted). If there is provision for polygamy in law it does not mean that all will take more than one wife and if there is ban on polygamous marriages it does not mean no one will take more than one wife. It is basically a problem of male-dominant culture than that of religion.

It is also not true that all Muslims beget large number of children and do not practice family planning. Family planning is also more related to literacy and income levels. All studies in India by demographers show that poor people of any religion tend to have more children and people of middle class (whatever the religion) tend to have less number of children. Among Muslims too, studies in Malegaon, Kanpur and other places clearly show that educated middle class practice family planning and poorer, illiterate Muslims do not. Thus it is poverty-related and not religion-related problem.

If there is relatively less family planning among Muslims it is because of poverty and lack of awareness than religion. Those Mullahs who come from poorer strata (and most of the mullahs come from this strata) do invoke religion for opposing family planning but it does not mean all Muslims necessarily listen to them. In states like Kerala there is more family planning among Muslims than Hindus in U.P. as Kerala Muslims are more educated than Hindus in U.P. Thus, sterilisation among Kerala Muslims is 42.7 per cent whereas among Hindus in U.P. it is only 18.2 per cent. It is obviously poverty and literacy related phenomenon.

One should not go by politically motivated propaganda and examine reality, which is much more complex and multi-dimensional. It is in the interest of whole nation to work for uplift of Muslims and raise their income and educational levels. It will ensure better national integration and national progress. Mere hostile propaganda motivated by narrow political ends would prove to be a drag on national development.

1

Historical Drawback

Inter-Faith Relations in Medieval India

The communal history emphasises confrontation between Islam and Hinduism throughout medieval India. In fact, communal historians tell us that it was war between Hindus and Muslims from Muhammad bin Qasim's invasion down to contemporary India. They also maintain that partition of India in 1947 was the natural consequence of this religious war. In other words, partition was inevitable and natural result of this inter-religious war. Needless to say this is grossest distortion of Indian history. Besides being grotesque it is harmful for the process of nation building. Such a history is written to serve needs of contemporary communal politics.

In fact history is much more than mere narration of events. A historian has to analyse these events and try to understand complex processes behind them. No event can be adequately understood without understanding complex processes and motives of the actors concerned. The simplistic theories like spread of Islam by sword can hardly hold water and no discerning historian who is aware of complexities of historical processes. In any society different trends co-exist.

What happens at the level of ruling classes does not necessarily reflect the social processes at people's level. Political confrontation does not necessarily translate into religious confrontation too. The communal historians depict war between two rulers - one Muslim and thep other Hindu - as war between

Islam and Hinduism. They completely ignore the fact that these were wars for political power and not for religious supremacy.

Also, these historians completely ignore the fact that various other trends existed at social levels. There was close inter-action between Islam and Hinduism and several syncretic traditions came into existence. Several communities had amorphous, and not sharply defined identities as Hindus and Muslims. There came into existence sects like Husaini Brahmins, Pranam Panthis, Meo Muslims and several others who were amalgam of Hindu and Muslim cultural and religious traditions.

The sufi saints and bhakti sants borrowed from each other as well as from local traditions and shaped new belief systems. Many low caste Hindus readily adopted these new beliefs and doctrines and gave birth to new communities which could not be identified as Hindu or Muslim communities. And many low caste Hindus and dalits converted to Islam to enhance their social status and human dignity. No coercion was involved. Since the Sufis adopted local dialects for communication and also local customs and traditions the low caste Hindus and dalits could easily identify themselves with the sufi idiom and embrace Islam. Most of the converted Muslims came from these social strata.

Also, there was constant dialogue between Hindu and Muslim saints and scholars. Hindus learnt Persian and Arabic and Muslims Sanskrit. Alberuni who came to India with Mahmoud Ghaznavi in 11th century, mastered Sanskrit language and studied Mahabharata and Ramayana and wrote is epitome on India. Mahabharat and Ramayana were translated into both Arabic and Persian languages by Muslim scholars as well as Hindus. Dara Shikoh also mastered Sanskrit language and translated Upanishads into Persian and named it as *Sirr-e-Akbar* (The greatest Mystery).

Dara Shikoh even wrote that Hinduism does not negate monotheism and found that the monotheistic verses contained in the four *Vedas* have been collected and elucidated in the *Upanishad*, which is an ocean of monotheism. Dara Shikoh, for this reason undertook a literal and correct translation of the work with the help of the Pandits and the Sanyasis of Benaras and accomplished the work in 1076 A.H. Dara Shikoh writes about Upanishads, "Any difficult problem or sublime idea that came to his mind and was not solved in spite of his best efforts, becomes clear and solved with the help of this ancient work, which is undoubtedly the first heavenly Book and the fountain-head of the ocean of monotheism and, in accordance with or rather an elucidation of the Kuran."

Dara Shikoh in his *Majma'ul Bahrayn* had done painstaking comparative study of Hindu and Muslim traditions and shows that content are same though languages are different. Islam uses Arabic and Hindu scriptures Sanskrit or other Indian languages. He compares Om with Ism-e-A'zam in Islamic tradition. He says that the Hindu monotheists (*muwahhidan-e-Hind)* do not agree on the exact meaning of Om as Muslims do not agree on exact meaning of Ism-e-A'zam. Some Hindu monotheists say that Om consists of three letters, i.e., 'a', 'w' and 'm' and 'a' stands for Aditya, 'w' stands for Warma and 'm' stands for Mitra. Thus it means God since these are names of God.

The Muslim scholars, on the other hand, differ on the exact interpretation of Ism-e-A'zam. Which name of the Allah out of His names is Ism-e-A'zam? Some say it is 'Al-Hay' and some say it is 'Al-Qayyum' is Ism-e-A'-zam and some say it is 'Al-Rahim'. Thus there is no agreement on Ism-e-A'zam as there is no agreement on the exact meaning of Om. Similarly there are three names of Ishwar in the Hindu tradition i.e. 'Satyam', 'Shivam' and 'Sundaram'. These three names of Allah are mentioned in the Qur'an too i.e. Haq (Truth), Jabbar (Mighty) and Jamil (Sundaram). The difference is of language, not of content.

There are many more examples of Hindu-Muslim togetherness or dialogue in India. Many Muslim sects adopted local traditions so as not to appear aliens to Indian cultural environment. The Ismaili Nizaris in Gujarat adopted local prevalent nomenclature for describing their religion. They called religion as Satpanth or Nizar Dharma or Mahamarg. The Bishnoi Panth of Rajasthan also appears to be amalgam of Nizari Isma'ilis and local Hindu tradition.

A Panjabi Sufi saint Bullhe Shah maintained that I am neither Hindu nor Muslim. He borrowed from both traditions and forged a new panth, which was essentially syncretic in nature. Dominique-Sila Khan rightly points out in her book *Crossing The Threshold – Understanding Religious Identities in South Asia*, "The Hindu-Muslim inter-face should not, however, be viewed as the convergence of two fixed straight lines, but rather as the encounter between various fluctuating sets of lines representing the religious movements which have their historical roots either in the Muslim countries (prior to penetration of Islam in South Asia) or the Indian subcontinent." (P-30)

Pran Nathis of Gujarat are an interesting sect resulting from coming together of Islamic and Indian beliefs. Pran Nathis believe that the Prophet of Islam is an *avtar* of Krishna. Krishna lived in *Satyug* and the Prophet lived in Kalyug. Their sacred book is known as Qulzum Sharif and contains verses from Geeta as well as Qur'an. They do not worship any idol but recite from the Sacred Scripture.

There are many instances of sharing of the sacred space by the two communities. Now of course the communal elements are raising political controversies but for centuries common people have believed in shared sacred spaces in several parts of India. The case of Baba Budangirni comes to mind. The Muslims worship their as a grave of a Muslim Sufi saint and Hindus worship it as Dattatray. Common people never made any distinction but now the Sangh Parivar politicians are claiming it as a Hindu temple and creating law and order problem now and then.

Dominique-Sila Khan has also given several examples from Rajasthan and other places in her above-mentioned book. She points out that in many villages of Shekhawati (Rajasthan), such as Mundawara, Losal and Kachriawas, near Sikar, Manihars (Muslim bangle-makers) and other artisan castes make vows and offerings to deities, such as Bherji or seven goddesses locally referred to as Sat Mamai, a particular clan of them established near Sikar even accept Shitla Mata, the goddess of smallpox, as their lineage deity and celebrate her annual festival in the same way as the Hindus. For these people Shitla is the protector deity of their clan.

One finds similar traditions in Ajmer among the followers of Mu'in al-Din Chishti (d,.1236). It is said, for instance that number of Hindu female devotees, who claim to have been granted the boon of a son, have vowed to visit the shrine each Friday, dressed in green saris. A Jain lady who was blessed with the son by the Chishti Saint has named her child as Chirag.

Shivaji's grand father was also supposed to have been blessed with two sons after praying at the dargah of Shah Sharifji in Ahmednagar and so he named these two sons as Shahji and Sharifji and Shivaji was the son of Shahji. No doubt than that Shivaji had great respect for Sufi saints and used to take blessings from Sheikh Yaqub, a sufi saint from Konkan area before going for crucial battles.

One can also give example of Abdul Quddus Gangohi a fifteenth century sufi saint wrote his *Rushdnama* which is also known as Alakhbani. He identified the doctrine of *wahdat al-wujud* (unity of being) with philosophy of Gorakhnath, one of the original founders of the Nath Panth. He identifies Alakh Niranjan (formless and immaculate God of the Naths) with Khuda of Islamic tradition in India.

There are several such examples of synthesis of Islamic and Hindu local traditions. It would thus be wrong to maintain that there was confrontation between Islam and Hinduism in India all through. They lived in peace and harmony and profoundly influenced each other. It is also wrong to say that Muslims have not been part of Indian mainstream. These instances prove that they very much have been part of mainstream.

Medieval History and Hurt Psyche

Two retired IAS officers who are known for their commitment to secularism and communal harmony recently wrote to me that will it not be in the interest of communal harmony and buying peace if the Muslims in India tendered apology for demolition of temples and rapaciousness, loot and plunder in India during medieval ages as it has caused deep hurt to the Hindu psyche. They feel that majority of Hindus feel hurt by demolition of their temples by the Muslim rulers during medieval ages and any such apology by Muslims today would work as healing touch. This will reduce communal tension and communalism will subside.

They also feel that secular interpretation of history does not help and what is needed is owning up the guilt. One of them also feels that as the justice and truth commission in South Africa healed the ruffled emotions and helped restore peace, the apology from Muslims would also help create goodwill among the Hindus.

Howsoever sincere these feelings may be and howsoever motivated by desire for peace, I doubt if it can prove efficacious. There are other questions of moral nature as well apart from legal ones. I would like to throw detailed light on these questions and also on methodology of understanding history. First, I would like to throw some light on the methodology of interpreting history.

As for understanding history it is not sufficient to take the events into account and even for every event several narratives are available and one has to chose one of these narratives. One often chooses the narrative in keeping with ones ideological bias. Every narrative is loaded one in as much as the reporter of the narrative himself has his biases or interests, if not biases.

The noted British historian E.H.Carr maintains that historians are like cooks and as cooks add their own recipe to the raw fish they cook and impart different tests to the same species of fish, the historians also add their ideological biases and create different narratives from the same event. And readers too bring to bear their own biases while choosing one of the narratives as true.

Also, one has to take holistic view of events and not selective view. Most of us often take selective view in as much as we tend to select those events, which are in keeping with our bias or interests and disregard those which go against our bias or interest. We cannot understand history with such bias. Not only history we cannot understand contemporary events with such bias.

There are major controversies about contemporary events, let alone about those events which have taken place hundreds of years ago. We cannot be sure about truth of many contemporary events as they are often surrounded by major controversies. And even commission of inquiries cannot establish truth of many events. How can we be then sure of controversial events of the past? Also, in understanding history and historical events, one cannot focus on event alone, motive is equally important, if not more. Our reading of history is often limited to description of events, often ignoring the motive behind them. Mere event without understanding likely motive behind it does not enable us to understand the event in proper perspective.

Even if a murder takes place before our eyes, we will not be able to understand the cause of murder without knowing the motive. Similarly, it is not enough to know that a temple was demolished unless we know why was it demolished? The motive makes all the difference. One cannot simply assume that the temple was demolished because idolatry is practiced there. It might have been demolished for other reasons say for plunder of wealth, for humiliating the ruler and give the message to his subjects that the ruler is impotent and cannot protect a temple. Also, it might have been demolished because it happened to be the temple of *Isht Devta* of the king or it might have been demolished to take revenge.

It is equally important to know the associated events and ignoring them can result in serious misunderstanding of the event. For example, when certain Muslim rulers demolished temples, often Hindu soldiers also took part in it. If the motive was to stop idol worship, in all probability they would not have taken part in such a project. If it was with the motive of plunder of wealth they could participate.

Also, it is important to note that those rulers who had demolished temples had also given jagirs to some other temples. Aurangzeb who is projected in our history textbooks as temple demolisher, has given jagirs to may other temples, in some cases in the same city. He also built a temple in Chitrakoot in M.P. and gave a piece of land with revenue for its maintenance. If he demolished temples only because he hated idol worship how could he give jagirs to other temples, or even construct temple in other place? Thus his demolishing some temples was not for hatred of idol worship but some other motive. This makes great difference.

All this is not mentioned in our history textbooks. Muslim rulers like Aurangzeb are projected as demolishers of Hindu temples ignoring all other things. Thus we often take selective view of history and not holistic, as pointed out above. To do justice to history we must take into account not only of few selected events but of all related events.

It is also important to note that temples were demolished not only by Muslim rulers but also by Hindu and Buddhist rulers. King Harsh of Kashmir (of 11th century) had appointed an officer in charge of demolition of temples (*devotpatan nayaka*) who used to select temples with lot of wealth. He would remove the idol and drag it on the streets and ask people to line up and witness it. He would then melt the idol (of silver or gold) and deposit the silver or gold in state treasury.

There are other instances of Hindu invaders demolishing temples in the region of the invasion. All this is not mentioned in our history textbooks. Only where Muslim rulers demolished temple it is highlighted in our history.

Now we would take up the question of hurt psyche and tendering apology by Muslims. Even if we assume that Muslim rulers demolished temples with the sole motive of stopping idol worship (which is not the case) how can Muslims today be held responsible for what their co-religionists did hundreds of years ago? Another important question to be taken into account is can we treat any religious community as homogenous? Can all Muslims be put in the same bracket? Were there not Muslim rulers or nobles who patronised Hindu places of worship? There were many Muslims who were even devotees of Hindu gods like Lord Krishna.

There were many sufi saints who even believed that Hindu gods like Ram and Krishna might have been prophets of Allah since Allah has said in the Qur'an that He has sent His prophets to all the nations. For example Sufi Mazhar Jan-I-Janan of 18th century held such a view and even considered Hindu idol worship as different from idol worship of pre-Islamic Arabs and justified it.

Thus all Muslims cannot be bracketed together and entire community cannot be held responsible for what some members of that community did. It would be morally wrong. How can all Muslims of even medieval ages could be responsible for what some of them did? And Muslims of today can certainly not be held responsible for any such events at all even morally, let alone legally. They are not even progeny of those rulers who demolished those temples. Most of them are converted from low caste Hindus. These converts were looked down upon with contempt by the ruling classes of Muslims who considered themselves as superior (*ashraf*) to these *ajlaf* (of low origin).

Most of these converted Muslims were far more integrated with the local low caste Hindus and followed their traditions and customs. They were far closer to the sufis and their belief of *sulh-I-kul* (i.e., peace with all). In no way they could be held responsible for what some rulers did. And it is also important to note that all Muslim rulers did not demolish temples. Among them were many like Akbar or Adil Shah or Zainul Abidin who contributed richly to local religions, traditions, customs, arts, architecture and music. There are very few rulers who have been accused of temple demolition.

And it is also important to note that who has created this 'hurt psyche'? It is not found among all Hindus. It is politically generated hurt, especially by the Sangh Parivar propaganda. The Sangh Parivar propaganda intensified during the last part of decade of eighties when they carried out intense propaganda for Ramjanambhoomi temple obviously for political purpose. It has also been partially generated by the history textbooks taught in or schools. These textbooks were originally written by the British historians of colonial India to divide us so that they can rule. Before British period it will be difficult to find such 'hurt psyche'. It has been generated for political reasons.

The common Hindus, especially in rural areas do not have such feelings even today. It is urban elite who entertains such ideas. Thus it is mainly political propaganda of communal variety and school textbooks which are mainly responsible for such feelings. And the remedy does not lie in apology by Muslims of contemporary India but in fighting communal forces who misuse history and in reforming our educational system.

Archaeological Excavations and Temple

The Archaeological Survey of India at last submitted its report to the Allahabad High Court a few days ago. It has come to the conclusion that a "huge structure indicative of remains, which are distinctive features associated with the temples of north India" existed there. This report by ASI has of course gladdened the hearts of members of the Sangh Parivar. However, the report will be subject to different interpretations and would not go unchallenged.

Different opinions are already being expressed by different archaeologists. Suraj Bhan, a noted archaeologist, says that the report has not "taken into account" certain features of the western -wall of the pre-Babri Masjid chamber. According to him the burnt brick wall of the pre-Babri Masjid structure had a carved stone laid in the foundation. "This has not been taken into account. If it was, this could have precluded the possibility of the structure being associated with Hindus, since they never used carved stone in foundation", he says.

He also maintains that the pillar bases are not of the same type, "which means they were used in different structures", he says. Also, it was just a few days ago that a senior archaeologist involved with the project had said that nearly five months of excavation near the site of the demolished Babri Masjid in Ayodhya, said no evidence of a pre-existing temple has surfaced. Speaking to *The Times of India* on condition of anonymity, the archaeologist stated categorically, "There is no evidence of a temple. In fact, as we go deeper, we are seeing more evidence of Islamic influence."

He also said other than "enriching our team's knowledge about the material culture of Ayodhya", the excavation had not helped the purpose the Allahabad high court had sought to address when it ordered the dig, the archaeologist said. When digging was ordered many historians like Irfan Habib had warned that excavation could not lead to a clinching evidence for existence of a temple. The artefacts could be interpreted differently. And this is precisely what is happening. The final report submitted by ASI seems to be highly controversial and is bound to be challenged.

On 22nd June *The Indian Express* had reported "The ASI, which has been carrying out excavations in Ayodhya, submitted its progress report for last fifteen days to the Lucknow Bench of the Allahabad High Court on Saturday, i.e., on 21st June, 2003. According to this AIS report, it found structural anomalies in some trenches during the digging, archaeologists argued that the anomalies did not indicate that a temple like structure once existed at that place."

In a six-page report, the ASI gave minute details about artefacts found at the site of the digging which included human figurines, pillar bases, animal structures, glazed tiles and small bone carvings. The report said structural anomalies were found in 46 of 86 trenches. The report also added that structural anomalies were found in some trenches near the sanctum sanctorum where the Ram Lalla idol is placed. Aniruddh Srivastava, former ASI archaeologist, said the findings so far did not suggest a temple like structure once existed there. "The pillar bases do not seem strong enough to be able to hold a big temple structure."

In some trenches some graves, terracotta and lime mortar and surkhi were also discovered which in fact indicated Muslim inhabitation and it was also surmised that there existed some mosque on the site and that Babri was built on the site of another mosque. Now we have final report of the ASI which says that there could have been a temple like structure below Babri Masjid? Is it not a glaring contradiction? All through the digging no definite indications of any temple like structure were found and suddenly the final report discovers temple like structure there.

R.C.Thankran of Delhi University, who also spent a long time in Ayodhya during excavation, says, "I have seen the material in the pillar bases. Pieces of early medieval bricks, thinner, smaller and less wide were found. Can it take a massive structure?" he asks. Supriya Verma of Punjab University, who spent months in Ayodhya as an expert of Sunni Wakf Board, has also pointed out glaring omissions in the report.

It is interesting to note that the ASI report talks about a shrine followed by a temple with different structural phases, it also talks of "animal bones recovered from various levels of different periods". If any shrine and a temple existed how can anyone account for the animal bones, Supriya Verma asks? She also maintains that stones and decorated bricks could have been used in any building, not necessarily only in a temple. Also, the carved architectural members have come from the debris and not from the stratified context.

According to Vinay Lal, B.B. Lal, the retired Director General of ASI had initiated a project on the archaeology of the Ramayana sites and in his reports that he submitted to the ASI in 1976-77 and 1979-80, he not only made no mention of any pillar-bases, he went so far as to say that though "several later-medieval brick-and-kankar lime floors(had) been met with", "the entire late period was devoid of any special interest". But later in 1990 Lal began to claim that certain brick bases he had excavated in the seventies were meant to support pillars and thus suggested, "the existence of a temple like structure in the south of the Babri Masjid."

Thus it will be seen from expert's opinions cited above that the ASI report cannot be treated as a final and authentic evidence of existence of a temple of 10th century at the site of Babri Mosque in Ayodhya. But the Sangh Parivar has already started treating the Report as a clinching evidence of existence of a temple. The RSS spokesperson Ram Madhav told *Indian Express* "The ASI report on excavation at Ayodhya site has confirmed and reinforced the existing historical and literary evidence besides the ground penetrating radar survey findings. With this final evidence forthcoming, the whole controversy should end. The judiciary should quickly dispose of the case and come out with its verdict, instead of allowing it to linger on", he said. He also said that "it is a slap on the face of our secularist friends and a section of the media which tried to spread the canard that the excavations had yielded no evidence to support the contention that a temple predated the Babri Masjid at the site."

However, the Sunni Central Board of Waqfs (SCBW) termed the ASI report as vague and self-contradictory. Abdul Mannan, a senior lawyer representing the SCBW termed it as a "saffron report". And another lawyer of BW Zafaryab Jeelani said, "it was prepared under political pressure". Zafaryab Jeelani also told reporters in Lucknow, "The report talked about massive structures at the depth of 50 metres, but how can the ASI say so when it had not even dug so deep." Jeelani also said, "we have a team of six archaeologists who will study the report and file objections."

But the Sangh Parivar is preparing to revive Hindutva politics in U.P. The fall of Mayawati Government also leaves no other choice for BJP. The ASI report will be used enthusiastically for coming elections in five states or may be even in U.P. if no government can be formed. In fact Ramjanambhoomi has lost much of its lustre but now this report has given some life to the issue and the Sangh Parivar will not spare any efforts in this direction.

In fact some BJP leaders have been reported saying that the bomb blasts in Mumbai and the ASI report together have given us emotive issues to be used in coming elections. It is very unfortunate for our democracy that such communal issues are being exploited repeatedly and every election results in more and more polarisation between Hindus and Muslims. Several general elections since late eighties have been fought on this emotive issue. Whatever the verdict of the Court the Sangh Parivar has found yet again an issue to fight elections with.

The expert archaeological opinion may not give much credence to the ASI report but as far as the Hindutva supporters are concerned they hardly care for expert opinion. For them the report will serve as a final verdict. Mr. L.K. Advani went to the extent of saying in New Delhi that the ASI report has gladdened the hearts of crores of Rambhaktas in the country. If the Deputy Prime Minister of the country so enthusiastically endorses the controversial ASI report without waiting for the Court's acceptance or rejection, what of ordinary supporters of the Sangh

Parivar. For them it is a sacred document and cannot be questioned.

The ASI should not have said in its report that a 'temple like structure, was found but should have placed before the Court all the artefacts and objects discovered in different trenches. It should have been left for expert archaeologists to interpret the findings in all the trenches dug at the site. Use of word 'temple-like structure' certainly arouses suspicion in the minds of dispassionate and non-partisan observers as to the integrity of ASI officials.

Thus the ASI report has created another controversy rather than solving the problem. There will be claims and counter-claims in the court yet again. Thus wisdom requires that the issue be resolved through negotiations. Both sides should make a gesture and bury the controversy forever.

The Role of Ulama in Freedom Struggle

Togadia's utterances have neither any truth, nor any restraint. They are full of ignorance on one hand, and of fanaticism, on the other. The other day he demanded ban on Darul 'Uloom, Deoband, a premier institution of Islamic learning in whole of South Asia. In support of his demand Shri Togadia said that Maulana Azhar Masood, a second in command of Osama bin Laden, Maulvi Umar, a principle accused of Godhra train arson tragedy and host of Talibani activists were all produced in Deoband.

He further said, "If at all Muslims are secular, then their leaders should condemn these terrorists and issue 'fatwa' to launch *jehad* against them". He also warned them that India was essentially a Hindu nation and Muslims could not think of safety without the help of Hindus. He made these utterances while speaking before a crowd of some 1000 Bajrang Dal activists at a much provocative 'trishul diksha' function held at Hardoi on 23rd March.

His provocative statements continue unabated. Yesterday in Bhopal, i.e., on 27th March he said referring to killings of 24 Pandits in Kashmir by terrorists and shooting dead Hiren Pandya of BJP in Ahmedabad that a Hindu army be raised equipped with AK-47s. Mr. Togadia warned Prime Minister Atal Bihari Vajpayee that an invasion of Pakistan was the compelling need of the hour to protect the Hinds from the worst. He also said that if this was beyond his capacity, the government should be mentally prepared to disburse one crore licenses to procure AK-47 guns. This would allow VHP, according to him, to raise an army of Bajrang Dal youths who would gun down terrorists on their own. "Otherwise, there will be civil war in every village."

These utterances, in my opinion, cannot be dismissed as mere empty threats or as utterances of a fanatic. The recent history of VHP clearly shows that what they say today becomes their plan of action tomorrow. In any other country he would have been arrested for disturbing communal peace but since there is BJP-led Government at the Centre, no one can touch him. On the contrary the BJP government benefits from such utterances of VHP-Bajrang Dal and RSS leaders. The VHP is very cleverly preparing a political atmosphere for forthcoming elections in the States like M.P. and Rajasthan. It is not without significance that he made this statement of raising Hindu army in Bhopal as elections are due in November in M.P.

The Sangh Parivar members, particularly likes of Pravin Togadia are penetrating villages and provoking Hindus there and creating communal tension. Communal violence was earlier an urban phenomenon but now RSS-VHP-Bajrang Dal cadres are fast spreading in rural areas and spreading hatred between religious communities. The rural areas were earlier by and large free of communal poison. Today these organisations have plenty of funds and can easily afford to recruit large number of hate propagandists. The whole atmosphere in the country is being disturbed for electoral gains. The Sangh Parivar is playing, to say the least, very dangerous game.

Here we want to throw some light on the role of Darul 'Uloom, Deoband which Pravin Togadia wants to be disbanded as it is producing terrorists. As pointed out before, Togadia should not be dismissed as mere fanatic. There is definite method in his madness. This applies to all the leaders of Sangh Parivar. What they say today, they plan to achieve it tomorrow.

The present generation is totally ignorant of the role played by the 'Ulama of this premier Islamic institution in freedom struggle and in opposing creation of Pakistan. The Sangh Parivar, through its vicious propaganda, has spread the half-truth that all Muslims were responsible for creation of Pakistan. The fact is that very few Muslims were responsible for it. In fact not more than five per cent Muslims voted for Muslim League in 1946 on the basis of which the decision for partition was taken.

It should be remembered that there was no adult franchise before India became independent. Adult franchise came into force only after independence when our Constitution was promulgated in 1950. But before independence the franchise was limited to not more than 10 per cent of the Indian population and it is these enfranchised people who voted in all elections before 1950. Of the 10 per cent Muslim population enfranchised about 60 per cent took part in voting and of which 60 per cent voted for Muslim League and 40 per cent voted for the Congress and other parties. Thus not more than 3.6 per cent Muslims voted for Muslim League in 1946.

Thus few elite Muslims – Zamindars, top civil servants, high ranking police and military officials were behind the Pakistan movement. The vast number of Muslim masses who had no voting right and had no interest in creation of Pakistan, could not influence the decision one way or the other. So was the case with the Hindu masses. They too had no voting right and remained mere spectators. If the Indian masses – both Hindus and Muslims – had right to vote, perhaps Pakistan would not have come into existence.

It should be clearly remembered that partition was brought about by the power elite from both sides. It was failure of power sharing arrangement between the elite of two communities, which brought about partition, not religion. Thus Pakistan was not creation of Islam but of vested interests of Muslim elite. Had Pakistan been creation of Islam the movement for Pakistan would have been led by Ulama like Maulana Abul Kalam Azad, Maulana Husain Ahmad Madani and others and not by Jinnah. But we find that Maulana Azad and Maulana Husain Ahmad Madani were staunch opponents of Pakistan and a modern educated and highly westernised person like Jinnah led the Pakistan movement.

It is interesting to note that Jinnah found it very difficult to enlist support of Muslim 'Ulama of great repute. They were all for composite nationalism. Maulana Husain Ahmed Madani, a great 'alim of his time and Nazim al-Umur (Vice Chancellor) of Darul 'Ulum Deoband, was great opponent of Pakistan movement. He wrote a book *Muttahidah Qaumiyyat Aur Islam*, i.e. Composite nationalism and Islam in which he opposed two nation theory and justified composite nation on the basis of Qur'anic verses and Prophet's sunna (sayings and doings).

The Maulana was a great champion of composite nationalism and he toured whole of India after two nation theory resolution was adopted on 23rd March 1940 at Lahore and appealed to the Muslims not to be misled by the Muslim League propaganda. He was repeatedly attacked by the Muslim League volunteers and his meetings were sought to be disturbed. But the Maulana remained firm and continued to oppose two-nation theory and creation of Pakistan.

In fact there is a long history of the 'ulama' making great sacrifices for the cause of Indian freedom since the British rule was established in India. They were also in the forefront of 1857 war of independence and many of them were exiled to Andaman-Nicobar (then known as *kalapani*). Most of them could never return and died there. They never apologised to the British rulers. Hundreds of them were executed by the British rulers after 1857 mutiny.

Maulana Qasim Ahmad Nanotvi, a very eminent 'alim of 19th century issued a fatwa urging Muslims to join Indian National Congress when it was formed in 1885 and said it was their religious duty to drive out Britishers from India. He also collected about 100 fatwas from other prominent 'ulama` of his time to this effect and published them under the title of *Nusratul Ahrar* (i.e. for helping the freedom fighters). It was Maulana Qasim Ahmad Naotvi and others who founded the Darul 'Uloom, in Deoband, a small town near Saharanpur in U.P.

This Darul 'Ulum became not only the centre of Islamic learning but also a centre of activities for freedom movement. It is these 'ulama' who supported the Khilafat Movement and came very close to the Indian National Congress. Even after the failure of the Khilafat movement (in fact Kamal Pasha of Turkey abolished Khilafat itself) these 'ulama' continued to support Indian National Congress and secular nationalism and do so even today.

It is this glorious history of Darul 'Uloom which, has to be kept in mind. It is absurd to demand ban on this important institution, which played such key role in freedom struggle. It is unfortunate that it is being attacked today by those who do not believe in composite and secular nationalism and want to create Hindu Rashtra. These 'Ulama' never supported a theocratic state and opposed vehemently creation of Islamic Rashtra as shown above. They supported and continue to support secular nationalism until today.

The Sangh Parivar believes in two-nation theory. The founder of Hindutva concept Veer Savarkar propounded two-nation theory much before Jinnah did. They never participated in the freedom struggle. Savarkar did participate in his earlier phase and won the title of veer (man of courage) but later on (i.e., after 1921) he not only apologised to the Britishers to obtain his release from Andaman jail but also became propounded of Hindu Rashtra which ultimately resulted in partition of the country.

And Savarkar's descendants like Togadia are once again destroying the unity of the country by attacking secular nationalism and playing majoritarian card which is totally undemocratic. The secularists should not underestimate the challenge of Hindutva today.

Ambedkar, Muslims and Partition

The Sangh Parivar keeps on raking up caste and communal issues since it has pro-people programmes. It thrives only on casteism and communalism and raking up issues pertaining to caste and communal controversies. After Gujarat carnage in which entire Sangh Parivar was involved now Mr. Katiyar of Bajrang Dal and president of U.P. BJP has raked up issue of Ambedkar and Muslims and that Ambedkar was anti-Muslim and anti-Pakistan.

Shri Katiyar maintains that his contention is based on Dr. Ambedkar's book on Pakistan entitled *Pakistan or Partition of India.* As all communalists basically perpetrate lies and falsehood and spread disinformation in order to establish their case, Katiyar is no exception. In fact Dr. Ambedkar was in no way against Muslims or Islam. But anyone can be quoted out of context to prove what one wants to. Ambedkar was no Muslim baiter as he was a very meticulous and careful scholar and would not indulge, like members of the Sangh Parivar, into community baiting.

Ambedkar's book on Pakistan is a work of great scholarship. I have reprint of its 1946 edition constituting the 8th volume of his writings and speeches published by Education Department of Government of Maharashtra. The plea of the book is such that one can easily extract some statements to suit ones purpose. But an honest scholar has to read the book in totality to understand Ambedkar's views on Muslims and on Pakistan.

Ambedkar has divided his above book into five parts. The first part deals with "Muslim case for Pakistan". Second part deals with "Hindu case for Pakistan". Third part talks about "What If Not Pakistan". Part four deals with "Pakistan and the Malaise" and part fifth discusses with issues like "Must There be Pakistan", "The Problem of Pakistan" and "Who can Decide?"

It can thus be seen that if one quotes Dr. Ambedkar say from first section in which he gives Muslim point of view on Pakistan one can prove that Ambedkar totally favoured creation of Pakistan and if one quotes Ambedkar from second section, i.e., "Hindu Case Against Pakistan" one can prove that Ambedkar was against Muslims. What Katiyar is doing is quoting Ambedkar from second section of his book to prove that Dr. Ambedkar was against Muslims.

It is interesting to note here that Ambedkar maintains in the third section, chapter VII that "Strange as it may appear Mr. Savarkar and Mr. Jinnah instead of being opposed to each other on the one nation *versus* two nations issue are in complete agreement about it. Both agree, not only agree but insist that there are two nations in India – one the Muslim nation and the other the Hindu nation." Further he says, "They differ only as regards the terms and conditions on which the two nations should be. Jinnah says India should be cut up into two, Pakistan and Hindustan, the Muslim nation to occupy Pakistan and the Hindu nation to occupy Hindustan. Mr. Savarkar on the other hand insists that, although there are two nations in India, India shall not be divided into two parts, one for the Muslims and the other for Hindus; that the two nations shall dwell in one country and shall live under the mantle of one single constitution: that the constitution shall be such that the Hindu nation will be enabled to occupy a predominant position that is due to it and the Muslim nation to made to live in the position of subordinate co-operation with the Hindu nation."

Thus it will be seen that Dr. Ambedkar has very fairly stated position of both the parties. He is not stating his own views in these two sections of his book. In fact Ambedkar is so fair and objective that he feels that one should not describe all invasions of India by Muslims as invasions against infidels or against India only. He says, "These invasions of India by Muslims were as much invasions of India as they were wars among Muslims themselves." "This fact has remained hidden", Ambedkar says, "because the invaders are all lumped together as Muslims without distinction. But as a matter of fact, they were Tartars, Afghans and Mongols. Muhammad (Mahmud?) of Ghazni was a Tartar, Mahommed of Ghori was an Afghan, Taimur was a Mongol, Babar was Tartar, while Nadirshah and Ahmadshah Abadali were Afghans."

Continuing this line of argument Dr. Ambedkar says, "In invading India, the Afghan was out to destroy the Tartar and the Mongol was out to destroy the Tartar as well as the Afghan. They were not a loving family cemented by the feeling of Islamic brotherhood. They were deadly rivals of one another and their wars were often wars of mutual extermination." This is very objective understanding of history and is not inspired by any communal attitude. However, one may differ from Ambedkar when he says, "What is, however, important to bear in mind is that with all their internecine conflicts they were all united by one common objective and that was to destroy the Hindu faith."

But here Ambedkar is clearly contradicting himself. When Tartars and Mongols and Afghans were out to exterminate with each other and were not bound by the feeling of Islamic brotherhood how could they be united by any common objective to "destroy Hindu faith". In fact these Muslim invaders had no such objective despite their rhetoric to the contrary. In fact many of them invaded at the invitation of Hindu rulers of India. But it must be said that Dr. Ambedkar is, on the whole, quite objective in assessing the history of Muslim rulers.

Dr. Ambedkar did not even support the Gandhian position that let the British quit India and then Indians would settle the matter among them and would sort out communal question. In fact in his introduction to the book Ambedkar says, "The British cannot consent to settle power upon an aggressive Hindu majority and make it its heir, leaving it to deal with the minorities at its sweet pleasure. That would not be ending imperialism. *It would be creating another imperialism.*The Hindus, therefore, cannot avoid coming to grips with Pakistan, much as they would like to do."

Thus Ambedkar is quite categorical in his assertion that the communal or minority question should be properly settled before the British leave India. He feels that the minorities cannot be left to the mercy of "aggressive majority" as he puts it. Ambedkar has thoroughly examined the Muslim (or rather Muslim League) point of view in the first section of his book "Muslim Case for Pakistan". Explaining Muslim League view he says, "...is it or is it not a fact that Muslims of India are an exclusive group? Is it or is it not a fact that they have consciousness of kind? Is it or is it not a fact that every Muslim is possessed by a longing to his own group and not to any no-Muslim group?"

And then he goes on to say, "if the answer to these questions is in the affirmative, then the controversy must end and the Muslim claim that they are a nation must be accepted without cavil." Can one quote this passage from Ambedkar to maintain that he was advocating the cause of Pakistan? Oh, certainly not. Ambedkar is explaining Muslim League's point of view, not his own.

Ambedkar had his own view of Muslims and Pakistan. He was totally opposed to the concept of Hindu Raj as well. In the section "Must There Be Pakistan" he says, If Hindu Raj does become a fact, it will, no doubt, be the greatest calamity for this country. No matter what the Hindus say, Hinduism is a menace to the liberty, equality and fraternity. On that account it is incompatible with democracy. Hindu Raj must be prevented at any cost."

Still Ambedkar did not want partition. He says, "How have the French, the English, and the Italians succeeded in preventing the Raj of the majority community being established in their country? Surely, not by partition: What is their method? Their method is to put a ban on communal parties in politics. No community in Canada, South Africa or Switzerland ever thinks of starting a separate communal party."

Ambedkar makes a very pertinent point in this respect and Indian Muslims should coolly deliberate over this. Ambedkar says, What is important to note is that it is the minority nations, which have taken the lead in opposing the formation of a communal party. For they know that if they form a communal party the major community will also form a communal party and the majority community will thereby find it easy to establish communal Raj. It is vicious method of self-protection."

Thus it is very clear that Ambedkar was certainly not anti-Muslim nor in favour of Pakistan. He wanted a just solution to the minority problem in India. He gives his suggestions in the last section of his book, i.e., part v. On page 359 of his book Ambedkar says that "Is not a fact that under the Montagu-Chelmsford reforms in most provinces, if not in all, the Muslims, the non-Brahmins and Depressed Classes united together and worked the reforms as members of one team from 1920 to 1937? Herein lay the most fruitful method of achieving communal harmony among Hindus and Muslims and of destroying the danger of Hindu Raj. Mr. Jinnah could have easily pursued this line. Nor was it difficult for Mr. Jinnah to succeed in it."

And Ambedkar was convinced that "..Mr. Jinnah is the one person who has all the chances of success on his side if he had tried to form such a united no-communal party. He has ability to organize. He had the reputation of a nationalist."

Thus a careful study of Ambedkar on the question of Pakistan makes it clear that he was far from being anti-Muslim as Shri Katiyar of BJP would like to project him. He was very balanced and just in his attitude towards Muslim question and suggested very constructive way out. One must read the full text of the book to understand Ambedkar's attitude towards the communal question in pre-independence India. Likes of Katiyar have neither ability nor honesty to study Ambedkar's writings before making public statements. He does so only to derive political mileage and polarise Hindus and Muslims on one hand, and Muslims and dalits, on the other, to monopolise Hindu votes.

Hindutva and Minorities

After the carnage in Gujarat and subsequent victory of Narendra Modi-led BJP in Gujarat has intensified threat of Hindutva forces. The Hindutva forces not only celebrated the victory in Gujarat but also declared their intention to repeat the Gujarat model in other states in coming elections. It is not so surprising after all that even the Prime Minister Vajpayee when asked about it, confirmed it. When reporters asked him would you repeat Gujarat model in other states he said, "Will Godhra be repeated"?

The implication of this cryptic reply is that if Godhra is repeated (or created?) in other states Gujarat model will be justified and the BJP Government will neither owe responsibility to prevent Godhra-like occurrence nor the subsequent events that followed in Gujarat. Thus the BJP owes no responsibility to enforce rule of law but rule of hate, blind revenge and violence.

Such hateful and revengeful Hindutva (which believes in even worshipping weapons on every Dasehra day) is bound to terrify minorities against whom its ire is directed. A question now is being asked what should be the response of minorities to the aggressive Hindutva? Should they submit to its demands for complete submission and accept the concept of Hindu Rashtra and status of *mleccha*? Or should they resist such demands and fight back with equal militancy?

I think no saner elements would advocate either course. To submit to such demands would amount to demise of democracy in our country and to fight back militantly would only strengthen the hands of Hindutva forces. What is better course then if both the above courses are not advisable? Before we discuss this we would like to throw some light on the stand taken by Jamat-e-Islami during sixties. It is again being advocated by some Muslims today.

The Jamat-e-Islami had advocated during the sixties that Muslims should not participate in the electoral process for two reasons: one, the Jamat was against secular politics and, second, it thought, as Sir Syed did in nineteenth century, it is in the interest of security and progress of Muslims to keep away from turbulent politics.

But both arguments go against the grain of democracy. Of course the Jamat has also accepted secular polity in India and no more advocates that Muslims keep away from electoral politics. Neither is tenable any more. Every one has realised that democracy can work only if it is secular. Hindu democracy or Islamic democracy prioritises religion over the notion of citizenship. In secular democracy citizenship is most fundamental, not religion. In Hindu *Rashtra* or Islamic democracy a Hindu or a Muslim will be more privileged than a non-Hindu or a non-Muslim. Thus such a course cannot be acceptable.

Not to participate in the electoral democracy is equally highly doubtful course. It clearly amounts to debunking democracy just because an aggressive section of majority community so demands or because it misuses electoral politics for forcing majoritarian values on minorities. Misuse of democracy cannot be negation of democracy. It amounts to throwing away baby along with bath water. Moreover, all Muslims cannot agree to such a course. They are 150 million in India and no leader of such a huge community can succeed in building consensus in the community on such a controversial course of action. Also, the Indian democracy will collapse if a community of 150 million keeps away from electoral process. There is no such precedent in any country of the world. If we add other minorities to this the problem assumes more massive dimension.

We have thus to evolve proper strategy for meeting the menace of Hindutva to the minorities. This can more easily be done by meeting this menace by winning the confidence of that major section of majority, which is aware of this menace or can be made aware of it. Hindutva forces, one should note, would ultimately set up an highly authoritarian regime and would undermine democracy. Thus the majority community should also understand that it is menace not only to minorities but also to majority itself. Its democratic freedoms would be in peril.

It is not true, as often claimed by the Hindutva forces, that Hinduism can't yield to theocratic or authoritarian set up and that only Hindus can be secular and democratic. Hinduism may not be a religion with one god, one prophet and one book but it does have many sects and *panths* with rigid shastric traditions and orthodoxies. The Hindutvawadis do talk of Manuvad and even advocated Manu's laws in place of modern Indian constitution. Originally the Constitution Review Commission was set up with a clandestine agenda to import Manu's laws back into the Indian mainstream. But thanks to hue and cry raised by democratic forces in the country that it did not succeed.

This shows that an aware secular democratic forces from the majority community can better stall Hindutva forces than an aggressive minority or minorities. However, most of the minority leaders either lack this wisdom or have ambition of their own to acquire instant leadership by using highly emotive issues. The Shah Bano and Babri Masjid issues, if handled with tact and wisdom by Muslim leadership, would not have had such disastrous implications they had.

There is need for think tanks at state and national level to tackle such controversial issues. The minorities should not respond to any emotional controversies impetuously without giving serious thought as to the consequences of taking a particular stand. Some ambitious leaders take hasty stand and put entire minority community in danger. The latest example is of an imam of the mosque in Gujarat appealing Muslims for coming out in large numbers to vote for the Congress and this appeal was published in a Gujarati paper *Gujarat Today*.

The BJP think tank immediately thought of exploiting it and various newspaper advertisements were issued appealing the Hindus to come out in large numbers and vote for the BJP to frustrate the conspiracy against the Hindus. This also helped the Hindutva forces in registering 2/3rd majority in Gujarat. I was told by some secular Hindus in Gujarat that the imam was close to the BJP and he did so at the instance of the Sangh Parivar.

Whether the imam was BJP agent or not it proves that how the Hindutva forces can exploit to hilt any mistake made by minority leaders.

Thus whenever such controversies arise – or are made to arise by the Hindutva forces – the minority leaders must restrain themselves and debate the issue preferably in a meeting of think tank from all possible angles and then take any stand. There are several issues like the Ramjanmabhoomi and Babri Masjid, which should be left to democratic and secular forces from majority community to fight it out. If this issue had not been projected majority versus minority and had been projected as secular democratic versus majoritarianism it would have had very different consequences.

The whole nature of fight would have been different. Of course the democratic secular forces also did not intervene effectively in the matter (the Congress Government led by Shri Narasimha Rao even allowing demolition of the mosque) and the whole nation had to face the consequences. The country would not have faced bloodbath in Mumbai in 1992-93 and in Gujarat if secular forces had effectively intervened in the matter.

The secular and democratic forces in majority community also have high stakes in strengthening secularism in the country. A pluralist democracy cannot survive without secularism. Our Constitution incorporated pluralism even without mentioning the word 'secular' as equal citizenship rights irrespective of caste, creed or race is not possible without secular politics. If the Hindutva forces win the greatest danger will be to our constitution and our pluralism.

Also, it is important for minorities, especially for Muslims to thoroughly imbibe democratic and secular values. A progressive and secular outlook is very necessary. Clinging to old traditions in the name of religion is not in the interests of the community even otherwise. There should be great stress on modern education and concerted efforts should also be made to modernise madrasas. Those who resist modern knowledge will have nowhere to go.

We should also convince the Hindu majority that the Qur'nic term *kaifr* does not apply to them. It had its connotation in the

Arab society in which the Prophet of Islam (PBUH) preached. Our ancestors like Mazhar Jan-I-Janan did precisely this. The RSS, the most important and ideological force behind Hindutva has convinced many Hindus that Muslims consider them as *kafirs* and the Qur'an requires all *kafirs* to be killed. This misinformation campaign has to be fought very effectively to carry majority of Hindus with Muslims.

It is also necessary for various minorities and weaker sections of society like dalits and tribals to come together along with secular and democratic forces of the majority community. One should not, however, form a separate block of minorities and dalits. It only provokes large majority to consolidate itself and goes to the advantage of Hindutva forces. In Gujarat the Hindutva forces have effectively used dalits and tribals against minorities. One has to deeply reflect on Hinduva's success in doing so.

On the whole it is very complex problem and minorities have to take various aspects of this multi-dimensional problem to tackle it effectively and successfully. It would also require constant evaluation of fast developing political situation and adopting effective strategies from time to time.

2

Socio–Political Context

Tribal-Muslim Dialogue

The Centre for Study of Society and Secularism has been engaged in for several years in organising inter-faith and inter-community dialogues in order to understand the nature of conflict; between various groups, castes and communities and to bring about reconciliation between them. The Centre is convinced that there is no future for pluralist India except in unity between its people of diverse faiths, languages and cultures. In a secular and democratic country both unity and diversity must be emphasised. One must seek unity in diversity and also try to build unity with diversity.

The Centre has organised several inter-faith dialogues on concrete issues like religion and violence, religion and women's rights, religion and democracy and so on and invited Hindus, Muslims, Christians, Sikhs, Parsees, Buddhists and Jains. These dialogues help promote better understanding between various faith communities and traditions. However, after the Gujarat carnage the Centre felt that it is also necessary to organise dialogue between Dalits and Muslims and Tribals and Muslims too. During the Gujarat carnage of 2002 Dalits and Tribals participated (or made to participate?) on a large scale. It, therefore, became necessary to gain insight into the dynamics of this large scale participation by them in the communal violence.

We thus first organised Dalit-Muslim dialogue in Ahmedabad in July 2004 in which large number of Dalit and

Muslim activists took part and frankly expressed their respective points of view. The result was better understanding of the causes of Dalit-Muslim clashes and both sides pledged to build bridges between the two communities. This was resolved not merely as a political slogan but as a serious attempt to bring them together on the basis of proper understanding of each others needs and inspirations.

In Central and North Gujarat tribals had also similarly taken part on large scale in anti-Muslim violence. It was, therefore, felt that there is great need for organising tribal-Muslim dialogue also. The Centre requested Fr. Lancy Lobo and Prof. Juzar Bandookwala of Baroda to take initiative on behalf of the Centre and both of them rendered very valuable help in organising very purposeful and constructive dialogue. Both are noted social activists and committed for the cause of communal harmony.

The dialogue was organised at St. Xavier Technical Training Institute near Baroda. Some fifty participants from both communities from different parts of Central and North Gujarat took part in the dialogue. Dr. Asghar Ali Engineer, Chairman, CSSS threw detailed light on the need for this dialogue. He said that the Centre had organised similar dialogue between Dalits and Muslims in Ahmedabad and it thought necessary to organise dialogue between Tribals and Muslims too, to gain insight into the nature of conflict between the two communities.

There are different theories about the nature of this conflict between the two communities. During the investigation of Gujarat riots of 2002 we were told that tribals did not take part in the violence of their own but were made to do so by the high caste Hindus. We were also told that the Muslim traders in villages charged high rate of interest from Tribals and thus they attacked Muslims when they got the chance during communal disturbances in February 2002. This theory was advanced by a noted tribal activist from Baroda. We were also told in Panwad village that some Muslim traders used to keep tribal girls in their houses and had sexual relations with them and the tribals took out their anger against them. However, this was strongly refuted by the Muslims in the refugee camp near Panwad.

It is only dialogue like this, which can bring truth out and bridge the differences and promote goodwill between these two groups. Dr. Engineer also emphasised that this dialogue is not meant to argue against each other but to understand each other, not to convert each other to ones point of view but to gain insight into the nature of the conflict. With these initial remarks the dialogue was thrown open to the participants.

Shri Jagdish Shah was requested by Shri Bandookwala, who was conducting the programme to give his point of view. Shri Jagdish Shah, a noted Sarvodaya activist from Baroda gave his own analysis of the situation. He maintained that of late there is increasing separatist tendency among the Muslims. They are trying to establish their separate identity and appearance. They want to become pure Muslims. U.P. Muslims are bringing this culture along them. Muslims are giving up their local identity. This creates social tensions as Hindus feel that Muslims are trying to separate themselves from others and they resent this.

As for tribals he made a point that they are trying to become the part of mainstream and in the process want to identify with the higher caste Patels. This is the inspiration of most of the tribals. They hardly care for their tribal identity. He also threw light on another pot of conflict. Muslims traders are not alone in exploiting Adivasis (tribals). Hindu Vanias, Parsis and others also exploit them. But Muslims are in transport business and tribals too are taking to transport business and there is keen competition between them. Muslims are becoming more prosperous and Adivasis resent this. Adivasis do not feel sense of solidarity with Muslims as they do with Hindus as Ram has always been popular among them and this brings them closer to Hindus.

Rohit Prajapati, a human rights activists has also worked among tribals in Modasa district. Muslims were not identified as Muslims but as traders but now they are identified as Muslims. Muslim traders do keep tribal women as their kept or even marry them. Earlier it was seen only as trader's exploitation. But the Swadhyay movement and Hindutva propaganda has made all the difference and tribals see them how as Muslim traders rather than only traders. Now Muslim traders' exploitation is seen as exploitation by Muslims, not as traders. Patels also keep tribal women and they also exploit them but they are not seen as Hindus. All this is result of Hindutva propaganda.

A strong delegation of Jamat-e-Islami had come to participate in this dialogue. The Jamat is doing good work these days for promoting communal harmony. Mr. Mohammad Hanif of Jamat-e-Islami from Modasa participated in the dialogue. He said that it is true that Muslims in Modasa were also treating Dalits as untouchables and when I did not they protested and threatened me with boycott as Hindus of the village would not like Muslims to treat Dalits as equals. Muslims have many drawbacks and they should come out of this and set better example for treating Dalits and tribals as equal. But how to do it in view of social pressures in the Gujarat villages. It is important question. It is not easy to get out of it.

Mr. Kazi of Jamat-e-Islami agreed with the analysis of Rohit Prajapati that it is Hindu traders not so much as VHP which incite tribals to eliminate Muslim competitors. These Hindu traders give bad name to Hindu traders. Thereupon an Adivasi leader from Godhra said that Adivasis are illiterate and unaware. They need to be educated and made aware of what is going on.

Ms. Amba, an Adivasi woman who has done M.A. – rather an exception as Adivasis are not highly educated – said that there are no Muslims in my village and so questions of animosity between Adivasis and Muslims does not arise. I have heard of Hindu-Muslim riots but never of Tribal-Muslim riots.

Mr. Patel, an advocate from Baroda maintained that Adivasis aspire to adopt Brahminical way of life as Brahmans are considered more civilised and more respected. For tribals it is struggle for survival. And like Brahmans tribals also want to be seen as anti-Muslim so that they have better chance of integration with Hindu society in their villages. Post 9/11 anti-Muslim hatred has increased. If one Muslim does something bad it is generalised as if whole community is responsible for it. It is also part of struggle for votes.

Kaderbhai Memon from Dohad area said that Adivasis were used for attacking Muslims. They were given Rs. 2500 each to loot a Muslim shop and were also allowed to retain the loot. He also said that Adivasis repented later as Muslims were selling things at reasonable rates. After eliminating Muslim competitors the Hindu traders started charging high rates and Adivasis realised their mistake. They came to Muslims and apologised and requested them to come back and said we stand guarantee for their safety and security. Poor and unemployed Adivasis were thus cleverly used by Hindu traders. Kaderbhai also suggested that Muslims should take part in Hindu festivals and become trustees in temples to promote better relations. They should not keep themselves aloof.

Ishaqbhai, an industrialist and a Sarvodaya activist felt that Gujarat riots were most barbarous. Such barbarities were never committed before. He said Hindu traders also charge interest, why then they were not attacked? It was all provoked by Hindutva forces. We should promote dialogue with Hindus and tribals and promote harmony. We must do continuous work in this direction.

Irfan Engineer who has worked for several years in Dang tribal area said that tribals are very poor and generally unemployed and for money they did all this. If paid money they can attack and loot. Tribals mostly voted for Congress but when BJP came to power many of them went with BJP for their survival. When one tribal friend joined BJP, I asked him whether you are Huzuria or Khajuria, he said I am none, I am only Zaruria (out of need I have joined BJP). He suggested that Muslims should take initiative in inviting more Adivasis to their functions and should participate in their functions as well to promote better relations.

Fr. Lancy Lobo felt that Adivasis are treated with contempt but now they are becoming more conscious of their dignity. They cannot be taken for granted anymore. They must be given better place in society. It is long overdue now. He felt there is high level of educated unemployment among Adivasis and they are being used by Hindutva forces for gathering information in villages against Muslims and Christians.

Dr. Engineer lastly made a few concrete suggestions to promote communal harmony. He said we should not have ambitious plans but concentrate on our own area and work with dedication to maintain peace in our locality. If we succeed in doing that it would be quite an achievement. We must come closer with each other, participate in each others festivals and in each others joys and sorrows and help each other with sincerity and it will make all the difference. This is the only way to frustrate communal design. Dialogue is the best way to understand each other. It is only through dialogue that we can understand each other better.

Dr. Juzar Bandookwala proposed a vote of thank and thanked all those who came from distant places to make this dialogue a success.

Muslim Intelligentsia and Liberalism

There is lot of debate in India about role of Muslim intelligentsia in India. It is contented that Muslim intelligentsia tends to be illiberal with few honourable exceptions and that it is illiberality of Muslim intelligentsia that has produced reaction among the Hindus and as a result we see illiberal Hindu intelligentsia today.

Mr. Ramchandra Guha in the edit page article in *The Times of India* (dated 23/03/04) "Nearly 40 years ago, Marathi writer Hamid Dalwai wrote a fascinating series of essays on the lack of a liberal movement among Indian Muslims. The leaders of the community, he argued, were incapable of critical introspection." Then he goes on to quote him, "When they find faults, the faults are invariably of other people. They do not have the capacity to *understand* their own mistakes..." Mr. Dalwai also maintained that "the moment they became liberals they lost the confidence of their backward and orthodox community."

What Hamid Dalwai says is hardly a revelation. It is a well-known truth and besides applies to many other communities. It is true that many of Muslim intellectuals have been reluctant to attempt critical introspection. But it is hardly peculiar to Muslims as such. If one seeks its social explanation, one would understand its underlying causes. The trouble with Mr. Dalwai and also with Mr. Ramchandra Guha who quotes him approvingly, is that they do not try to understand underlying causes.

First it is also necessary to state that Muslims produced eminent intellectuals in nineteenth and twentieth century before partition like Sir Syed Ahmed Khan, Maulavi Mumtaz Ali Khan, Maulavi Chiragh Ali, Justice Ameer Ali and several others who were highly critical of community traditions, practices and religious orthodoxy. They not only developed critical insights but had great courage to criticise these practices openly. Their Muslimness did not deter them from attempting critical reflections and blaming the community for what they saw as wrong.

And it was not only among scholars like them but also great litterateur (writers, poets and others) who were highly critical of orthodoxy and orthodox practices. Of course, in latter case they used poetry and fiction to attack orthodox practices. The progressive literary movement has glorious history of its own. The problem with likes of Hamid Dalwai is that they take very static and superficial view of the problem. Mr. Dalwai had very limited knowledge of Muslim affairs. His entire knowledge about Islam and Muslims was based on secondary sources. What he read was mostly in Marathi and very little authentic information on Islam and north Indian Muslim movements was available then in Marathi. Now of course more and more information is being made available.

Mr. Guha unfortunately and uncritically buys Mr. Dalwai's argument that lack of liberal intelligentsia among Muslims will create strong reaction among the Hindus and will produce illiberal intelligentsia among them too. Thus Mr. Guha quotes Hamid Dalwai, "...unless a Muslim liberal intellectual class emerges, Indian Muslims will continue to cling to obscurantist medievalism, communalism and will eventually perish both socially and culturally. A worst possibility is that of Hindu revivalism destroying even Hindu liberalism, for the latter can succeed only with the support of Muslim liberals who would modernise Muslim and try to impress upon these secular democratic ideals."

Then Mr. Guha says that Dalwai's "prediction has come chillingly true". Hindu illiberalism has emerged with vengeance. I do not think it is Mr. Dalwai's prediction which has come true. The causes of emergence of Hindu revivalism does not lie in absence of Muslim liberalism but should be sought in the RSS's unceasing efforts to bring about this revivalism and BJP political leaders' ambition to come to power climbing on the *rath* of Hindu revivalism.

It is a strange argument that Hindu liberalism will survive only on Muslim liberalism and will collapse if Muslim liberalism does not materialise. It seems to be quite an erratic view of social movements. This is not to say that Muslim liberalism should not be strong and that Muslim intellectuals should not be self-critical. But Hindu liberalism should not be expected to walk on the crutches of Muslim liberalism.

There are very good reasons for weak liberal movement among Muslims in India. Firstly, there never was a strong capitalist class among Indian Muslims. Muslim ruling class was basically feudal class and that was either ruined due to Anti-zamindari Act passed by the Congress Government or many of the zamindars migrated to Pakistan. Those left behind in India were mostly from artisan classes and most of whom were poor, backward and even illiterate.

A new middle class began to emerge again after partition from amongst the low caste artisan classes then referred to as *ajlaf*. The middle class which migrated to Pakistan mostly came from amongst upper classes known as *ashraf* who were highly educated and cultured. The new middle class which is emerging in India has seen much insecurity due to frequent occurrence of communal riots since early sixties of the last century, besides rough and tumble of economic uncertainties.

This new middle class has been much less sophisticated for lack of traditional culture and liberal values. The Hindu middle and upper classes, on the other hand, suffered no such loss due to migration. On the other hand, it drew all the benefits of capitalist development since independence and have had the best available education. Also, the Hindu upper classes did not have to suffer any sense of insecurity due to communal riots. There is no reason why their liberalism should be weakened and also such weakening be blamed on lack of Muslim liberalism. It seems to be strange logic by any account.

The reasons for weakening of Hindu liberalism and emergence of revivalist movement should be sought elsewhere, particularly in the politics of Sangh Parivar. If at all the weak Muslim liberalism kind of argument is to be applied it could be applied (with little justification) to North India. What about Gujarat where Muslim presence has never been strong historically and Muslims have never been competitors either in political or cultural field there. The Hindu revivalist movement has been strongest today in Gujarat.

Also, as pointed out earlier, one should not take static view of social and cultural movements. The Muslim scenario is also changing, particularly post-Babri demolition period. A new awareness has emerged among the Muslims in general and Muslim intelligentsia, in particular. The trend for education is growing and liberalism and secularism is much more acceptable among Muslim intelligentsia today. The Shah Bano-like movements are a history now.

But I do not think the Sangh Parivar's revivalist ideology is going to be much influenced by this positive development among Muslims in general, and Muslim intelligentsia, in particular. Again, it was the Sangh politicians who challenged the Nehruvian concept of secularism and dubbed it as 'pseudo-secularism'. Even orthodox Muslim 'ulama in India had never challenged the concept of Nehruvian secularism, despite their illiberalism. One can argue that the Muslims accepted Nehruvian secularism as it guaranteed their security in India. This argument is also not historically correct. The members of Jami'at-ul-'Ulama including Maulana Husain Ahmed Madani had accepted concept of secular nationalism much before partition and never deviated from that line.

The RSS, Hindu Mahasabha and their related organisations never accepted secular nationalism whether before or after partition. They consistently opposed it. Only thing is that before partition and until late seventies after partition, they did not succeed in widening their social base. They succeeded in doing so only from beginning of eighties when the Indian politics took a new turn in the post-emergency period and Mrs. Gandhi also appealed to the Hindu card. Also, the Rajiv Gandhi period, Shah Bano movement, corruption scandals like the Bofors, Ram Temple controversy, all these were cleverly exploited by the

Sangh Parivar to win over Hindu middle class intelligentsia, which was tired of the Congress rule and was seeking political change.

There is one more important reason for emergence of the revivalist movement among Hindus. The BJP, in order to widen its political base tried to win over the backward class Hindus from all over India and this class among Hindus was neglected and was seeking for fulfilling its political aspirations. The BJP gave it an ideology of Hindutva through which it could seek its political aspirations. This is one of the very important causes of strengthening of revivalist movement in contemporary India. Its cause should not be sought in weak Muslim liberalism as Ramchandra Guha does. Socially and politically it would not be correct.

These backward caste Hindu leaders like Vinay Katiyar, Uma Bharti, Pravin Togadia and others are most vocal revivalists and supporters of Sangh Parivar and have become high achievers in political fields, holding high positions in the Parivar hierarchy as well as in political field. Thus one has to survey entire socio-political panorama to understand the causes of Hindu revivalism rather than simplistically blame it on lack of Muslim liberalism.

Dilemmas of Democracy

Democracy in a multi-cultural, multi-lingual and multi-religious country like India poses difficult problems and dilemmas not easy to resolve. We began to face these dilemmas much before independence. Different castes and communities make demands, which are often difficult to accommodate. Also, some castes and communities from ages have been holding disproportionate power and they are not easily persuaded to give it up and accept more egalitarian set up which democracy seeks to usher in.

Before independence also two serious problems arose when still democracy had not been fully ushered in. These problems arose in anticipation of the enactment of full fledged democratic structure. The Muslims demanded their share in power under the leadership of M.A. Jinnah and so did the dalits under the leadership of Dr. Ambedkar. While the later problem could be resolved by giving them reservation the Muslim problem could not be as it was far more complicated and involved many complex issues not to be discussed here. As a result of non-resolution of the Muslim problem our country was ultimately partitioned.

Both problems remain in different forms and many more have arisen during the course of working of democracy during last more than half a century. India is a bewilderingly diverse democracy and several castes and communities bracketed with major castes and communities are splitting into their own autonomous groups and making their own demands. The backward classes and castes had not asserted their separate identities during independence but began to make their own demands once democracy began to deepen during course of time.

Kaka Kalelkar Commission was appointed to meet their demands and then Mandal Commission and after deferring decision for their reservation for several years the Central Government had to announce implementation of Mandal Commission in 1990. Its implementation threw Indian society into turmoil, as the upper castes were not prepared to give up their privileges so easily. What happened after enforcing Mandal Commission is now matter of history.

Several castes and communities still feel that they are not getting their share of power and government jobs as compared to tiny number of upper caste privileged groups. Similarly the minority communities like Muslims feel that they have been given a raw deal. When these castes and communities assert themselves for justice the upper caste and class privileged groups cry foul and begin to say national integration is in danger. And more so, if those making demands, happened to be Muslims. It happened in earlier decades of our independence. When in early sixties some Muslim leaders after the Jabalpur riots in 1961 formed Majlis-e-Mushawarat across political parties it was seen as great danger to national unity.

But during eighties when dalit leaders across party lines came together it was thought to be the only way to solve dalit problems. Anyway this is only a side point. What we are trying to drive at is that democracy in a diverse country like India creates certain problems, which pose dilemmas for ruling classes and ruling parties. Before independence Muslims and dalits had demanded their share but now several castes and communities are making their demands. Earlier caste-based parties did not exist. Today several caste-based parties are coming into existence.

Earlier regional parties did not exist and all India parties used to be voted to power. The only regional party, which asserted itself during sixties was in Tamil Nadu. Now several regional parties have come into existence and only alliance of these regional parties can form a government at the Centre. No single party can rule over India. It is all because functioning of democracy brings more and more awareness among people of diverse origins and they begin to assert their respective identities and organise themselves.

In the North-East earlier only Naga problem existed right from pre-independence days. After seventies Assam problem erupted and then in almost all seven states of North-East experienced armed struggle. Thus, on one hand we desire national integration and greater national unity but on the other, under democracy more and more people agitate and even demand separation apparently causing disunity.

This is because democracy cannot work without justice and justice denied under democracy agitates people and in extreme cases they begin to demand separation, thinking justice would never be done under the present dispensation. Kashmir also remained quiet for some time after independence but the Kashmiri youth took to arms under similar assumption. The youth looses patience earlier than others. In entire North-East too it is students and youth who took to arms.

The right wing communal forces further aggravate the problem of religious minorities. The Jan Sangh thus for years condemned assertion of any religious identity and demanded that all Indians should have only one Indian identity and should not assert any other identity. Whenever Muslims asserted their religious identity Jan Sangh (and later BJP) condemned it strongly. Regional identities though not condemned as strongly as religious identity, was disapproved of. Tamil identity too appeared separatist.

Only the North Indian Hindu identity was considered as the core identity and symbol of Indian unity. All other identities either disapproved of or strongly condemned. The Jan Sangh (and later the BJP) was merely an upper caste North Indian party. It had not penetrated into south or had extended its base among the low caste Hindus. It is only during eighties that it realised its upper caste north Indian credentials cannot see it in power. It then exploited the Ramjanambhoomi issue to entice low caste Hindus to its fold and thus could widen its vote base.

However, during that decade the BJP, though apparently caste away its communal garb and had taken oath for secularism on Gandhi's Samadhi for secularism, became much more stridently anti-Muslim in order to garner Hindu votes of all castes and classes. For the first time it adopted stridently anti-Muslim Hindutva agenda, i.e., imposition of uniform civil code, construction of Ram Temple in Ayodhya and removal of Article 370 granting Kashmir a special status. The BJP itself called it a Hindutva agenda to attract more and more Hindus in its fold by inciting anti Muslim feelings.

As a result of this anti-Muslim politics the BJP who always swore by 'patriotism' and *akhand Bharat* (united India) created greater degree of social disharmony and tried to weaken the unity and integrity of India. And all this to reach the seat of power. Thus, democracy can be misused greatly by vested interests. Democracy demands, as pointed out above, justice to all sections of society and using majoritarian anti-minority discourse a serious attempt was made by the BJP leaders to perpetrate injustice against religious minorities reducing them to second class citizens.

In Gujarat too the BJP, under the leadership of Narendra Modi, a hardcore Hindutva demagogue, planned to organise anti-Muslim genocide in 2002 using the unfortunate Godhra incident in order to create anger among all class of Hindus to win the assembly elections and he won those elections with overwhelming majority. Thus, democracy was seriously misused by the Hindutva zealot to retain power in Gujarat. The central BJP leadership, at that point of time, not only approved of this genocide but also began to say that the Gujarat model would be repeated in other states.

But the BJP was rebuffed in Himachal Pradesh and lost elections very badly and they forgot all about the 'Gujarat model'. They began to re-think their strategy. Now the BJP has come full circle and is trying to woo the very Muslim minority its leaders had despised all along. They had used hate propaganda to come to power all these years. But again it was strength of Indian democracy that hate politics lost all its appeal and of all the states in U.P., which was part of the Hindu core nationality.

The rise of caste politics in U.P. and emergence of Dalits and Yadavs as great political force, seriously weakened the upper caste Hindu political appeal and the BJP, going against its core agenda had to strike an alliance with the Dalit party of Mayavati. Even this alliance proved to be riddled with problems for the BJP and it could not rise to a significant political force in U.P. The Muslim vote in U.P. is crucial for any political party. The Congress lost its primacy in U.P. as it lost both the Muslim and Dalit vote. The Muslims began to vote now either for the Samajwadi Party of Mulayam Singh or Bahujan Samaj Party of Mayavati.

Ironically the BJP is wooing Muslims in this coming general elections as there is no other way out for it to come back to power. It has enticed some Muslims into its fold and is apparently diluting its Hindutva agenda. It now says it would construct Ram Temple through negotiations with Muslims and the uniform civil code will be brought as a measure of gender justice, not as an anti-Muslim measure and has quietly dropped the issue of removing Article 370 from its agenda.

Let us hope that the BJP sincerely realises (not merely as an election winning stunt as it appears to be doing today) that it cannot in any case rule over India by antagonising a minority as large as Muslims numbering over 13-14 crores. Even the bloodshed like the one in Gujarat is possible once in a while and reconciliation with Muslims is the only solution.

Dalit-Muslim Dialogue

The Gujarat carnage of 2002 once again showed that Dalits and OBCs are widely used by the Sangh Parivar to kill Muslims.

In several localities especially in Ahmedabad like Kalupur, Darapur etc. Muslims and Dalits live side by side and whenever communal violence breaks out attack each other. It is unfortunate that the strategists of Sangh Parivar easily win over poor Dalits to attack poor Muslims. However, it will be wrong to assume that all Dalits play the Sangh Parivar game.

Dalit and Muslim leaders at the same time talk of Dalit-Muslim unity to counter the Sangh strategies. However, the ground realities are very different. In all major communal riots it has been observed that Dalits participate in Hindu-Muslim riots on behalf of Hindus, especially the Dalit youth. In North India the Valmikis are invariably used against Muslims. In Maharashtra of course Mahars who follow Ambedkar's ideology by and large resist the Shiv Sena attempt to assume anti-Muslim posture.

However, in Mumbai riots of 1992-93 though followers of Ambedkar kept away from supporting the Shiv Sena engineered riots, the Dalits from Gujarat in Tardeo and other areas attacked Muslims. This clearly shows that ideology can play major role. In Gujarat the Dalits have repeatedly taken part in anti-Muslim violence. When anti-Dalit riots had taken place in Ahmedabad in 1981 on the question of reservation, Walji Patel, one of the Dalit leaders had told us that now Dalits have understood the Sangh game and they will not become handle in their hands to kill Muslims.

However, in 1985 riots in Ahmedabad again, the Dalit youth were used by the Sangh Parivar to attack Muslims. When I questioned Waljibhai about it he expressed his helplessness and said that these youth do not listen to us. We can hardly influence them. This continued during subsequent riots in Ahmedabad and in 2002 Gujarat carnage Dalits were used in large numbers to attack Muslims. Many people even told us during investigation that Dalit youth were paid for this and even supplied liquor to drink.

It was because of this repeated disturbing trend that Centre for Study of Society and Secularism decided to organise Dalit-Muslim dialogue to understand as to why the Sangh Parivar every time succeeds in using poorest of poor to kill poorest of the poor from among the Muslims. It was quite heartening that large number of Dalit intellectuals and Muslims responded though Muslim presence was rather not very encouraging. The reason, Sophia Khan told me, was that she could not get enough contacts of leading Muslim intellectuals. Anyway overall presence was more than encouraging.

I threw light on the purpose of the dialogue and also stressed the importance of Dalit-Muslim unity and discussed some of the possible causes of Dalit-Muslim hostility. One major cause is, I said, poverty, backwardness and large-scale unemployment both among Dalits and Muslims. Another important cause is mutual rivalries as any Muslims and Dalits are in illicit liquor and gambling business, die again to poverty. These rivalries get accentuated during outbreak of communal violence. Sometimes these factors help accentuate communal violence.

Mr. Chanderbhai Meheria, a Dalit writer, said that such dialogues are highly necessary to enhance understanding between the two communities. It is mainly the RSS and the BJP who have created serious misunderstandings between the two communities. He felt that Muslims are somewhat better in economic and educational status and they should take initiative for education of Dalits. Some Muslim communities in Gujarat like the Bohras, Khojas and Memons are well off and run many educational institutions and they can reserve some seats for Dalits. It will have very mollifying effect on relations between two communities.

The Dalits are too poor to have such institution. But the problem is that Bohras, Khojas and Memons themselves are too inward looking and very identity conscious and do not give place to other Muslims in their institutions. Though the suggestion was made in good spirit and really could help.

Mr. P.K. Valera, a retired IAS officer, felt that Muslims, like upper caste Hindus, have never accepted the Dalits. Muslims have been rulers in this country and do not consider them their equals. He also felt that Dalits do not feel secure among Muslims. Muslims should give Dalits opportunities in jobs to win them over. Much of this again is based on misconceptions. Muslims themselves are divided in different *biradaris*, if not castes. The social hierarchy very much exists among Muslims too. Though it may not be as intense like among Hindus, it nevertheless does exist among Muslims. It may be true that upper caste or upper class Muslims may not accept Dalits, but low caste poor Muslims have no such attitude. And in India by and large, Muslims have accepted the idea of Dalit-Muslim unity and there is certainly no rejection of Dalits even among upper class Muslims. Like upper caste Hindus Muslims would not treat Dalits as untouchables. Also very few Muslims have means to offer jobs to Dalits or educational opportunities. Most of the Muslims in India today are almost on par with Dalits. Whatever limited economic data is available indicates that clearly.

Mr. J.V. Momin, on the other hand, had a complaint that Islam and Muslims are considered as *jihadis.* Even in the Congress there are people with the RSS mentality. They treat Muslims with hostility. Mr. Afzal Memon of Gujarat Sarvajanik Welfare Trust and who did lot of work during the riots for rehabilitation of Muslims agreed that many Muslims do not accept Dalits. He felt that the Congress in Gujarat is also to be blamed for communal situation. He even felt that the Dalit elite who achieve high status also neglect poor Dalit and hardly do anything for them.

Mr. Kannur Pillai, a retired I.G. Police said that Muslims are also Dalits. They are also suppressed. A section of Dalits converted to Islam because they were harassed by upper caste Hindus. He felt that communal propaganda by the Sangh Parivar affects Dalits too. The anti-Muslim propaganda among Dalits by the Sangh Parivar is to prevent Dalits from being converted to Islam. They want to keep hostility alive between Dalits and Muslims for variety of reasons, Mr. M.K. Parmar felt that the RSS is creating hostility between Dalits and Muslims on one hand, and between Muslims and OBCs, on the other. All those who attacked Gulbarga society in which 40 Muslims along with Ehsan Jafery were killed were OBCs and not Dalits. In fact OBCs (Other Backward Castes) Hindus are far more hostile to Muslims. It is true that OBC Hindus committed far more atrocities against Muslims than Dalits. The RSS is systematically working among both and is trying to give them sense of being Hindu.

Mr. Mukesh Patel, an advocate felt that the administration and judiciary both do injustice to Dalits and Muslims. He also revealed that Dalits were supplied weapons by upper caste Hindus to kill Muslims and threatened that if they did not kill Muslims they (Dalits) themselves will be targeted. Many Dalits killed Muslims out of fear for their own security. He laid stress on joint committees and training the youth to counter Hindu communalism.

Prof. Jafer Husain Laliwala, an economist said that Dalits and Muslims have been divided since independence and several Muslims themselves fall in the category of Dalits. It is quite a complex situation and Dalit-Muslim unity is a must to counter upper caste communal forces. In history too few instances of demolition of temples are generalised by the Sangh Parivar to create Hindu-Muslim hostility. The instances of Hindu-Muslim cooperation are deliberately ignored. In Shivaji's army 35 per cent soldiers were Muslims. This also needs to be projected.

Mr. Prakash Benkar a Dalit advocate pointed out that Muslims also attacked Dalit houses and burnt them. Raju Solanki, a young Dalit activist and a poet maintained that in 20 mohallas where Dalits and Muslims lived together, no Dalits are found in them today. They migrated to other places as they felt insecure in those mohallahs. They feared attack by Muslims. The Dalit leadership, it must be admitted, failed to stop Dalit youth from going to RSS and VHP. It is Ambedkar's ideology alone which can forge unity between Dalits and Muslims and this unity is needed to stop communal violence.

In the later half session Dr. Engineer suggested that in order to counter Sangh Parivar propaganda among Dalits it is necessary to constitute Dalit-Muslim Council on All Gujarat level to be followed by such councils in every district. There is great need to continue this dialogue to remove various misunderstandings from each other's mind. A newsletter should also be published on Dalit-Muslim problems. And, if possible, a resource centre should be established in Ahmedabad to provide research facilities on this question.

It was also suggested that there is great need to work among the youth of both the communities. The Dalit youth are getting attracted by the RSS-VHP ideology. This has to be stopped and older Dalit leadership has lost all influence on the youth. Thus they should go and make them aware of Ambedkar's ideology.

In Gujarat there is no Ambedkarite movement Mr. Irfan Engineer pointed out. The Shiv Sena failed to attract Mahars because of Ambedkar's influence, he said. Gujarat needs such a movement.

A decision was taken to constitute Dalit-Muslim Council and work for spreading the Ambedkar's ideology in Gujarat. It is the only effective weapon to counter RSS ideology.

Education, Secularism and Human Values

Education is highly valued in modern society. One cannot survive without it in this world. One must attain higher educational levels if one has to progress and be economically well off. Thus in modern times education is more a means for higher economic status than search for truth or search for meaning of life. It means equipping oneself with more and more information than knowledge what we traditionally called *gyan or 'ilm.*

No wonder than that information technology has acquired such importance in contemporary world. It is also referred to as knowledge industry thus dragging knowledge to the level of information and reducing it to an industry, a profit making venture. Thus knowledge has lost its sanctity and it is no more a quest for truth, but for money. It is no more a goal but an instrument, not an end but a means.

Also, as the well-known American philosopher Herbert Marcuse aptly said our universities are no more centres of knowledge but have become centres of acknowledgement and they are no more centres of cognition but are centres of recognition. Excellence in knowledge and learning is no more encouraged in these institutions. Competition for jobs has become its aim.

Today education is controlled by the government on one hand, and by the rich, on the other. Both have their own objectives and agenda. While government tries to promote its political ideology the rich tries to enrich themselves. In country like India the government is still a major player in the field of education. It determines what to teach and prescribes text- books. Thus, the education is largely controlled by government, both central and state. Its role is most crucial in deciding the quality of education.

We are a secular state in India but our education is far from being secular in content. Our textbooks both at primary and higher levels are thoroughly contaminated by communal outlook. We often blame the British rulers for their divide and rule policy but our textbooks even 57 years after independence is divisive in character with some honourable exception. It systematically cultivates communal outlook and creates hatred against minority communities.

It is regrettable that despite such sustained controversy against communalised textbook there are no concerted efforts to change them so that these textbooks can become a dynamic instrument for promoting secularism and secular values and respect for all religions, languages and cultures. Our textbooks represent majoritarian outlook and fail to strengthen pluralist values. Pluralism needs to be promoted with vigour today in our country to fight communal ethos.

Today in most of the schools we find pictures of Hindu gods and goddesses and *slokas* from Hindu scriptures. Recently I visited a school run by Mumbai Municipal Corporation and found entire atmosphere suffused with of Hindu religion. There was no representation of any other religion at all. Not a single picture or quotation from Bible or Qur'an or Sikhism. This obviously discourages children of other communities to study in such atmosphere where they feel totally alienated.

Our aim through education should be to cultivate critical thinking. No school even remotely reaches this goal of education. All our schools cultivate conservative unthinking outlook. The students are encouraged to imitate traditions rather than develop faculty to critically evaluate. The teachers themselves come from highly conservative environment and pass it on to their students. Most of them do not even teach, just read out from textbooks so that students can memorise and pass the examination.

The Latin American educationist Father Paul Ferear stressed interactive method of teaching so that students can discuss and raise questions on a subject. This method can develop students thinking and critical faculty. What our teachers do is to deposit information in the minds of their students and totally discourage any critical discussion. Also, real learning involves quest for truth, quest for knowledge. Our educational institutions are simply not equipped to promote this kind of learning.

Our educational institutions do not cultivate universal humanitarian outlook. They perpetrate narrow sectarian thinking. These institutions promote majoritarian ethos and a sense of superiority in majority culture and majority religion. It holds good for our entire subcontinent which includes India, Pakistan and Bangladesh. We simply take pride in our past and fail to build our future. We stress cultivating superiority of our respective religion and culture rather than universality and humanity. We do not even stress core values of our religion and its spirituality. We simply promote certain rituals, customs and traditions. We do not promote love but hatred of others.

Our textbooks still promote caste superiority and contempt for low castes. The exposures recently of some Gujarat textbooks were shocking, to say the least. A crow was likened with a *safai kamgar*, i.e., with dalits. Thus, dalits are presented as ugly. How can we ever cultivate humanism in our students. At every step in our education institutions we stress discrimination on the basis of caste and creed.

No wonder than that educated people are more communal than poor and illiterate persons who are found more humane. All these prejudices and stereotypical thinking is acquired through educational system. When the BJP government came to power it tried its best to inject pride in the Hindu past and demonised the Muslim past. Past associated with one particular religion is glorified and the one associated with other religion is demonised. This is not history, it is its mockery.

Human society, past or present, has always been full of conflict and violence. It is not religion which makes a society good or bad as often thought. It is human beings who promote good or evil, depending on their interests. There has not been a single era in history, which was without conflict whatever religion it was associated with. It is human interests which determine the dynamics of a society. Unfortunately it is human interests, not religious values which occupy the centre stage of history.

If we have to build modern India our education system must be thoroughly reformed. Unfortunately no government has such political will, whatever their proclamations. Without such thorough cleansing we cannot promote genuine man outlook among our people. There is so much communal polarisation today in our society thanks to our education system and communal propaganda.

Today we find fundamentalism and communalism among lower middle classes as well as upper classes though for different reasons. Among lower middle classes and backward castes and dalits as they go to municipal and government schools and acquire narrow and sectarian outlook through the textbooks and prevailing atmosphere. And as far as upper classes are concerned they concentrate more on their career through acquiring degrees and building professional future. They have neither time and aptitude for spiritual quest for philosophical truth.

These people do not mind exploiting fundamentalism for their own interests. Many highly successful professionals are today joining communal organisations in their search for power and self. They exploit lower class and lower caste people through their narrow outlook and religious sectarianism. This is what happened on large scale in Gujarat. The upper caste and rich Hindus used dalits and backward castes for their political objectives and won assembly elections.

The political exploitation of caste and religion has reached its apex in the quest by the rich and powerful for power. We had the ideal of a casteless society but no one even dreams of it today let alone try to build such society. We have no more desire to combat communalism, let alone build a secular nationhood. Those in search for power leave no opportunity to exploit caste and communal ethos. Babri Masjid-Ram Mandir controversy is its classical example.

We, with all our modernity, are not prepared to give equal status to women. Our textbooks still glorify women as ideal housewives and good mothers. Our laws, Hindu or Muslim, are unable to give women justice in the name of religion and tradition. Tradition is more dear to us than justice. Our traditions must be upheld even if they result in grossest form of exploitation. Muslim personal law board refuses to abolish triple divorce or accept *nikahnama* whatever the suffering of Muslim women.

And our educated people uphold such injustices in the name of identity and our politicians refuse to change laws for fear of loosing political power. Politicians would not reform education system either as rational and humane outlook will make people more aware of their rights and will strengthen desire for better and more just society. But to ensure better future and just society where pluralist ethos and minority rights are respected there is no other go but to thoroughly overhaul our education system. We are otherwise doomed to live with violent conflicts and bloodbath destroying our future and keep us stuck in the quagmire of our past.

Religion, Identity and Democracy

Most of the countries of the world are now. becoming multi-religious thanks to faster means of transportation and employment opportunities in western countries and oil rich Middle Eastern countries. The western countries were mostly mono-religious until early twentieth century. It was in the post-colonial society that migration from former colonies began towards metropolitan countries that these countries became multi-religious. Most of the European countries were Christian (Catholic or Protestant) in medieval ages. Only languages were different.

Later on the nation states came into existence on the basis of languages and most of the countries with few exceptions became monolingual as well in Europe. Thus, the European nation states were quite homogenous. The USA was mainly populated by the Europeans and had common religion, i.e., Christianity. But they were speakers of the different languages. However, Anglo-Saxon group was dominant and English became the national language and other linguistic groups from Europe adopted English and America became linguistically also homogenous. Thus, the problems of religious and linguistic identities did not arise in most of the western countries.

However, Asia in general and South Asia in particular was always multi-religious and multi-lingual. As the politics in the medieval ages was based on feudal system and feudal system depends on monarchical and dynastic power and hence non-competitive, no problems arose. All religious and linguistic groups were loyal to one or the other dynasty. The politics in colonial South Asia with consolidation of the British rule became competitive. Different religious and linguistic groups, and particularly religious groups began to compete with each other for share in political power and government jobs.

Thus religion became a source of identity for political mobilisation and hence became a source of conflict. The power elites of Hindus and Muslims began to assert religious identities of their followers so that they may bargain for power on the basis of their respective numerical strength. Many groups among Hindus and Muslims had no clear religious identities being halfway between Hindus and Muslims. Hence purificatory movements like Shuddhi and Tablighi movements were launched to establish 'proper identities'.

The electoral system introduced by the colonial powers proved more divisive. Political leaders began to generate religious identities to bargain for share in power. The South Asians stressed caste and regional identities before such as Bengali, Rajput, Pathan and so on. But the electoral politics in colonial India changed all this and Indians began to assert their religious identities such as Hindu, Muslim, Christian or Sikh.

On one hand, our freedom fighters were trying to forge a sense of common nationhood and unite various religious and linguistic groups for common struggle against colonial powers and on the other, the power elite from these religious groups were trying to divide on the basis of religious identities. Thus the efforts to form a common nationhood in a multi-religious society was quite challenging. The British rulers, on the other hand, were creating more fissures between Hindus and Muslims so as to consolidate their colonial rule. The British rulers and the Indian political elites thus reinforced each other in widening the gap between the two communities.

Thus it will be seen that communal politics was borne not on account of religion per se but by use of religion for political ends. Both Hindu, and Muslim political elites invoked religious sentiments to further their own political interests. As the Hindus were in majority the Hindu communal leaders began to exploit majoritarian sentiments for creating Hindu Rashtra and a section of the Muslim leaders began to invoke minoritism and that led to two-nation theory.

Thus religious identities became powerful force in democratic politics and religious identities are posing a great challenge even today in all the South Asian nations. Our sub-continent was divided into three countries thanks to politics played by the power elites on the basis of religion and language. All the three countries have religious majorities and religious minorities and despite the division the problem continues.

In fact religion and democracy are not incompatible with each other if both function in their well-defined spheres. Religion is a spiritual force and democracy a political one. But serious problems arise when religion transgresses its limits to interfere with politics and democracy transgresses its limits to use religion for political ends. Religion should be used for spiritual growth and for inner needs of the soul.

Democracy should address the problems of the people and solve their worldly issues in a participative spirit. Both can benefit from each other in a positive sense. Democracy can infuse into itself the moral values provided by religion and religion can imbibe democratic spirit as religious leaders also tend to be quite authoritative. However, our experience shows that when religion is used only for identity politics and democracy only for power politics. It results in confrontation between the religious communities.

In the modern globalised world one cannot have mono-religious societies and one has to live with multi-religious and multi-lingual nations. Thus religion as a basis of nationhood will never create a peaceful society. It would lead to confrontation between different religious communities real people's problems will always be sidelines. It should also be noted that majoritarianism is very negation of democratic spirit.

A true democratic country would ensure equal rights to all irrespective of religion, caste and creed. Religion, ethnicity or linguistic origin should not come in the way of fundamental rights. The rightist forces in all countries try to create religious chauvinism and equate majoritarianism with democracy. Majoritarianism, as pointed out above, is very negation of democracy. Not only that democracy has no place for majoritarianism but, on the contrary, a true democracy ensures additional rights to religious and linguistic minorities to protect their religious and cultural traditions. The Indian Constitution, for example, ensures these rights to minorities through articles from 25 to 30.

However, the communal and majoritarian forces call enactment of such provisions in the constitutions as 'appeasement' of minorities and try to incite religious feelings of the majority community. The BJP in India is wedded to the concept of Hindu Rashtra and through its chauvinistic propaganda creates basis for removing these articles from the Constitution. And makes minorities feel quite insecure. It is as a result of such aggressive majoritarian politics that Gujarat like situations arise. Gujarat carnage is a great shame for a liberal democracy like that of India.

India was the first liberal democracy in whole of Asia and it produced a model constitution ensuring rights to all sections of society despite well-entrenched social hierarchies and age -old horizontal differentiations. But the Jansangh now renamed as the BJP closely wedded to the RSS ideology is bent upon destroying the very spirit of liberal democracy. Religion, in a liberal democracy, cannot become the basis of governance. In fact majoritarianism does not benefit entire majority community; far from it. It benefits only a section of the community.

Aggressive majoritarianism also leads to minority communalism and then both feed each other. Aggressive majoritarianism strengthens religion-based identity and mobilisation among the minority communities as well and both together seriously weaken foundations of liberal democracy. Religion becomes a powerful source of political mobilisation among majority as well as minority communities.

Since late eighties Ramjanambhoomi, a religious symbol, became a powerful tool for mobilising the Hindu masses in the hands of the Sangh Parivar and it exploited it to the hilt to come to power. The Sangh Parivar politics has also weakened traditional toleration found in Indian society. Modern democracies cannot work effectively without tolerance. One can say that tolerance is the very foundation of modern liberal democracy. The Sangh Parivar, using religious issues like the Ramjanambhoomi has systematically cultivated intolerance towards minority communities in India.

Common nationhood in a multi-religious society is not possible if Hindu Rashtra or Islamic or Khalistani states are made the basis of politics. In a democracy, religion should never become the basis of politics. If religion becomes the basis of politics it would lead to worst of both the worlds. Religion will become more and more sectarian than spiritual and democracy will tend to be vehicle of majoritarian rule. The common people will be the ultimate losers in this game of political power.

Those who have real regard for the sanctity of religion would never allow it to be politicised or ideologised. Religion then ceases to be a morally and spiritually guiding force but becomes a powerful tool of power politics. As a result of this power politics Hinduism becomes Hindutva and Islam becomes a source of *jihadi* violence. Both Islam and Hinduism are sources of peace and non-violence.

Thus, we should not allow religion to be politicised at any cost and democracy should remain a source of people's participation in decision making and for welfare of common masses. One must understand the difference between religion as a faith and religion as a political ideology.

Religion, Religious Institutions and the State

Religion plays very important role in our lives, at least in the Asian and African countries. It has become an integral part of our lives. But the important question is what is religion? This question is important, as there is great deal of confusion as to what exactly constitutes religion. For most of us what we have inherited by way of beliefs, dogmas, customs and traditions and institutions. For us all this together constitutes religion. And what is problematic is that we consider religious priests and leaders called by various names like rabbis, fathers, pundits, ulama etc. as true representatives of religion as they are considered as having knowledge of theologies of these religions.

Also, every religion develops powerful institutions and there develops politics of controlling these institutions. Be it church, temple or wakf institutions, they amass considerable wealth and priests and trustees wield considerable influence due to amount of money they control. Take for example the Sankaracharya who has been accused of involved in murder. His Mutt is reported to have wealth amounting to Rs. Five thousand crore. This is by any standard huge amount of money and misuse of such wealthy and powerful institutions is quite understandable.

Another example is that of the Bohra high priest and his powerful establishment. There is no estimate of his wealth available but it is not likely to be less than 5,000 crore; it may be more. No wonder than that he wields, like Sankaracharya SriJayendra Saraswati of Kanchi Kamakoti Peethum, considerable clout in social and political life of the country. Such priests, rather than protecting religion and religious beliefs, are more interested in protecting their powerful vested interests. They resort to all that is most irreligious in order to protect their properties and income.

They do use smokescreen of religion in doing so and to project their acts as legitimate. And to protect their interests they collude with politicians or politicians, having an eye on their resources and influence, try to politicise them. The BJP protest on arrest of Sankaracharya is hardly a genuine expression of religious faith in Sankaracharya. They are agitating with a view to win sympathy of followers of the Sankaracharya. However, it is heartening to note that ordinary Hindu, though having full faith in religion, has not given much importance to the BJP agitation. He has dismissed it as BJP's political ploy.

The Bohra high priest does all sorts of things under the garb of Islam. He has amassed, as pointed out above, great deal of wealth and owns big prime properties and gives money liberally to politicians of all hues, including those of BJP and Shiv Sena to protect his worldly interests. He is reported to have not only given huge amounts to Narendra Modi for his election campaign but also held felicitation for him in Surat (which is alternate head quarters of the Bohra high priest) after the Gujarat carnage. When the whole world was condemning Modi for his utter failure to stop mass murder of innocent people, he had no hesitation in felicitating him. Why? Syedna Saheb, the Bohra high priest, has huge properties in Gujarat to protect.

The BJP is demanding that Sankaracharya should be immediately released and is also saying that he should not have been arrested at all as if a religious leader is above the law of the land. No one, however, respectable and highly placed a person is, can be above the law of the land. No one is saying he is guilty, he is only accused and can be exonerated by the court after examining all the available evidence or convict him but no one can claim being above the law.

Syedna Tahir Saifuddin, the father of the present Bohra high priest, also had claimed in 1918 in the Chandabhai Gulla case filed by the then Solicitor General in the Bombay High Court, that he has his own laws and he does not follow law of the land. Justice Martin of the Bombay High Court reprimanded him saying no one however, exalted, can claim exemption from the law of the land. Ever the Arch Bishop of Canterbury cannot, if he commits any crime, though he would conceivably not.

The Bohra high priest ex-communicates any Bohra, who raises any question not about his but about any of his functionary's conduct; and all this in the name of religion. Islam has no concept of church yet the Bohra priesthood has developed a churchlike hierarchy and claims absolute authority and what is more problematic, absolute infallibility. Anyone questioning the concept of infallibility is severely punished by ex-communicating him. And once ex-communicated, no one can maintain any relationship with him/her and anyone even talking to ex-communicated person, is excommunicated and subjected to same humiliating treatment.

Last month Mr.Fakhruddin Khorakiwala, owner of Akbarally's Departmental Store just chatted with this writer in an Iftar Party in the American Consulate and he was immediately ex-communicated. He is in deep trouble and is trying to get high priest's pardon. We were not talking about the Bohra matter but about movement for communal harmony. Why the Bohra priesthood is so afraid of any one talking to this writer. Does it in anyway endanger religious beliefs? Not at all. It endangers his iron-like grip over the community and institutions of the community, which he tightly controls.

To play politics with religion and to create powerful establishments in the name of religion is the very negation of the spirit of true religion. A truly religious person would ever like to control powerful establishments and become subservient to vested interests rather than to God, Ishwar or Allah. All those who control such institutions are anything but religious. They do, however, try to legitimise their actions by invoking religious terminology. They can hardly deceive any discerning mind.

A truly religious person is first of all most humble and gives topmost priority to service to humankind. All Sufi and Bhakti saints never remotely touched wealth and ever associated with any ruler. Nizamuddin Awliya saw times of five Sultans but did not pay court to a single one and when Jalaluddin Tughlaq sent a message that if Nizamuddin does not come to my court I will go to his hospice, he said if Sultan enters my hospice from one door I will walk out from the other. Such was the distance saints and seers maintained from power centres and never allowed religion to be misused for political purposes.

Unfortunately religion today has not only been politicised but also commercialised. Religious leaders identify themselves with one or the other politician or political parties. They amass wealth by exploiting religious beliefs of people and lead life of luxury. They enter into profitable bargains with powerful politicians and politicians go to them for money and votes. Both together thus exploit religious beliefs of common people.

We do need religious values in politics but certainly not politicisation of religion. Moreover, a state should never prioritise one religion over the other, particularly in a secular country like India. But most of our politicians while paying lip service to secularism grossly misuse religion for political purposes. Our constitutional provisions are violated with impunity. It is only lately that the Election Commission has started enforcing rules but still it is too soft to make politicians behave. The irony is that these politicians take oath for secularism while filing their nominations but having filed that beg for votes openly in the name of religion and caste. The Election Commission opts to look the other way.

A political party, which openly agitates against the arrest of Sankaracharya just because he is Hindu and seeks to incite Hindu religious passions, should never be allowed to contest elections in a secular country. It is strange that the ex-Prime Minister of India leads such agitation demanding that law of the land not be applied to a person simply because he is a Hindu religious leader. How such a person can be expected to govern impartially, if again elected to power. The BJP has failed to entice even Hindus by taking up such a lost cause. As Shri Swaminathan, an eminent agricultural scientist, has pointed out that the government of Tamil Nadu by serving food to Sankaracharya cooked by a Brahmin, has also violated the spirit of Indian Constitution. Our Constitution has abolished untouchability and any cook, Brahmin or a Dalit can cook food in the jail run by the secular government.

Religion in our society has not only been politicised and commercialised it has also become greatest obstacle for any meaningful change. Religion, unfortunately is identified with status quo. Most of the religious leaders oppose any change as violation of religious beliefs. This attitude does not arise from religious beliefs per se but by the interest associated with status quo. Every religion in the world brought social change and changed the face of the world.

However, soon the religion came to be controlled by vested interests who benefited by maintaining status quo. A truly religious person would always fight against status quo and try to change society to make it more just and meaningful. Religion is basically a transcending force and fights against all sorts of vested interests. Priests who are associated with vested interests can never be truly religious people. A religion should be a revolutionary force, bringing healthy change in society.

When a religion becomes a powerful establishment it looses its spirit to struggle for justice. All the Prophets and saints devoted their lives for fight for justice and compassion for suffering humanity and came from poorer sections of the society. It is this spirit of religion, which we have to uphold if it is to be disentangled from powerful interests.

Religion, Law and Governance

Secular governance in a modern society throws up many problems, particularly in developing societies. Developing societies can be divided into two categories: those countries which were colonised and those though not directly colonised but impacted by modern western societies. Those colonised were directly influenced by western concepts including modern legal concepts and practices.

When these countries became free the process of decolonisation began but it was almost impossible to completely decolonise all the legal and administrative practices. At best some compromises could be worked out. Also, the impact of modern legal and sociological concepts was also very deep and no developing society could escape these influences. Such a deep impact of modern legal institutions created tensions between traditionalism and modernism in countries like India.

The British colonial rulers governed India and imposed their own laws and legal institutions on the country. They right away abolished certain legal institutions and continued with some to avoid aggravation of social tensions. For example, they abolished the traditional criminal law and imposed the western criminal procedure code while retaining personal laws of different communities. All communities of India including the Muslims accepted this arrangement. Even the Muslim 'ulama did not protest against imposition of modern western criminal law. Not only this Maulavi Nazir Ahmad translated it into Urdu and was bestowed the title of Shams-ul-'Ulama (The Sun of Theologians) by the Britishers for his services.

The colonial rulers avoided imposing secular laws in the domain of personal laws as they were very well aware of the sensitivity of the issue. In matters of marriage, divorce and inheritance no community would have accepted modern secular laws. Any imposition of such laws would have created unmanageable conflict in the society. The British rulers did not want to take that risk. However, even for personal laws they introduced modern legal procedure and it was the British judges who decided these cases. The traditional qazi and other courts were abolished.

India of course decided to be a modern secular country. Its leaders like Jawaharlal Nehru were greatly influenced by western secularism and modernism. Nehru in particular was a great modernist and committed to the political philosophy of secularism and secular governance. Thus, secularism became the anchor-sheet of Indian political philosophy. However, even a secularist like Nehru could not abolish personal laws in India.

It was not only Muslims, as often maintained by many, who opposed imposition of modern secular laws known as common civil code. Traditional Hindus were even equally, if not more vigorously, opposed to change in their personal laws. In fact the Hindu Code Bill was introduced in the Parliament even before independence, i.e., in early forties but it could not be passed due to vehement opposition from traditional Hindus. Nehru again tried after independence to reform the Hindu personal law and requested Dr.B.R.Ambedkar to frame a Hindu Code Bill and introduce in the Parliament. The Congress ministers themselves opposed the Bill introduced by Dr. Ambedkar and the Parliament was gheraocd by Sadhus and Hindu religious leaders. The Bill had to be withdrawn and Ambedkar resigned as Law Minister.

It was only a watered down version of the Bill that was passed in three different acts. It is important to note that such reform was urgently needed as traditional Hindu laws did not give nay rights to women in matters of marriage, divorce and inheritance. These rights, however, were available to Muslim women in traditional Shari'ah law. Some modernists tried to make uniform civil code as part of the Constitution as the Constitutional Assembly debates clearly indicate. However, there was great deal of opposition from leaders of various communities and it was for this reason that a compromise was worked out and personal laws were allowed to continue while uniform civil code was made part of Directive Principles, not enforceable but desirable.

It was hoped by the modernists that in near future uniform civil code would become acceptable to Indian people. However, it was not to be for variety of reasons. First of all religion very much remains an integral part of our lives. It could not be wished away as many modernists thought. Rationalism and humanism could not replace religion which provides a sense of sacred to human beings. Rationalism is an intellectual process and does help in critical inquiry but fails to produce any sense of ultimate Reality and relationship with that higher Reality.

Also, religion appeals to our emotions and becomes part of our culture and cultural traditions. It is so difficult to separate the two. We cannot live in cultural void. Even western culture is influenced by Christian traditions and beliefs. It is after all not totally secular as some would like to believe. Western culture was considerably secularised over a period of two centuries. But our cultures are far more under the influence of religious beliefs, customs and traditions though the process of secularisation is having its impact on our cultures too. But our cultural institutions remain far more complex. Even rationalists and atheists cannot escape the vicelike grip of traditional cultures.

Thus, in developing secular countries like India secular governance poses many complex problems, particularly in the field of law. This causes many anomalies, which is very difficult to remove. On one hand, it is difficult to enact changes in the law and, on the other, women are fast becoming aware of their rights and demand changes in the law. Even the courts, more often than not, become helpless as they have to operate within the given legal structure. The Shah Bano case is an important example of such anomalies.

The Shah Bano case, besides illustrating such anomalies, also throws light on the identity problems in a multi-religious but modern secular countries. The competitive religious identities pose serious political problems and gender justice takes a back seat. Religion, in a developing and multi-religious but democratic country, becomes part of power struggle between various religious groups. Democracy is supposed to ensure minority rights be they religious, cultural or linguistic. However, democracy is often reduced to majoritarian ethos and minorities suffer discrimination.

The Shah Bano case was not so much fight for Shari'ah as for minority rights. The Muslim responded to the call for agitation by Muslim leaders fearing their Muslim identity is in danger. The fear was expressed that if they do not fight against the Supreme Court judgement Islam may be wiped out from India. The Supreme Court judgement unfortunately pontificated that Islam is unfair to women and that government should enforce uniform civil code.

The majority communal forces, on the other hand, though hardly prepared for justice to their own women, began to demand enforcement of uniform civil code and accused the ruling Congress of not implementing UCC as it appeases the Muslim minority for its votes and condemned its secularism as pseudo-secularism. Thus, a purely legal issue was politicised and was used to intimidate the minorities. The role of Muslim leaders was far from desirable but due to BJP's anti-minority politics their role at that time was seen by Muslims as that of saviour of minority identity.

Thus, the modern secular but multi-religious democracies have their own problems. The competitive struggle for power between different religious communities deflects the country from its ideal secular course. It would be too much to expect that ideal secular course will prevail in muti-religious set up. In fact, power interests are more basic than the secular ideals.

The media, both print and electronic, play no mean role. It also falls victim to majoritarian attitude with some honourable exceptions. Some newspapers display almost chauvinistic attitude and condemn minorities outright without appreciating their problems. This further aggravates the situation and ultimately helps the reactionary minority leadership. And in all this the cause of women suffers. Gender justice becomes increasingly difficult to realise. Any progressive change in laws in favour of women is seen as interfering with religious matters and becomes danger to existence of religion.

Thus, at the level of the state any change in personal laws is becoming increasingly difficult. However, it does not mean that situation remains static. Modernisation and secularisation is bringing sometimes perceptible and sometimes imperceptible changes and these incremental changes become qualitative changes in the status of women. Increasing degree of education among women is creating new awareness about gender justice and is creating more and more pressure for change in traditional laws.

The state has obvious limitations in enacting gender just laws but it is civil society in general and women as part of civil society in particular, which will be a catalytic agent in ushering in needed changes. The role of NGOs in promoting gender justice has also been quite remarkable. These NGOs promote awareness among women for sexual equality. Equal democratic rights enshrined in the Constitution for both sexes and ever deepening democratic processes also sharpen awareness among women for sexual equality. In the given circumstances our best hope is not state but civil society, which is getting increasingly modernised and secularised. No political interests can stop this process. Not state but the civil society should be the leader. And in the modern civil society women will play more actively than ever before.

Sociology of Communalism

One cannot understand phenomenon of communalism without understanding the very nature of society. Society plays very important role in genesis of communalism. One cannot divide unless society is divisible along certain fault lines. These fault lines get further aggravated in certain conditions. In feudal societies too these fault lines exist but do not play politically divisive role as do in a colonial or capitalist society, which are much more competitive.

It is important to note that Indian society was never homogenous throughout history. It was highly diverse religiously, culturally, caste-wise and linguistically but there was hardly any tension between these groups. It all began with establishment of

British rule in India and so most of the scholars agree that communalism is a modern phenomenon and not a medieval phenomenon.

Why the social cleavage got so aggravated with the advent of British rule? The cleavage did exist all through but it turned hostile only in the British colonial period. The explanation for this is quite complex, as there are host of reasons for this. However, three reasons are quite predominant which are as follows: The British divisive policies, competitive nature of colonial, political and social structure and backwardness of colonial society with stunted economic growth.

The British rule was shaken with war of independence in 1857 as Hindus and Muslims united to challenge British hegemony. It was easier to divide as fault lines were sharpening and communal consciousness was emerging among Hindu and Muslim elite. It is further to be noted that communal phenomenon is basically an upper class elite phenomenon. The Hindu elite welcomed the British rule as a 'liberative' one and began to aspire for higher administrative jobs.

The Muslim elite – mostly feudals – on the other hand, considered British rule as unmitigated disaster as not only they lost power but also because they suffered most during the retaliatory action by the British after 1857 uprising. They developed a sort of aversion for the British rulers and were quite reluctant to take to modern education introduced by the Britishers.

Sir Syed Ahmad Khan, a great thinker and educationist urged Muslim elite to go for modern education to better their future. Thus, the Hindu and Muslim elite began to compete for British jobs and political favour. This widened the cleavage between the two elite. The British fully exploited this in their favour. The formation of Indian National Congress in 1885 also made the British more apprehensive of rising aspirations of the 'Hindu nationalism' and now began to manipulate Muslim feudal elite and play them against the Hindu elite.

Thus, the colonial society sharpened communal consciousness and the British further fuelled separation through political manoeuvres. The Hindu and Muslim masses remained aloof from these controversies and coexisted without such hostilities. Among them neither there was competition for jobs nor for political posts. However, there was some trickling down effect.

The communal hostilities intensified with passage of time and controversies about sharing power between Hindu and Muslim elite and constitutional arrangement for sharing power. It must be noted that communalism is product not of religious hostilities but of political and economic struggle for share in power and resources between the educated elite. It is not a subaltern phenomenon either as they are not involved in such struggles.

Jinnah, a product of Lincoln's Inn in London, represented Muslim elite, not Muslim masses. The orthodox 'Ulama, on the other hand, were closer to the masses and represented their aspirations. No wonder than that Jinnah and the Deobandi 'Ulama never saw eye to eye on political matters. They were closer to Indian National Congress than to Muslim League, which was the party of the Muslim elite. They supported the composite nationalism than Muslim separatism.

The British society was essentially a colonial society and masses had no say in political matters, as there was no universal franchise. After independence universal franchise was introduced and masses of people began to participate in the political processes. For few years after independence the Congress got elected to power. Its leaders like Nehru and others enjoyed tremendous prestige and people of all castes and communities continued to vote for it.

However, the political scenario began to change sharply at the end of sixties. Few general elections had brought more political consciousness among different castes and communities. Each caste and community began to develop heightened consciousness and began to demand greater share in power. Among Hindus only upper castes had all the political or economic benefits so far. Now increased participation in political processes made minorities and lower caste people understand importance of their vote and they began to make increased demands thus changing the dynamics of political change.

This gave new dimension to communalism, which we had inherited from the British period. Economic changes also added to the social strife. With land reforms middle castes in various states acquired more social clout and they demanded greater share in political power. The Reddys and Cammas in Andhra Pradesh, Patels in Gujarat, Marathas in Maharashtra, Yadavs in Uttar Pradesh and Bihar etc. acquired much greater clout and political parties began to woo them.

During early eighties Mrs. Gandhi realised the potential of these newly emerging castes and sought their support for electoral purposes. For these castes communalism provided an easier route to power in some cases. Thus Patels in Gujarat flocked around BJP to claim greater share in power. Also other backward castes found it very attractive to support communal outfits.

A sociological study of castes supporting VHP will be quite an interesting phenomenon. Most of the backward caste people finding no place in established secular parties found ready acceptance in outfits like the VHP. And to be in VHP, one has to compete with others in displaying communalism. The communal rhetoric helped them doubly: it helped them rise in the esteem of upper caste Hindus and also ensure them quicker rise in political power hierarchy.

The BJP which earlier had narrow upper caste base found it extremely difficult to win few parliamentary seats. It felt the necessity to widen its base. Initially it opposed implementation of Mandal Commission in 1990. But soon it realised its political potential and began to woo the OBC's to its fold. For these OBCs it was not easier to rise to the higher ranks of the political hierarchy. They thus flocked to VHP, which was a militant Hindu organisation. The extreme communal rhetoric made them more acceptable to the Hindu nationalist organisation.

It is such extreme rhetoric, which ensured quick rise of OBC leaders like Kalyan Singh who rose to became chief minister of U.P., Uma Bharti, Sadhvi Rithambara, Acharya Dharmendra Acharya Giriraj Kishor, Pravin Togadia and others. Ramjanambhoomi became their peg to hang their political aspirations on. It was confrontationist politics all along for them. More extreme the rhetoric quicker the rise. The Shiv Sena too attracted those castes which were below Mahars in the caste hierarchy in Maharashtra. The Mahars already had acquired political clout due to struggles by Ambedkar but those below Mahars had no such clout. It is Shiv Sena looking for expanding its political base gave them political importance and attracted them.

The Muslim politics too underwent similar change. In pre-partition days Muslim politics was monopoly of upper class Muslims known as *ashraf.* Most of the *ashraf* from minority areas like U.P. and Bihar migrated to Pakistan leaving behind low caste and poor Muslims known as *ajlaf.* Most of these Muslims were artisans and belonged to lower professions.

It is these Muslims who began to acquire economic clout in post-independence India. They began to rise in class hierarchy and upper class status and began to aspire, like OBCs among Hindus, for more political power and this drove a section of them to religious and fundamentalist rhetoric. The confrontationist postures some of them acquired during Shah Banu movement and Babri Masjid issue also has to be seen in this light. This confrontationist postures from both sides led to sharpening of communal consciousness and eruption of communal violence became more intense and widespread during eighties and early nineties.

The Indian society will continue to experience such violent caste and communal eruptions as long as it does not find political and economic equilibrium in terms of castes and communities. The rise of OBCs on one hand, and impact of globalisation on Indian economy on the other, will continue to cause occasional eruption of violence in Indian society for quite some time. Caste and communal polarisation will be with us as long as we are not able to create more egalitarian society.

Religion and Communalism

This is an ongoing debate among the scholars whether religion is the main cause of communalism. Often many scholars maintain that main 'culprit' is religion and some even go to the extent of saying that if there is no religion there will be no communalism. Of course it is quite hypothetical formulation.

Human beings cannot live without religion or some kind of ideology which gives human life a meaning and direction and whatever the nature of ideology or thought or value system it creates its own 'other'. And some form of struggle starts between followers of one or the other ideology.

First, we would like to define what is religion? Do different religion clash with each other? Is the clash between religions or between human communities and why? These are important questions, which need to be answered for this debate to be meaningful.

Religion can be defined as a system of beliefs and values with associated rituals to give these beliefs and values a concrete form. When these beliefs and values are held in common and rituals are performed in congregation it gives rise to a sense of commonality and a religious community comes into existence. This community is also product of a pre-existing social structure and this social structure deeply influences the religious community and its practices. No religious community can totally transcend this pre-existing social structure.

A religious community induces a sense of belonging in its members what we call identity in modern political discourse. This identity, for its members, in course of time, becomes more important than the beliefs and values. And it is this sense of identity, which creates problems rather than religion *per se.* It is important to keep this in mind in the whole debate. It is equally important to note that a community exists in this world and hence represents worldly (or secular?) interests of its members. These worldly interests become as important, if not more, as religious beliefs, rituals and values.

One more thing we need to state in this debate. A religion must be understood on different levels – ritual, social and cultural and on level of values. There are often marked differences on ritual and partially on social and cultural levels between religions but much commonality on the level of values. When many reformers and those advocating inter-religious dialogue assert commonality, it is on this level of values. Thus all religions teach to be truthful, compassionate, honest etc. It is this commonality of values, which is often asserted to promote communal harmony.

But, as pointed out above, there are marked differences between religions in terms of rituals and cultural practices. Those who wish to promote their agenda of creating conflict between communities they assert these ritual, social and cultural differences. Over assertion on these differences often lead to social or political confrontation.

Now the main question of this article: Is religion main cause of communalism has to be seen in the light of above discussion. Firstly, it is important to note that we often refer to communal conflict, and not to 'religious conflict'. There is obvious difference between the two. The conflict is between two communities and not between two religions. Then the question arises: Is there difference between the two? Yes there is. The religious conflict would mean conflict between theologies and rituals and conflict between two communities indicate conflict between worldly interests of two communities.

However, many people use these words religious and communal quite loosely as if there is no difference between the two and confusion arises. Strictly speaking they are not interchangeable. There is problem with our social discourse. In fact today the media uses communalism, religious fanaticism and fundamentalism as if they are one and the same. A rigorous social scientist would always take care to make proper distinction.

Of course one can find something in common between religious fundamentalism, fanaticism and communalism. The feeling of hostility towards the other is the common link between them. However, hostility can also be passive or active. Passive hostility, though not desirable, does not express itself violently. However, active hostility is often violent. Active hostility needs external push and this external push often comes from political and not religious motives.

In fact there is no direct relationship between religion and communalism, if we understand religion in its proper sense and not use it very loosely. Even a firm believer in religion or an orthodox believer may not necessarily be communal. And even one who does not care for his/her religion or might not have ever practised it may be communal. Many of our orthodox leaders in freedom struggle were quite supportive of secular democratic India and many otherwise liberal modernistic leaders tended to be communal or separatist. One can cite examples of Mahatma Gandhi and Savarkar on one hand, and, of Maulana Azad and Jinnah, on the other.

Whereas Gandhiji and Maulana Azad were orthodox believers in their respective religions yet both were strongly supportive of secular democratic India and both fought communalism with great vigour. Savarkar and Jinnah, on the other hand, were quite modern and liberal in matters of religion and yet both believed in Hindus and Muslims being separate nations. It is also interesting to note that the Deobandi Ulama, quite orthodox believers in Islam, opposed two-nation theory and firmly stood by the concept of composite nationalism.

These examples clearly show that there is no direct relationship between religion and communalism or religion and political separatism. It would thus not be wrong to say that fundamental cause of communalism is not religion but political. How? And what is then relationship between religion and communalism, if any?

As pointed out above, communalism is something related to religious community, not to religion itself. A religious community or its members have their own worldly interests and politics is based on these worldly interests. Hinduism and Islam had survived in India for thousand years peacefully. There were no serious problems, no inter-religious clashes or no communal riots. But we see that in modern India, i.e., from nineteenth century onwards there were serious clashes between the two communities. What went wrong? While in medieval India there was no political or economic competition between the two communities, in nineteenth century there was both political and economic competition between the elite of two communities. The medieval politics was feudal and non-competitive. Power was wielded through sword, not through ballot. In modern society, on the other hand, power was wielded through ballot.

It was this competition for power between the elite of two communities, which created communal consciousness among some members of both the communities. As pointed out above, religion creates a sense of belonging and sense of identity and it is this sense of identity, which is appealed to by the politicians for gathering their political support. The politicians cleverly mix up political discourse with religious discourse to mobilise support of their fellow religionists. Thus, the question of Ramjanambhoomi temple, basically a religious issue, was cleverly exploited by the BJP politicians to gather Hindu votes. Also, recently Narendra Modi, with the active support of top BJP leaders, provoked communal violence, mixing religious discourse with political one and won the Gujarat elections with overwhelming majority.

Thus, from this it can be easily seen that it is politics which uses religion than religion using the politics. Thus we can argue that in a democracy, politicians exploit religious identity for political power. They, by clever mix of religious beliefs and worldly interests, win the hearts and minds of people. Here it is important to note that these politicians who evolve this clever but highly explosive mix of religion and political power, do not represent interests of entire community but only its elite. The masses who are really religious are left high and dry.

Some liberals and atheists believe that the antidote of communal politics is anti-religious political discourse. This is in correct approach. One can be atheist, if atheism appeals to him/her but the real antidote of communalism is not anti-religious discourse. It will only strengthen communalists. One can hardly disregard religious feelings of millions of people in the society.

There are two alternatives for fighting communal politics. One alternative is to evolve carefully a secular discourse around real developmental issues and mobilise people around these secular issues. The other alternative is to use religious discourse in a creative manner making religion an option for the poor rather than for the powerful elite. Every religion has certain traditions, which can be used for empowering the poor. The vested interests exploit certain problematic traditions for their own interests. Why can't then those traditions, which empower people be used for pro-poor and pro-people politics?

Of course there is no cut and dried solution but with creativity and imagination either of the alternatives can be used for countering communal and separatist politics. Our social reality is very complex so our response also has to be as complex. Religion is not only part of problem it can also be part of solution, if handled imaginatively. As far as our society is concerned religion has not outlived its utility. Of course I do not maintain that religion is the only response but it could certainly be one of the responses.

3

Muslim Women, Police and Society

Muslim Women and Modern Society

The question of women's rights in general and those of Muslim women's in particular have remained at top of agenda in developing countries. Muslim women continue to face many problems in not only Muslim-majority countries but also in democratic secular countries like India and even in western countries where Muslim personal law cannot be practised. Their Islamic rights are also denied to them in the name of shari'ah law which is supposedly divine.

One reason for this is ignorance of Islam in general, and Qur'anic pronouncements in respect of women, in particular. There are two extremes among Muslim women: one, who accept Shari'ah pronouncements in respect of women totally and uncritically being totally unaware of circumstances in which the Muslim jurists made those pronouncements. Most of these women are either illiterate or educated in traditional Islamic sciences. Second category is of those women who are totally indifferent to religion and consider religion an impediment in realising women's rights. They even reject religion aggressively like Taslima Nasrin.

Both these extremes do not help as far as average women women are concerned who, ignorant or otherwise, take their religion seriously and also are struggling against traditional shari'ah pronouncements about women. These women are in overwhelming number and one has to help them realise their rights in the Muslim society. This can be done only through the medium of Islam and by re-examining the Shari'ah pronouncements in the light of Qur'an and its normative verses.

There is enough in the Qur'an favouring rights of women but these Qur'anic pronouncements have so far been ignored or interpreted in ways loaded against women. It is, therefore, necessary to critically examine the Shariah pronouncements in respect of women in the light of Qur'an as understood by modern Muslim women in a democratic set up. We should bear in mind that cultural mediation affects our understanding of scripture.

Thus, two things are important in this respect: reading the Qur'an from women's perspective and secondly from democratic cultural perspective since medieval cultural perspective has seriously affected our understanding of the Qur'an. It is heartening that some Muslim women are making serious attempt in this direction. Some of them are organising seminars and discussions and re-reading the Qur'an from women's perspective and are invoking the doctrine of Ijtihad which is dynamic principle of Islam. Ijtihad has been sanctioned by no less a person than the Prophet (PBUH) himself. Thus Ijtihad is integral part of Islam and has played a very important role in the entire history of Islam. The corpus of Shari'ah laws would not exist but for Ijtihad. It is unfortunate that after 11th century A.D. the 'ulama began to frown upon Ijtihad for various reasons.

I have before me a compilation called *For Ourselves-Women Reading the Qur'an*. This is an important compilation by Women Living Under Muslim Laws. This is a serious attempt by believing Muslim women from various Muslim and non-Muslim countries to re-read the Qur'an and re-interpret it. It is also important to note that there are different translators of the Qur'an and translation, howsoever honest and liberal, does tend to be interpretation and translator's ideological dispensation sneaks in. For example, a presenter in the seminar points out, "Among translators there is a range from ultra-conservative to ultra-liberal, and Abdullah Yusuf Ali is a liberal translator." There are translators whose translations almost indicate as if women are secondary to men. The word qawwam in the verse 4:34 has been translated in number of ways as ruler, as manager, as protector, supporter, in charge etc. you find 30 different translations.

In this key verse men have been described as *qawwamun* by the Qur'an and conservative translators translate as "men are rulers over women" and prove the superiority of men over women. However, liberal translators do not accept this translation and translate it as 'in-charge', or 'protectors' or 'managers' and so on. But even this carries a sense of superiority and others have translated it as those who run around to earn and nothing more. This reduces the degree of superiority and also they add that being *qawwam* is a function, not any biological superiority or inferiority and a woman can also be *qawwam*, if she earns and many women earn today in modern society and hence she also becomes *qawwam*.

Thus the Qur'anic text *per se* cannot be decisive but how it is understood by the jurist or theologian, is equally important and as pointed out before, cultural mediation, plays an important role. The Qur'anic text cannot be understood in the same way today as it was understood centuries ago in feudal cultural ethos. Thus one great impediment in bringing about change even today is absence of democratic ethos in Muslim world. The women still continue to play subordinate role in these countries as in authoritarian societies the jurists and theologians too tend to be authoritarian and totally lack democratic perspective.

Thus, a great struggle is going on in the Muslim countries for rights of women. More and more women are getting educated and becoming aware of their rights, Islamic or otherwise, and demanding changes in law. Something will definitely emerge from this great churning. Women scholars like Fatima Merssini from Morocco, having both Islamic and modern secular education have also shown the way. She has pointed out in her work *The Veil and The Male Elite* how to understand Qur'an and Hadith literature. She has critically examined the Hadith literature which is one of the main sources of Shari'ah formulations.

It is of course, not easy to challenge traditional sources of Islamic jurisprudence. It would require not only great Islamic scholarship but also sustained efforts in that direction. After all we have inherited a rich corpus of laws which have been integral part of Islamic practices for centuries. They carry weight of great learned 'ulama behind them. It is so difficult to disregard this juristic heritage.

But one need not despair. Much greater changes have taken place in the world in last two centuries. Until yesterday it was unthinkable that a Muslim woman can step out of four walls of her house and be active earning member of the family. But today it is an accepted practice even in countries like Saudi Arabia though with lot of restrictions. In other Muslim countries she can move freely, go out and earn and also hold important public positions. When Benazir Bhutto took over as Prime Minister of Pakistan many conservative 'ulama objected quoting a hadith that if a woman becomes head of the state it would be a disaster for the country. Fatima Merssini effectively demolishes authenticity of this hadith in her scholarly work and the Muslim world also ultimately accepted women premiers in Pakistan and Bangladesh. In Bangladesh two women have been alternating as Prime Minister for last several years.

Despite the fact that there have been women Prime Ministers in Bangladesh and Pakistan it does not mean that women in these two countries are not suffering. Quite to the contrary, the Pakistani and Bangladeshi societies are very complex in structure and Muslim women are suffering a great deal. In North West Frontier Province tribal customs and traditions are going very strong and honour killings are quite common. Women enjoy very inferior status in tribal areas. In Sindh too, there are practices like *karo kari* (local Sindhi term for honour killing) and marriage with the Qur'an. The later practice is meant to prevent women from marrying outside family and thus keep the land within the family itself since a Muslim woman can inherit land also as per Islamic law of inheritance.

The mechanical interpretation of *hudud laws* (punishments for crimes like murder, theft and rape or adultery etc.) in respect of adultery and rape normally goes against women especially when she becomes pregnant or she goes to lodge complaint against man who raped her. This is taken as self-confession of illegitimate sexual intercourse and is arrested and jailed or even sentenced to death by stoning as it was the case of Amina Lawal in Nigeria.

The *hudud* laws also need to be properly interpreted in the light of the Qur'anic pronouncements and translators like Maulana Muhammad Ali, Abdullah Yusuf Ali, Muhammad Asad and others have tried to do that. Stoning to death is certainly not a Qur'anic punishment as there is no such verse in the Qur'an but is based on hadith literature and it is necessary to critically examine the entire hadith literature. Even Imam Bukhari whose collection of hadith is considered most authentic had rejected thousands of ahadith while collecting them. Some of the ahadith that he accepted as authentic also are problematic and should be re-examined; in the light of the Qur'an.

We have to re-codify the Shari`ah laws pertaining to women on the basis of the liberal, modern interpretation of the Qur`an and some ahadith which are in conformity with the Qura`nic spirit. Such an approach, it is hoped, will be an instrument of struggle for women's rights for believing Muslim women. This requires a great deal of research in authentic Islamic sources. This would need great Islamic scholarship on the part of Muslim women activists in various countries, especially Pakistan, Malaysia and Indonesia and some Arab countries like Egypt, Jordan etc. They may have to face opposition from conservative 'Ulama but there is no other way.

I think this is the only way in the given situation. Rejecting religion altogether is not the way out nor total submission to what exists. A new way will have to be carved out by women themselves.

Indian Muslim, Identity and Modernity

Both identity and modernity are important parts of socio-political discourse today and more so in case of Muslims. Muslims, needless to say, are considered much more concerned about religion and religious identity and supposed to be rejecting modernity. It is assumed that they prefer madrasa education to modern secular education and refuse to accept any change in their personal law. These are considered as indicators of rejection of modernity and pre-occupation with religious identity.

What is the truth? In fact social questions are quite complex and cannot be reduced to black and white ignoring grey areas in between. Another important thing is that we cannot subject the Indian Muslim community of more than 130 million to uniformity and homogeneity. Indian Muslims are immensely diverse not only in terms of sects, languages and cultures but also in terms of classes and socio-political attitudes. There is hardly any issue about which there is complete consensus in the entire community, not even issues like change in Muslim personal law. It is really dangerous to apply stereotypes on such immensely diverse community.

It would also be equally wrong to think, as we often do, that all non-Muslims in India have accepted modernity and all that goes with it and that only Muslims resist it. Modernity, in such discourses, is never defined properly and is used in rather highly generalised sense. Some scholars have sub-divided modernity into 'hard modernity' and 'soft modernity'.

What is meant by 'hard modernity'? It is science and technology and in this sense all Indians, including Muslims have accepted modernity. No one rejects benefits of modern science and technology any more. If there was any resistance to it, it was in nineteenth century. In nineteenth century there were debates whether sun goes round the earth or vice versa. Hardly anyone debates this, not even semi-literate mullahs and pesh-imams. And no one ever rejected benefits of modern technology.

Soft modernity implies philosophical issues and critical examination of traditional beliefs. Here one can say there are significantly differing attitudes among Muslims. Soft modernity also includes secular education and acceptance of secularism. It is true there is comparatively more resistance to soft modernity among Muslims in general and Indian Muslims, in particular.

Secularism is integral part of soft modernity and it is also important to note that secularism implies discourse of rights whereas religious discourse is discourse of duties. All authoritarian societies adopt discourse of duties rather than that of rights. During emergency in our country from 1975-1977 concept of duties was added to our Constitution. Indian Constitution otherwise always talked of rights. Religious authorities also always talk of duties and never of rights. Religious authorities never concede rights to their followers. Their duty is only to obey the authority or traditional beliefs.

Secular discourse, on the other hand, is entirely discourse of rights. A modern thinker asserts, not only political rights but also right to examine traditional beliefs critically. But this right can be availed of only when there is widespread high standard education. Muslims, for various reasons, chief among them being poverty, lack widespread high degree of secular education and hence there is general resistance to discourse of rights, including right to critical examination of traditional beliefs.

But it should also be admitted that education is one factor among many. Socio-political interests also play an important role. Thus, both among Muslims and Hindus we find some highly educated ones aggressively promoting traditional beliefs and vehemently opposing any attempt to critically examine them. The members of VHP and Bajrang Dal and even those of BJP advocate old beliefs and traditions and even imply violence against those asserting their secular rights.

Similarly among Muslims organisations like SIMI adopt violence against those who promote rational thinking and Muslim Personal Law Board only promoting concept of duties among Muslims and rejecting their right to critically examine certain age-old traditions followed by Muslims. They often invoke the concept of divine immutability to oppose any change. The other reason is fear of aggressive communal campaign from a section of majority community.

Whatever the reasons, women have to pay heavy price for rejection of soft modernity by men of the community. Women are entirely subject to the discourse of duty. The discourse of duty is, it can be said, doubly applicable to women in all the communities in India. Women are subject to this discourse both in the name of religion as well as in the name of age-old customs and traditions.

Women are much more unequal as they are denied benefits of soft modernity. Even among Hindus very few women are truly 'liberated' in this sense. Among Muslims women are even more unequal. The aggression shown by Muslim leadership during the Shah Bano movement was good example of this. Though such aggressive movement is no longer possible the situation of women has not improved much. They suffer from many disabilities more due to customs and traditions than religion. Islam is far more just to them than the traditions. But in traditional societies religion itself is subject to customs and tradition. Often it becomes important to liberate religion from traditions.

In modern Indian society question of religious identity has become far more important. A religiously plural country like India throws up complex problems in a democratic set up. A secular democratic society throws up the question of rights for different religious communities and also promotes competition for political power and economic resources. The elite of the communities mobilises masses by using religious identities and hence religious identities becomes quite important.

Communal problems came into existence in modern society, as concept of rights because more important than that of duty. Every community asserts its religious identity to put pressure on the system to wrest greater share in power. Our experiences in post-independence period shows that minority community finds it difficult to match aggressive mobilisation by majority community. Though before independence too, Nehruvian theory of communalism emphasised that majority communalism could be more dangerous but in post-independence period majority communalism did prove to be much more aggressive than before independence.

Thus, for minority community religious identity becomes even more important. It becomes a mental refuge. Communal solidarity is seen as effective compensation for external pressure. And this communal solidarity puts its own demands on individual liberties. Individuals have to fall in line under the weight of communal pressure and individual rights are compromised.

It is an irony of the situation that on one hand the majority communal discourse puts Muslims under pressure for uniform civil code and makes it part of political agenda and on the other hand, creates conditions making it increasingly difficult for the community to accept change and 'soft modernity'. In fact the Sangh Parivar itself rejects soft modernity and opposes secular discourse of rights and loves concept of duties. It attacks those who emphasise individualism and individual rights.

Here it should also be noted that it is wrong to depict one's religious community as more liberal and progressive and another community as more regressive and backward. It all depends on socio-political conditions particularly in multi-religious societies. If Muslims are less under majority communal pressure and find political atmosphere more congenial for their economic progress they will be more prone in a democratic society like India to accept change and soft modernity.

It can be demonstrated from Kerala experience of the Muslim community. The Kerala Muslims, living under comparative sense of security are ahead of other Indian Muslims in accepting modern secular education, family planning and social change. The rate of family planning among Kerala Muslims is higher than that of Hindu women in U.P. Also, the rate of literacy among them is far higher than their counterparts in other parts of India.

Also, more educated Muslims more easily opt for soft modernism than less educated and less secure Muslims. Some sects like the Bohras and Khojas accept change more easily than other sects. These sects are economically and educationally better off though not all Bohras and Khojas. There is poverty and illiteracy among them too. Thus, there are regional, sectarian and economic factors influencing Muslim behaviour. Religion is invoked by these sections to accept or reject change as legitimising factor.

Thus it will be seen that a sense of physical security and economic status can be far more influential than is generally recognised. However, communal discourse tries to blame it only on religion and that itself is communal approach to the complex problem of change and progress. The rationalists too err in this matter and tend to blame religion rather than these material factors for lack of acceptability of change.

Roots of Communal Violence

Communal violence has been increasingly taking place in India for last several decades. There has hardly been any respite throughout period of independence. To understand the phenomenon of communal violence and its roots in our society is highly necessary to find solution if any. Many rationalists reduce it to religion and for them religion is the main culprit. Such reductionism would not help. It is not only oversimplifying an issue it also means ignoring the complexity of a social phenomenon.

Religion, at best, is one factor, among many. Religion, it should also be noted, is an instrumental rather than fundamental cause. Religion is used as a powerful instrument to achieve political, economic and social purposes for its powerful mobilizatory power. Religion has powerful emotional appeal and hence it is easy to exploit clouding real interests. What appears to be clash of religions is, really clash of interests.

Even partition was not result of clash between Hinduism and Islam as popularly thought. Jinnah was quite indifferent to religion and religious practices. He was a constitutionalist and was fighting for constitutional arrangements for the Muslim power elite. Had it been resolved satisfactorily our country would not have been partitioned. The theory invoked by communal forces that since Muslims were not loyal to the country they saw it partitioned, can hold no water.

Jinnah represented interests not of all Indian Muslims but only of elite Muslims. He had no concern for low class, low caste Muslims and overwhelming majority of Indian Muslims belonged to, and belong even today, to this category. The interests of poor Muslims left Jinnah quite cold. When the noted poet Dr. Iqbal wrote to Jinnah about acute poverty among the Muslims of Punjab and to do something about it to make Muslim League popular among them, Jinnah quietly dropped him from presidentship of the Punjab Muslim League. Muslim League was party of Muslim power elite.

In understanding the roots of communalism one must understand that communalism neither represents religion nor patriotism, it represents interests. Secondly, it should also be understood that no religious community is homogenous as communalists make it out to be; every religious community is divided along several lies – caste, class, culture and language. These are the fault lies of any religious communities. Muslim

League, as pointed out above, did not represent the entire Muslim community nor Hindu communalists represent interests of all Hindus. The Hindu community is irreconcilably divided along caste lies apart from class and linguistic-cultural lines.

In any case Hindus are much more stratified (though Muslims too are) than any other community in India and no single formation like the Sangh Parivar or Muslim League (in pre-partition days) can represent entire community. However, since who knows this better than communal forces that they employ religious rhetoric much more aggressively to compensate for lack of political unity in the community.

The Muslim League tried to arouse religious passions to fanatical pitch as Muslims in pre-partition days were far from united. The low caste and lower class Muslims as well as Muslims from regions like North West Province and South (particularly Tamil and Malayalam speaking Muslims) were opposed or indifferent to Muslim League and supported Indian National Congress or even left parties. The Muslim League used aggressive religious rhetoric precisely to make up for this lack of unity.

The Sangh Parivar transcended even pre-partition Muslim League in unabashedly exploiting Hindu religious rhetoric to promote its own political interests and to make up for total lack of unity among the Hindus. Since the caste consciousness is very deep among the Hindus and now every caste is pressing for its political interests, the task of leaders of the Sangh Parivar became even more challenging any time. And hence they are compelled to use much more aggressive rhetoric and also much more organised violence against the other community to try to forge unity among Hindus fragmented along so many lines.

Greater the fragmentation higher the tendency to attack other community to create illusion of unity. High pitched rhetoric and maximum degree of communal violence reaching proportions of carnage help 'unite' disparate groups of Hindus though this 'unity' itself is extremely fragile and temporary.

It is also important to note that the real carriers of communal virus are those belonging to educated middle classes. And most of these middle class people happen to be not so enthusiastic about religion and religious orthodoxy. The carriers of Muslim communalism were educated Muslim middle classes of colonial India. These middle classes become, through their education, more conscious of their caste and communal identities and then they articulate these identities in caste and communal idiom. Their whole political discourse veers round caste and communal issues.

It is in this sense that communalism is product of modern British colonial period, and not of medieval period as made out by the communal forces. It is not only the British colonialists who divided Indians to rule over them, the Indian elite too was equally divisive in its own interests. It got easily divided, as basically its interests were divisive.

The Sangh Parivar (The Hindu Mahasabha in the colonial period) created illusion of patriotism by employing rhetoric of '*Bharat Mata*', '*Akhand Bharat*' and so on but it was no less divisive of the country as Muslim League politics itself. Both Savarkar as well as Jinnah employed similar communal discourse and both talked of Hindu nationalism and Muslim nationalism. Savarkar also maintained that Hindus and Muslims are two separate nations as Jinnah did. Only difference is that majority communalism leads to hidden inner division and minority communalism to visible external division. But minority communalism also does not lead to external visible division in all cases; it can lead to such division only if it is concentrated in some areas; but not if it is dispersed.

In independent India majority communalism slowly and gradually became much more aggressive and ultimately almost subdued the minority communalism. Jawaharlal Nehru maintained even during pre-partition period (when minority communalism was comparatively more aggressive) that majority communalism is aggressive and reactionary and minority communalism is defensive and borne out of feeling of insecurity.

The majority communalism showed its aggressiveness in post-independence India first in Jabalpur riots of 1962. Nehru never thought in post-independence India such aggressive communal violence can break out. He was greatly shocked. However, Nehru and Maulana Azad were great pillars of secularism and did everything to protect and even promote it.

The subsequent generation of Congresspersons hardly had such commitment to secular ideology and secular politics. They were more interested in power than ideology. The gradual de-ideologisation of politics further strengthened politics of communalism. The de-ideologised 'pragmatic approach' then began to deteriorate into opportunism and even unabashed use of caste and communal rhetoric by the Congress 'secular' leaders to capture power.

What mattered now was to win elections rather than promote politics of secular and socialist ideology though the rhetoric of socialism and secularism continued. Nehru's socialist-secular discourse now became an empty rhetoric. Indira Gandhi continued this discourse but for a short while. For her too power superseded ideology in less than a decade. And, she was much more of a secularist than other leaders of the Congress.

This weakening of secular commitment injected much greater degree of dose of opportunism, if not outright communalism, in Indian politics. The decade of eighties proved to be much dangerous from this point of view. The weakened secular commitment of the Congress and much more aggressive communal rhetoric of the Sangh Parivar brought about greatest spurt if communal violence in the decade of eighties. The Sangh Parivar raised new issues and began to seriously question the very concept of Nehruvian secularism as 'psuedo-secularism' based on 'appeasement' of minorities. Such overtly communal discourse was never employed before as part of secular political discourse.

The result was not any serious debate from the Congress leaders but a feeling began to take roots in the Congress circles that we are getting alienated from majority community in order to court minority votes. Though such a stance was never officially adopted by the Congress, it was never seriously challenged either. The Congress commitment to secularism became so weak during the eighties that it even surrendered before minority leaders to overturn the Supreme Court judgement in the Shah Bano maintenance case by enacting another law for maintenance for Muslim women. Rajiv Gandhi then went to the extent of laying foundation stone for Ramjanmabhoomi Masjid and got completely alienated from the minority community and lost subsequent elections.

Had the Congress maintained its commitment to secularism like Nehru and Azad communalism would not have been emboldened to such an extent and India would not have seen eruption of communal carnage in Gujarat. The Lohite socialists also wavered in their commitment to socialism often making compromises with the Sangh Parivar. It is only the Communists who remained steadfast in their commitment to both socialism and secularism.

Politics, Values and Power

Our politics today is purely power-oriented and values are thrown aside as if values are shell and power the core. Politics without values become monstrosity as Gujrat has proved. Gandhiji, in early twenties, had felt this danger and had then written that politics without religion (read values) is like breathing without nose. Gandhiji later modified the word religion as he realised its use could be misunderstood. He was quite clear that state should remain secular.

Thus in 1942 he clarified when he said "Religion is a personal matter which should have no place in politics." He even went further and told a missionary: "If I were a dictator, religion and State would be separate. I swear by my religion. I will die for it. But it is my personal affair. The State has nothing do with it."

However, our politicians have completely reversed this approach. They mix religion with politics with vengeance and throw away values in the air. Religion without values like justice, equality, compassion, love, non-violence, truth and sensitivity to others suffering is mere dead ritual and if such empty rituals, and not values, are associated with religion, which our politicians do, it can be very deadly. This is what we have been witnessing since independence.

Not that power is not important in politics; it is. But the question is power is a means to achieve certain goal. Power should to be a goal but a means to an end. But for our present day politician's power has become the goal and outright foul or unethical means are employed to achieve this goal. And all this is done quite unabashedly. Also, the struggle for power has become quite ruthless.

Such struggle existed in medieval ages too as power has terrible attraction for some people. It often leads to patricide or fratricide too. But then we do not approve of medieval methods of seizing power. Democracy is important both for means employed and goals to be achieved. But it appears our medieval mindset has hardly changed and our methods of achieving power have even worsened.

I do not want to idealise the freedom fighters. They were also human beings and had their own weaknesses and had also faltered at times but at least those who were at the helm of affairs and were leading the fight for freedom made great sacrifices and avoided wrong means and did care for values. They made mistakes but did not play foul. They kept certain ideals before them and secular democracy was one among them. Also, Gandhiji felt strongly and practised non-violence so much so that when in 1922 some policemen were burnt in Chorichora he withdrew the movement. Although the movement was at its height he did not compromise on the doctrine of non-violence. For Gandhiji even movement was not an end, only means to achieve certain ideals.

Gandhiji knew if violence is not controlled at this stage whole freedom movement will become violent and the ideal of non-violence will be seriously injured. Thus Gandhiji sacrificed the momentum of the movement for the sake of values he stood for.

Today the politicians do not mind inciting communal violence if it helps them in achieving power. Our freedom leaders had even believed that there will be no communal violence in post-independence India and when the Jabalpur riot took place in 1962 it shook Jawaharlal Nehru. The Congress swore by secularism and never compromised with it theoretically but never practiced it satisfactorily. Most of the Congressmen have had communal attitude. When Jawaharlal Nehru sent Subhdra Joshi to Jabalpur in 1962 as his own emissary to M.P. Congressmen did not co-operate with her. The then Congress Government did hardly anything to stop the riots.

Apart from the fact that many Congressmen have communal attitude they do not act for fear of antagonising the 'majority community'. And this for fear of loosing power. Secular values are not important, power is. When the BJP began questioning the Nehruvian secularism as 'pseudo-secularism' and 'appeasement of minorities', there was hardly any hard-hitting reply from the Congressmen. They took totally defensive posture. Mr. Gadgil, a Congress leader from Maharashtra, even said that there is something wrong with the Congress secularism as it is alienating the majority from us. Though Shri. Gadgil's view did not prevail in the Congress Working Committee but the very fact that this question was raised was disturbing enough.

This attitude of the Congress is being reflected in Gujrat again. The Congress leaders, for fear of antagonising the majority community failed to take strong stand against communal violence in Gujarat. They were even afraid of speaking out. When the *Dargah* (mausoleum) of Vali Gujarati was bull-dosed and levelled and replaced with road the Congress Mayor of Ahmedabad refused to intervene.

And when Mrs. Sonia Gandhi wanted to visit the widow of Ahsan Jafri, the former Congress member of Parliament from Ahmedabad who was brutally killed and burnt in the communal carnage, she was advised by the Gujarat Congressmen not to do so as it would alienate the majority community and the Congress would loose in the forthcoming election. The Congress in Gujarat is very much shy of fighting the BJP for fear of loosing the elections. Thus, ultimately power is more important than ideology.

The Gujarat Congress is planning not to campaign in the forthcoming election on the issue of communal carnage for fear of alienating the majority community. It plans to focus only on developmental issues and failure of the BJP to govern. It is shocking to say the least. Such a carnage has shamed India in the comity of nations and the Congress strategists do not want to take it up even as an election issue.

Thus, it will be seen that democracy is being used not for transparent governance but as a means for coming to power by using religious sentiments. The Sangh Parivar is doing it most unabashedly. It is quite ironical that on one hand it talks of moral conduct and lays emphasis on Hindu religion for character building, particularly the RSS, but it kills thousands of persons belonging to minority, on the other hand, without batting an eyelid. The Sangh Parivar has been guilty of inciting raw passions of Hindus throughout the period of independence but it crossed all limits in butchering them in Gujarat in most cruel ways. It incited most brutal violence in the name of Hindu nationalism. But all available evidence shows that it did so only to grab power by monopolising the Hindu votes.

The communalists, it must be remembered, use religion and culture most cynically and ruthlessly for seizing power in democracy. If we go by religious values, not rhetoric, they are most anti-religious people. Only a communalist will use religion for inciting violence. The communalists trample upon all religious and human values and instrumentalise it for power politics.

A democracy can work successfully only if it remains secular and keeps off all religious controversies. We declared India to be a secular democracy immediately after we became free from the British rule but even today are unable to practice modicum of secularism. In more than fifty years we should have consolidated secularism and should have freed our politics of all traces of religious controversies and communal trappings. But fact is that our secularism today after fifty-three years of our independence is much weaker than it was in early fifties. In fact it was never so weak as it is today.

Our leaders never tried to disseminate secular values, much less practice secular politics. Power, at an cost, was the obsession of these leaders. They had no spirit of true nationalism, not to talk of humanism. Our whole political discourse is unsecular and we, as a people of India, have not risen above sectarian controversies. While describing ourselves as a modern secular nation, we unhesitatingly employ communal discourse in our politics. The extent and intensity of communal discourse has been continuously on increase.

The gap between secular democracy and communal politics is ever widening and we are heading for great disaster, if we continue to regress into past with such consistency. Modern secular politics should have made us look to the future and our political discourse ought to have been future-oriented it has become, particularly since mid-eighties, consistently past-oriented.

If our secular democracy has to survive, all efforts should be made to eradicate communalism from political arena. To ensure minority rights, is not appeasement of minorities, it is test of real democracy. Minority rights are part of human rights and no democracy is worth its worth without ensuring minority rights and human rights. Unfortunately the Sangh Parivar dubbed minority rights as 'appeasement of minorities' and communalised the whole political discourse since mid eighties to exploit sentiments of majority community.

All secular parties, particularly the Congress, should do every thing possible to cleanse our political system of communalism and communal discourse and prepare the Indian masses for value-oriented secular democratic politics. Political opportunism of some 'secular parties' has already considerably weakened our democratic fabric. Let us not tear it apart any further.

Religion in Secular Society

Role of religion is quite controversial in modern society and much so in a secular society. During the modern period rationalism ruled and religion came to be rejected by rationalists as superstitious and irrational. Rationalists not only rejected it but even ridiculed it. Communists, on the other hand, described it as opium of the people taking a sentence from a powerful paragraph from Marx's essay out of context. Marx had much better understanding of religion than many Marxists.

Secularists were also rationalists and maintained that religion should not have any role in modern society and at best it should be strictly a private matter to be practised at home. It should not have any role outside home or any private premises. This attitude, whatever its relevance in our culture, was an imitation from the western liberal society where individual, and not a community, was at centre stage.

In post-modern society, however, religion has been once again rehabilitated in the name of pluralism. A post-modern society lays emphasis on pluralism, and not mere rationalism. Religion can co-exist with other ideologies in a pluralist society. Religion, in post-modern society, is not to be rejected, but accommodated.

In modern society science was supposed to answer all questions of the origin of universe and other related questions. In post-modern society it is assumed that science cannot answer all questions, especially questions related to meaning and direction of life.

Also, in our culture religion has been its integral part. Even western society, which is highly developed and has quite secular culture, is rediscovering religion in one or the other sense or at least has become much more tolerant of it today. We here think that entire western society follows secularism in one sense only. It is not so. Its meaning and practice differ from country to country.

In France though religion never disappeared, secularism is followed more strictly and ideologically than other European countries thanks to long-lasting impact of French Revolution. State is strictly a-religious and keeps strictly away from Catholic Christianity which is the majority religion there. Government educational institutions do not allow any religious practices or rituals to be performed. It is for this reason that there was great hue and cry in the media when a Muslim girl went to her class wearing scarf (termed *hijab* by the press). She was not allowed to enter into her class by her teachers.

In Germany, on the other hand, religion is taught and there is debate in certain circles whether it should be taught or not. Those living in East Germany particularly oppose religion being taught in schools. The German Government also deducts religious denominational tax and passes it over to different churches from which many NGOs get their funding. In Norway, government even maintains churches and provides them with funds for their upkeep. In England State still has a religion – Anglican Christianity and the king or queen is supposed to be head of the church. Of course now it is only in symbolic sense. But still Anglican Christianity is a state religion in the UK.

Thus, there is no uniform concept of secularism and its role in society. Our culture is much more closely associated with religion, religious practices and rituals. Also, unlike western society, public manifestation of religious practices like religious processions is part of our culture. Festivals like Durga Puja, Ganesh Chaturthi, Ram Navmi, Prophet's birthday procession and *taziyas* in Muharram are all celebrated publicly and often become occasions of communal trouble.

Even Nehruvian model of secularism is not averse to celebration of these festivals publicly provided they do not become nuisance. Nehru had strongly criticised a *havan* which, was being performed in Kanpur in early sixties but he never banned it as it was his personal view. He criticised it more for waste of thousands of kilo-litres of pure *ghee* which was being poured into the *havan fire* than anything else. Constitutionally also there is no restrictions to performance of religious rituals publicly as the Article 25 allows profession, practice and propagation of religion to all persons living in India, subject of course to social order and public health.

However, when it comes to state no religion can be prioritised by it in a secular society or a country. State should have no religion. Here there seems to be sort of contradiction, i.e., an intensely religious society and a state governing the society to be without religion. However, in a democratic society, it is not a serious or unresolvable contradiction.

In UK it is quite otherwise: the society is highly secular, people are indifferent to religion (now of course number of Indians and others from Asian and African countries who are intensely religious is increasing but still it is quite small compared to the English people who are quite secular and a-religious). But state still has a religion though of course in quite symbolic sense.

India is a pluralist democracy and it was pluralist even before it became democratic. Its ethos happens to be pluralistic and have been its strength for centuries. Our secularism thus carries more sense of pluralism than an atheistic political ideology. Secularism in the later sense cannot be acceptable to India and its socio-religious culture. Since its society is so religious it is all the more necessary for the state to remain quite secular in the sense that it should not prioritise any religion.

When the state so prioritises any religion in a highly religiously pluralistic society minorities are bound to suffer whether they are religious minorities or sectarian minorities within the fold of one religion. In Pakistan, the state is associated with Islam and different Islamic sects like Sunnis and Shiahs are at logger-heads. There is conflict between other Islamic sects also.

Indian state has been by and large secular but it is unfortunate that now under the Sangh Parivar, government is getting closer and closer to the Hindutva ideology, which prioritises Hindu religion over others. This is disturbing the fine balance which the Indian state has maintained so far.

A secular democracy is bound to have majority religion and minority religions and they can co-exist without any conflict if state remains either equi-distance from all religions or equally protective of all religions. State should not develop majoritarian ethos as far as governance is concerned. Unfortunately this majoritarian ethos is becoming stronger and stronger in last several years.

Once this majoritarian ethos grips the minds of those governing the country minorities cannot feel secure. Our Indian society was quite secular in the sense that it has had several religions co-existing in our country and it has developed the tradition of tolerance and respect for all religious traditions. The sufis and sants emphasised tolerance and developed a culture of religious tolerance in our society.

Baba Farid, Nanak, Kabir, Chishti, Eknath, Gyaneshwar and others are part of our religious heritage and they all promoted culture of tolerance and peace. They attacked hypocrisy and emphasised genuine religious and spiritual outlook. Religious conflict in our country is more of colonial origin. In medieval ages we see more religious tolerance than in the colonial and post-colonial society.

Thus one can say it is politicisation of religion which is real problem than religion *per se.* It is very important to understand this in order to promote communal harmony in our country. Some people begin to attack religion itself rather than its politicisation, which takes us nowhere. One must oppose instrumentalisation of religion for political end. Our country was divided not because of religion but on account of exploitation of religion for political purposes.

Even today the cause of Hindutva is not championed by Hindu religious leaders but by those Hindus who are far from religious in their conduct and are grossly misusing Hindu religion for Hindu votes. Persons like Narendra Modi, Chief Minister of Gujarat, even tried to polarise Hindus for getting their votes by permitting communal carnage or looking the other way when such carnage was taking place.

Thus, in a bewilderingly diverse country like India one has to meticulously shun religious politics. It can do immense harm than good to any religious community. Hindutvawadi politics does not benefit all Hindus nor Muslim communal politics has ever benefited all Muslims. The Pakistan project was meant for the upper class Muslim elite (then called *Shurufa*). It only brought communal disaster for the poor and lower caste Muslims (then refered to as *ajlaf*). They are paying price for it even today in India.

The Hindutvawadi politics does not benefit poor and low caste Hindus, particularly dalits and backwards. They are only used as instruments by upper caste Hindu elite for their own political power. Thus it is poor of all communities who ultimately become victims of communal politics. What is needed is secularisation of politics in India rather than the society. State needs to follow tenets of secularism, and civil society in India needs to cultivate the culture of tolerance and respect for religious order, which has been its historical heritage. Secular culture in Indian civil society should be equated with pluralist culture.

Police and Minorities

Recently few trainee police officers in UK were suspended for their racial remarks against Asians. The BBC had made a secret film on these trainees officers and they were passing racist remarks against Asians. It came as a shock to the authorities and immediate action was taken against the concerned officers. According to the newspaper reports four British police officers have been suspended following allegations of racism prompted by undercover reporting in a BBC documentary.

These officers three from Manchester in north-west England and one from North Wales, were suspended after police chiefs viewed the programme "The Secret Policeman". According to the documentary a police officer was dressed in a Ku Klux Klan mask at a training centre in north-west England. According to the undercover BBC reporter he also recorded some racist comments by some officers.

The Police department took action against these officers even though the BBC had not supplied them the copy of the programme. These accused were suspended immediately as they heard about it from other sources. A thorough inquiry will be conducted against these officers. The Home Secretary David Blunkett called on the forces "to take decisive action", a spokesperson of the Home Office said.

This was the biggest survey of the forces ever undertaken. Nearly 13000 officers were scanned for sexual and racist attitude among the police. The study led by Prof. Gus John, a key adviser to Home Secretary David Blunkett on race, found evidence that at virtually every stage of the prosecution process Asian and black people appeared to suffer discrimination.

The Britain is becoming a pluralistic society and the authorities are worried that police may not have right attitudes to handle law and order in the new pluralistic set up. A couple of years ago the Home Secretary had visited Mumbai along with few members of House of Lords to study how a city like Mumbai with its tremendous plurality is managed and how law and order is maintained. A few prominent citizens of Mumbai with experience with the police were invited and I was one among them, to find out how the police handled the situation.

The fact that such secret survey was done with the help of the BBC undercover reporter speaks volumes about the concern the British authorities have towards law and order problem in the growing multi-religious society in Britain. It is also interesting to note that the authorities took immediate action against the officers involved even without seeing the undercover BBC programme.

It is in sharp contrast with the behaviour of authorities towards those policemen who publicly display their anti-minority bias. No action has ever been taken by any erroneous police officer. Every communal riot has its own story of police behaviour towards minorities. The PAC in UP displays crude anti-Muslim sentiments and deliberately kills innocent Muslims and yet no action has ever been taken against these guilty policemen despite all available evidence. The classical case is that of PAC commandant Tripathi who ordered killing of 23 Muslim boys pulled out of their houses in Hashimpura in Meerut on 23rd May 1987 and their bodies thrown in the nearby canal after shooting them dead. Only two boys survived to tell the story.

These officers have not been brought to book until today, no case has been filed against them, let alone suspend them or remove them from service. In UK the guilty officers were suspended immediately just for passing racial remarks.

In 1970 riots in Jalgaon a police sub-inspector Kadam led the mob and set fire to the house of a Muslim widow in which her children were burnt alive. Hajra Begum whose children were burnt had to meet Prime Minister Indira Gandhi to get the concerned sub-inspector suspended. Madon Commission of Inquiry also passed severe remarks against the police behaviour during Bhivandi-Jalgaon riots. The police even tampered with the daily diaries and Madon Commission was very upset about it. It arrested Ibrahim Maddu and others falsely implicating them in 'conspiracy' to engineer riots without any iota of evidence against them.

No action was taken against any officer; on the contrary many of them were promoted and enjoyed high status. The strictures by Madon Commission also did not move the authorities to take any action. The story is no different as far as Mumbai riots of 1992-93 are concerned. The Srikrishna Commission too, like the Madon Commission, passed severe strictures against the then Additional Commissioner of Police Mr. Tyagi and 31 other officers and yet hardly any action was taken. After long agitation by some NGOs and filing of PIL in the Supreme Court Tyagi was nominally arrested and immediately released on bail. After the riots he was promoted as Commissioner of Police, Mumbai and he retired 'honourably' and nothing happened to him. He was accused of ordering killing of 9 bakery workers near Minara Masjid.

In Bhagalpur riots of 1989 a police officer dumped the bodies of several riot victims in a village well and then buried them in the field and began to cultivate cauliflower to hide his crime. Another officer was suspended in Bhagalpur City and had to be reinstated by Rajiv Gandhi, the then Prime Minister, as he was gheraoed by the policemen demanding his reinstatement. And Rajiv Gandhi obliged them.

What is happening in Gujarat need not be repeated here. A large section of the Gujarat police was part of the mob, burning, killing and lynching poor and helpless Muslims. It displayed open bias even in launching prosecution. It even refused to take down FIRs or even openly changed the FIRs and did not record the names of the culprits given by the victims.

And just see what happened to the accused for killing a Sikh in New York mistaking him for Muslim after the attack on New York trade towers on 9/11, 2001. He was sentenced to death though he was white male. And see the contrasting behaviour of the authorities in Gujarat after the Godhra incident? More than 1000 persons were done to death most brutally and yet not a single culprit has been brought to book. In the Best Bakery case in which 14 persons were burnt alive all the culprits were let off by the fast track court. It is only the Supreme Court, which came to the rescue of the victims.

There are several such stories of police bias against minorities, which I do not want to repeat here. It is quite clear from what is stated above that the Indian police is, in general, with some honourable exceptions at higher echelons, is strongly biased against minorities. So is the UK and USA police. But there is stark difference between how authorities behave in UK and USA and how they behave in India. The Home Ministry took immediate action against the guilty police officers only for passing a racial remark whereas in India the police men can get away even if they shoot a number of people belonging to minority community.

What is needed is to sensitise the police to communal and racist situations in a multi-racial and multi-religious society. India is bewilderingly diverse and a police officer should be thoroughly aware of this social situation. His thinking should be purged of all majoritarian ethos or a majoritarian arrogance. A qualitative democracy should ensure equal rights for all, whether belonging to majority or minority.

However, there is no such training, sensitising the police is imparted and authorities themselves display such prejudices and even election campaigns in India are based on caste and communal basis. The BJP openly indulged in anti-minority propaganda in its election campaigns. The policemen also listen to these speeches and acquire these prejudices.

At least to neutralise the police a thorough training is needed. But there is no such effort and the training module for the police does not include any such material. I have been conducting workshops on communal harmony for the police regularly and the police trainees display very raw prejudices during discussion. In one such workshop when I asked police constables what comes to your mind when I utter the word 'Muslim', one of the constables said 'criminal' and the other constable said 'violent person' and others clapped indicating support for the two constables.

If the policemen at lower levels display such crude prejudices how can they be expected to be impartial while handling a riot situation? It would be in the interest of our multi-religious and multi-cultural society to train policemen to appreciate diversity and respect it. Such training would ensure much better law and order in the society. We do have multi-religious and multi-caste society but we have still to develop a multi-religious cultural ethos. Such bloodshed would not have taken place in our country in post-independence era if we had developed such culture.

We are unfortunately still quite reluctant to develop such culture. Our politicians aggressively promote majoritarian ethos and thus put up comfortably with such police attitude. The whole culture has to change if we want India to become one of the leading democracies in the world.

The police has often been accused of having anti-minorities attitude in general and anti-Muslim attitude in particular. Various inquiry commissions like Madon Commission and Srikrishna Commission have also passed strictures against the police. Enough has been written on this by many scholars and others.

Fundamentalism and Terrorism

Fundamentalism and terrorism are widely used term in the media as well as academia. And, more often than not, they are loosely defined terms. Many people describe anything religious as fundamentalism and any act of killing as terrorism. There is great necessity to define these terms properly and prevent their use in loose sense. In fact the term fundamentalism is hardly applicable to Indian religions on one hand, and to Islam on the other. It is American media, which started using 'Islamic fundamentalism' when Islamic revolution was taking place in Iran in late seventies. We hardly see this term in the media or academia before that. Our media also then started using the term and soon it was being very widely used.

The term 'terrorism' too has its origin in American media after 9/11. We have had violence from across the border since nineties of the last century but never used 'terrorist violence' for it. We called it either extremism or militancy. But now call it 'cross border terrorism' after 9/11. Thus it will be seen that American rulers and American media set the term for us to be used.

I would, therefore, like to define these terms though not with academic rigour. We can only try to put some sense in these terms so that we do not confuse them with something else or something not intended. America devises terms to reflect its own interests and not to make any academic sense. We should resist temptation to use the terms loosely.

First, let us try to define fundamentalism. It should not certainly be confused with fundamentals of religion. Even in America this term was not used in that sense in early twenties of last century. In fact those who believed that every word of the Bible is literally divine word were called fundamentalist. One, it did not refer to fundamental teachings of Christianity and second, it was never used in derogatory sense. But now the term is used in derogatory sense and specially 'Islamic fundamentalism'.

As it is used in derogatory sense we must separate it from religion *per se.* Thus to follow Islam or Hinduism should not be described as 'fundamentalism'. Even to follow orthodox traditions of religion should not be dubbed as 'fundamentalism' tough one may not agree with orthodox practices. There are millions of people in every religious tradition who follow these orthodox traditions without being any nuisance to any one in the society. Their practices could be quite harmless.

Thus, one must distinguish between orthodoxy and fundamentalism. Fundamentalism in the sense in which it is being used in the media is, in fact, political misuse of religion in a narrow sectarian manner. In this sense there is not much difference between communalism and fundamentalism. Both the phenomena are based on political interests. But still there is subtle difference between the two. While communalism is all about political or economic interests of a particular community, fundamentalism is enforcement of sectarianism with all rigidity for political mobilisation of a community for the power-goals of its elite. Thus, while communalism is exploitation of sentiments of a religion based community for a secular goal (i.e., political power) fundamentalism is enforcing narrow sectarian practices for strengthening religious orthodoxy on one hand, and, achieving political power, on the other.

Thus, while BJP will be closer to communalism in this sense while the VHP-Bajrang Dal will be closer to fundamentalism. However, it must be said at the same time that the distinction is getting more and more blurred of late as VHP is setting the agenda of the BJP. Similarly the pre-partition Muslim League was closer to communalism and the Jamat-e-Islami was closer to fundamentalism.

Thus, communalism is more about secular interests (mainly political) of a religion based community. Fundamentalism, on the other hand, is enforcement of narrow sectarian religion by misusing political power and for political end, i.e., with a view to consolidate political power.

Now let us define terrorism. One must admit, while defining terrorism that it is very difficult to reach any consensus about it. Even the UNO failed to evolve one despite great deal of debates. It is often said, and rightly so, that ones terrorist is others freedom fighter. Thus those for Palestinians are freedom fighters, for Israelis they are 'terrorists' to be killed and eliminated. And in Kashmir those who are 'terrorists' for us are, for Pakistanis and even for some Kashmiris, are freedom fighters.

The word terrorism is being widely used by the media after 9/11. It was rarely used before. In Kashmir we describe those who use violence as terrorists and no more as extremists or militants, as pointed out before. Again the change of terminology is in keeping with American interests. Though it is difficult to define 'terrorism` those who kill innocent and non-combatant people on large scale could certainly be categorised as terrorist. Many Pakistan-based organisations like Lashkar-e-Tayyiba who kill innocent citizens in not only in J&K but also in other cities of India are terrorists.

Now let us see whether fundamentalism necessarily leads to terrorism and what is the link between them. Though logically fundamentalism should not necessarily and inevitably lead to terrorism, it often does. Fundamentalism, as already pointed out, involves enforcement of narrow sectarian practices using political power and for consolidation of political power – extreme coercion becomes necessary and extreme coercion involves violence.

People do not easily accept such enforcement willingly (except a few) while the authoritarian forces use violence. Also, when it involves political power, political rivalries and secessionist movement violence is inevitably used as democratic alternatives take far too long a time and tries out patience. But it should also be noted that all terrorist movements are not fundamentalist in nature though fundamentalism may also lead to terrorism. For example, the LTTE movement is terrorist one but not fundamentalist one.

Another important thing to be noted is that terrorists may use religion or religious terminology like *jihad* or *dharma yuddh* or holy war but their objective may have nothing to do with religious teachings as such. It would, therefore, be wrong to describe a terrorist act as religious terrorism just because of religion of a terrorist and his use of religious terminology. Thus Osama bin Laden being a Muslim his attack on New York twin towers does not become an act of 'Islamic terrorism'. Unfortunately the media used this term quite unthinkingly.

Osama bin Laden has his own agenda and his acts by no means represent Islamic teachings. No religion in the world, much less Islam, teaches terrorism or inspires any one to kill innocent people. Though some Muslims may have expressed sympathy for Osama (so did some non-Muslims also who resent American policies and its pro-Israeli stance) he never had any official sanction from any Islamic establishment behind him. It is true there is no priesthood or church in Islam and no *fatwa*, howsoever eminent the institution issuing *fatwa* be, cannot be binding on any Muslim.

And in case of Osama no such institution has issued any such *fatwa* supporting his act of terrorism. It is, therefore, not justified at all to describe 9/11 attack by Osama's men as an act of Islamic terrorism. Even if any eminent *Mufti* (one who issues *fatwa*) had issued such an opinion it would not have been binding on all Muslims. And in this case no one issued such a *fatwa*

Osama bin Laden and his al-Qaida organisation does not pretend to have any mass base and in fact no terrorist organisation has any mass base anywhere in the world. It would otherwise seem to be a terrorist organisation. Osama does use Islamic terminology to gain sympathy of Muslim masses but use of such a terminology does not make it an Islamic organisation. It remains basically a terrorist organisation. The religion practised by masses of Muslims is more spiritual than political and religion practised by likes of Osama is more political than spiritual.

The Qur'an clearly lays down that killing any person without a just cause amounts to killing whole humanity and saving one person's life amounts to saving entire humanity. This is truly humanistic and spiritual dimension of Islam and of any religion for that matter. Killing hundreds of innocent people cannot qualify for being a religious act by any stretch of imagination.

In fact whether fundamentalism and terrorism (in the sense in which they have been defined above) are linked together or not both are curses for humanity. No truly religious person should approve of such gross misuse of religion. A religious attitude has to be of humility, distance from political power and of non-violence. The Sufi Islam which was truly spiritual Islam always maintained its distance from power centres and believed in the doctrine of what is called *sulh-i-kul*, i.e., peace with all.

True religion is one, which does not get politicised. Political Islam or political Hinduism became great danger for peace and tranquillity in the society. It is political Hinduism (Hindutva) which caused havoc in Gujarat and many other places and it is political Islam which has resulted in bloodshed in New York or in Kashmir or in Algeria, for that matter. Muslims and Hindus should fight against politicising of their respective religions.

Muslim Women on the Move

There is widespread perception that Muslim women are among the most backward, illiterate and oppressed in the world. In media they are always shown clad in *burqa* or wrapped in *hijab* (veil). They are also perceived to be confined to the four walls of their homes totally cut off from outside world. While partly it is true but reality is much more complex and also not static. Generally we tend to oversimplify and assume reality to be static. In a fast changing world reality cannot taken to be static. We should always pay attention to changing and emerging reality.

What happens in the Muslim world is usually blamed on Islam. The underlying assumption is that Muslim behaviour is always determined by religious belief and since Muslim women are backward and do not enjoy rights like other women it is because of Islamic teachings. This impression is further reinforced by the pronouncements of some orthodox 'ulama that want to see Muslim women wrapped in *hijab*.

It has to be borne in mind that firstly all Muslims do not behave according to what theologians or 'ulama say or even according to the teachings of Islam; secondly, social customs, traditions and social milieu exert their own pressure. It is difficult to ignore all this. Thirdly, there are multiple interpretations of Qur'an. Fourthly, modern world-view also plays an important role in determining one's point of view as well as behaviour.

The question of Muslim women, their social status and rights cannot be understood without keeping these things in mind. First of all it must be kept in mind that Qur'an makes clear pronouncement in favour of equal rights for both sexes (2:228). However, this vision of Islam for sexual equality could not find practical implementation for number of reasons. Those who embraced Islam, however sincere they might have been, were product of a fiercely male-dominated society. The Qura'nic pronouncement on the other hand, was an ideal which required very different cultural milieu. From sociological viewpoint it was not immediately implementable.

The scriptural understanding is always mediated through culture. The Arab culture was patriarchal and had set its own understanding of women's position. Thus the Qur'anic pronouncement of sexual equality was understood and implemented through mediation of Arab culture. What is worse Islam spread through deeply feudal societies like those of Iran, parts of Roman empire and India. The 'ulama certainly could not transcend cultural norms of these societies. Thus shari'ah formulations came into existence mainly in Iraq, Egypt and of course Madina. Iraq and Egypt were confluence of ancient cultures with age-old traditions of their own. These milieux greatly influenced the Muslim theologians in their understanding of Qur'anic pronouncement of sexual equality.

To meet the demands of their societies they selectively used Qur'anic verses and certain sayings of the Holy Prophet (PBUH) to formulate shari'ah approach to women problem, their status and rights. This became medieval religious heritage, which no one could question. However, under pressure from modern social norms these Qur'anic pronouncements are being rediscovered by modernists and a debate is raging in the Muslim world today about rights of women in Islam.

Meanwhile the Muslim women are on the move in various Muslim countries. In every Muslim country and countries with considerable Muslim population like India education is spreading fast among Muslim women. This certainly brings increased awareness among women themselves and they press for their rights both Islamic as well as secular. There are both types of movements among Muslim women in Islamic world. In some Muslim countries Muslim women theologians have emerged with thorough knowledge of the Qur'an, Islamic theology and shari'ah. There are women theologians like Fatima Mirsani from Morocco, Amina Wadood and Riffat Hassam from USA and several others. Also there are women's organisations like 'Sisters in Islam' from Malaysia.

These Muslim women theologians and organisations are questioning the traditional interpretations of the Qur'an in respect of women's rights and developing new feminine oriented theology ensuring equal rights for men and women. Sisters-in-Islam from Malaysia is challenging the orthodox 'ulama from Malaysia. They are even trying to get the concept of 'marital rape' accepted as a valid law.

As pointed out above reality is not static in Muslim women`s world. The women in as orthodox society as that of Kuwait are demanding right to vote which is being denied to them by the Kuwait ruling elite. It is hoped they will win this right sooner than later. In Pakistan the women agitated in early fifties itself against the Pakistani Prime Minister when he married his secretary and took her as second wife. The agitation continued until Ayub Khan who had captured power in 1958 brought Muslim Family Ordinance in 1961, which put certain restrictions on polygamy and oral divorce. This ordinance could not be undone even during Zia-ul-Haq's period when the orthodox 'ulama were closest to state power in Pakistan.

The Pakistani society, despite its ups and downs as far as project of 'Islamisation' is concerned, is on the move in changing women's social status. Recently seven Pakistani woman diplomats have been appointed ambassadors. An official of Pakistani foreign ministry said that it is for the first time so many women have been appointed ambassadors in important world capitals. They are all career diplomats and have been posted to European capitals. One woman Asma Aneesa, who was ambassador to one of the Central Asian countries, has been appointed on directing staff of National Defence College. No mean achievement.

Bangladesh, though otherwise quite poor and backward, is not far behind. There recently twenty female officers have completed two year gruelling military training and passed out from Bangladesh Military Academy (BMA). This training was for the post of second lieutenant and their passing out ceremony was attended by Bangladesh Prime Minister Khaleda Zia.

The Saudi society too is by no means as static as we think of. The Saudi women too are facing complex choices. There is no doubt compared to other Muslim countries they are subjected to stricter traditions. But there is no reason to assume that they are passive and inert to modern changes in the society. The Saudi society as a whole is conceived as governed by purely traditional Islam and totally shut out to modern world. The Saudi society is undergoing pangs of modern change and this is causing social convulsions and these social convulsions occasionally assume violent forms. This is subject of another article and cannot be discussed here.

We will discuss here only other issues related to women in Saudi Arabia. The women in Saudi Arabia are taking modern education. The princess called Umm Abdul Aziz, for example, said (see www.amanjordan.org) "We have our own traditions, but they do not prevent women seeking education." Though there are obviously separate educational institutions for women and there is no co-education in Saudi Arabia. They strictly follow the tradition of sexual segregation.

The News Letter of Pakistani women's organisation *Shirkatgah* of April 2003 says about changes among Saudi women, "Trying to balance the challenges of modernity with the demands of traditional past has meant that change is cautious and slow, but women insist that change is afoot." Mona Megalli says in her article "Saudi women face complex choices" in the above news letter, "Saudi women now outstrip men as graduates and other specialised colleges, making up 58 per cent of a total of nearly 32000 students in 2000." The female students listen to male instructors through closed circuit video an audio system.

There are many restrictions Saudi women have to grapple with. Women are not taught engineering and law, for example. They have to compete in touch job market in Saudi society.

Similarly though women own 40 per cent of private wealth and thousands of businesses from retail to heavy industry, they face frustrating legal and cultural restraints and they have to rely on male agents to deal with government offices.

It is also encouraging news from Jordan that it has amended law to give women equal rights. This was announced by Queen Rania. She made this announcement on the opening day of Arab first ladies dedicated to improving the conditions of women in the male dominated Arab world.

In Iran of course though women have to wear chador but chador has not been a constraint for them as far as work is concerned. Iran has very active women's movement in whole of Islamic world. They are active in practically every field of work and are present in large numbers in Iranian parliament too. In Indonesia too women have entered in educational field in a big way. There are large number of women in Islamic universities too and there is strong movement developing for women's rights.

Thus one must realise that reality is multi-layered and complex. Muslim women too are undergoing through throes of change the world over. The orthodox 'ulama can hardly restrain this forward march. More and more Muslim women are either challenging medieval theological formulations or simply ignoring them. They are trying to carving out their own niche in this male dominated world.

Hijab Controversy in France

Again a controversy has been ranging in France on the question of wearing *hijab*, i.e., head-scarf in schools by Muslim girls. This controversy had erupted a few years ago but had died down. Again France is agitated as some Muslim girls, particularly the Algerian Arab girls insist on wearing head scarf in schools too, apart from wearing it at home or in private functions and public places.

Though the government authorities have no objection to these girls wearing *hijab* in public places, it wants to ban wearing it in schools as the French government maintains it has to protect its secular traditions. It is going to ban wearing of crosses by the

Christians and skullcaps by the Jews in schools. The French Government feels these are religious symbols and hence should not be allowed to be worn in schools.

This issue needs to be discussed at different levels and should not be treated as mere threat to secularism. We would like to throw light on various aspects so that one can understand the real issues involved.

Firstly, one has to decide whether wearing a head-scarf really threatens secular tradition of France? What does secularism mean in a modern democratic multicultural society? Is religion a threat to secularism? Is wearing *hijab* a religious or a cultural practice? Even if it is religious practice (actually it is simplistic to treat it as a mere religious practice) should it be banned? In fact like other things the concept of secularism should also not become a mere dogma. It should remain as dynamic political and social process to be continually discussed, debated and updated.

The European societies are changing very fast and are attracting people from all over the world. These societies were almost mono-cultural before World War-II but today are highly multi-cultural. Secularism in multi-cultural societies cannot be same as in Christian mono-cultural societies. Today America has also evolved a different multi-cultural identity model. Until recently America took pride in melting pot model of identity as almost all migrants to USA were from western countries. But today when migration to USA has been taking place from all over the world including Asian and African countries, this model has become outdated and new model known as mosaic model of identity has emerged. Now white Americans no more take pride only in American identity.

The American whites have adjusted themselves to multi-cultural model and recognise other identities. For example, the blacks are no more referred to as blacks in America but as African Americans. Those who have migrated from India are called Indian Americans and those from Arab countries as Arab Americans and Chinese Americans and so on. But it seems France is yet to come to terms with its growing multi-culturalism and still sticks to its mono-cultural model.

In post-modern societies pluralism and multi-culturalism has been accepted by all social and political theorists. In fact cultural pluralism is the norm and not exception in the post-modern society. The notion of secularism in multi-cultural society is bound to differ from that of mono-cultural society. Unfortunately France is still stuck with its mono-cultural model of nineteenth century and has, therefore, adopted rather rigid and dogmatic approach towards secularism.

France had a predominantly Catholic Christian population when it adopted its secular model. Its culture was certainly influenced by not only Catholic Christianity but also by elements of western society. There is no doubt that French Culture is quite rich but this does not mean it is the only culture in France today. There is large number of Arabs from Algeria in addition to people of other countries and France, like any other European nation is a multi-cultural nation.

The notion of dress varies from culture to culture. Covering head is more of a cultural than religious practice, as pointed out above. In Eastern cultures hair is considered sexual stimulant and covering head is a common practice in many Asian and African countries. In India even Hindu women cover their heads with *saris* in presence of elders and strangers. The Qur'an also suggests covering head though it is not very clear whether it is recommendatory or obligatory. The Muslim theologians of course consider it as obligatory.

It is also not true that all Muslim women wear headgear even in Muslim countries except in Saudi Arabia and some gulf countries. In Syria, Egypt, Algeria, Pakistan, Bangladesh and some other Muslim countries many women go about bare-headed and consider wearing head gear as either sign of 'backwardness' or simply unnecessary. In France too all Muslim women do not wear *hijab*.

Also, all multi-cultural societies take very liberal view of secularism. India has been multi-religious and multi-cultural for centuries and here understanding of secularism is much more liberal and far from anti-religious as in France. Here of course secularism has been weakened as a result of onslaught from Hindu rightist forces. But secularism as such is quite liberal and tolerant of religious and multi-cultural practices. Who wears what, is hardly a question in India and its educational institutions? We see several Muslim women in *hijab* covering not only the head but also the whole body and no one bothers about it. Similarly many girls wear dresses of their own choices without attracting any adverse notice. The RSS and VHP boys tried to prescribe their own dress code but was never accepted by people in general. It was never adopted.

In fact secularism is always considered quite liberal and tolerant and concedes full freedom to all individuals. The French model of secularism is unfortunately quite dogmatic and intolerant. Generally orthodox religion is generally dubbed as intolerant of individual freedom. It is beyond ones comprehension how few Muslim girls wearing *hijab* can threaten overwhelming secular society of France. In fact any such law banning wearing of *hijab* would promote religious fundamentalism among those Muslims who want their female children to wear headgear.

Turkish military too imposes such rigid and dogmatic form of secularism. There too women wearing scarf are dismissed from service or even disqualified from membership of Parliament. But this made Islamist forces more popular in Turkey and the reformist party came to power. In a modern secular and democratic society everyone should be free to make his/her own religious or cultural choices. To impose anything from above including the dress code would prove self-defeating.

The Shah of Iran also tried to impose western dress for Muslim women and failed miserably. In fact to defy the ban even those women who had willingly taken to western dress started wearing *Islamic hijab.* Even their mothers who used to wear western dress were shocked to see their daughters wearing *hijab* in defiance of Shah's order. By imposing any dress code we violate individual rights and even sense of dignity. A person forced to wear a particular form of dress against his/her will feels great resentment his/her self-dignity is injured. It is quite against notion of human rights in a liberal democracy. One should be free to choose mode of dressing or any religious or cultural practice, of course without threatening the social order.

There is yet another dimension, which has to be taken into account. Every community – religious, ethnic or cultural – has certain identity symbols visible and invisible in a multi-religious and multi-cultural society. And those communities, which are in minority, guard their visible symbols of identity more jealously. They feel overwhelmed by majority religion or culture and deliberately make their identities visible. *Hijab* too is a part of visible identity for Muslim women.

The UK today is better disposed of to put up with these symbols of religious and cultural identities. It tried to ban Sikhs wearing turban while on duty. But the Sikhs resisted and the Government of UK had to bow down and accept their headgear as part of their religious duty. UK has a large Indian community Hindus, Sikhs, Muslims and Buddhists. They all are free to wear their respective cultural dresses. Now there is absolutely no problem.

In fact in France too Algerian Muslim girls have been wearing head-scarf for some time now and not that it has really threatened French secularism. The reason why the French Government is trying to ban wearing of *hijab* (cross and skullcaps to balance banning of *hijab*) is more political. The right wing party is gaining more popularity and is likely to get greater percentage of votes in coming elections. This right wing party is attacking foreigners and foreign cultures. The French Government wants to stem the tide of right wing popularity by banning wearing of *hijab*.

Thus the controversy about wearing *hijab* has to be seen at several levels. The right wing parties always oppose foreign immigrants and their culture. It is a universal problem and every government has to work out its own strategies to face this challenge. While understanding these political compulsions one would insist that the fundamental principles of multi-religious and multi-cultural society should not be compromised. France should enter this brave new world in 21st century.

4

Contemporary Politics

The BJP's Twenty Five Years and Communalism of Indian Polity

The BJP is celebrating silver jubilee of its existence. It claims it was born in 1980. The fact is that it changed only its name in that year and not its direction or ideology. For it the old adage 'what is there in name' applies in its entirety. Though it changed its name but continued with its Jan Sangh ideology. However, it made the world believe that it has discarded its Jan Sangh ideology and adopted 'secularism' and 'Gandhian socialism'. In fact when the Jan Sangh merged with the Janata Party in 1977 immediately after emergency it had oath at Gandhiji's *samadhi* for secularism and Gandhian socialism for qualifying for merger into the Janata Party which was formed under the leadership of Shri Jai Prakash Narain.

Jan Sangh was indeed a communal party and its pledge to adopt secularism and Gandhian socialism was only a strategy, not a change of heart. The subsequent events proved it abundantly. Jan Sangh's sole aim at the time was to gain more acceptability and to defeat the Congress at the hustings. The Janata Party which included Jan Sangh swept the polls in 1977 inflicting crushing defeat on the Congress and the Janata Government assumed power with Morarji Desai as Prime Minister and Mr. Vajpayee as Foreign Minister.

The Janta Party however soon plunged into a crisis on the question of duel membership raised by socialists like Raj Narain, Fernandes (today of course he is ardent supporter of BJP) and Madhu Limaye. Though the Jan Sangh leaders like Vajpayee, L.K. Advani and others took oath for secularism and Gandhian socialism, they never broke their ties with the RSS. RSS was their very ideological *raison d'etre.* This itself was sufficient evidence to show that there was no change of heart and their adoption of secularism and Gandhian socialism was merely a matter of political strategy. In other words it was a political deceit.

Since the Jan Sangh members refused to break their ties with the RSS the Janta Party broke and Morarji Desai had to resign. The RSS made it clear to the Jan Sangh leaders that they cannot survive without it and to register this with them (Jan Sangh leaders) it organised riots in several places like Aligarh, Varanasi and Jamshedpur in which hundreds of innocent people were killed. Minorities, angry with the Congress policies during emergency had reposed their trust in the Janata Party but were grossly disappointed with the behaviour of Jan Sangh and the riots that broke out taking toll of large number of Muslims.

They voted Indira Gandhi back to power. The Jan Sangh now re-christened itself as Bhartiya Janata Party (BJP) in 1980 and again reiterated its commitment to 'secularism' and 'Gandhian socialism' and elected A.B. Vajpayee as its president as Vajpayee is supposedly Sangh Parivar's 'liberal face'. However, as usual its integral relationship with the RSS continued and its new *avtar did not convince* anyone, much less the voters and it lost 1984 parliamentary elections very badly. It could win only two seats in Parliament.

With this new *avtar* it could neither win secular votes and also lost its traditional supporters too. Thus soon it went back to the basics and now with vengeance to recover the lost ground. It not only removed its secular mask (*mukhota*) but began to attack it with all ferocity it could command. It dubbed it as a western ideology not suited to India and Indian culture. It also attacked the Congress secularism as 'pseudo-secularism' and accused it of 'appeasing' the minorities.

This was the new strategy adopted by the BJP leaders to win over the Hindu middle classes who were disillusioned with the Congress performance and were looking for viable political alternative. The decade of eighties was a decade of complex challenges for Indian democracy. Ethnic movements had assumed serious proportions throughout North East and Punjab. The Assam Students Union (ASU) movement was at its height and militancy in the Punjab was claiming several lives every day. Communal violence too was recurring now and then. The Bihar Sharif riots of 1981, the Meerut and Baroda riots of 1982, Neli (Assam) riots of 1983 had claimed several thousand lives and then anti-Sikh riots broke out after the assassination of Mrs. Gandhi in November 1984.

Then came the Shah Bano movement, which heightened the communal feelings among Hindu middle classes. The BJP had not only caste away its secular mask but was trying to exacerbate communal feelings to regain the Hindu votes. In these circumstances disillusionment with the Congress role grew and then V.P. Singh also launched Bofors movement against Rajiv Gandhi which further discredited the Congress. In these circumstances the BJP grew stronger and stronger and then came the Ramjanambhoomi movement which it encashed unashamedly for its politics.

It is interesting to note that the BJP accused the Congress of 'vote-bank' politics i.e. 'appeasing' Muslims to reduce it to its vote-bank but itself played similar politics and tried to create its own vote-bank among upper caste Hindus by placating them through issues like the Ramjanambhoomi and also by arousing their anti-Muslim sentiments. It exploited the Ramjanambhoomi issue to the hilt to arouse communal sentiments and blatantly distorting Indian history.

Unfortunately Mr. V.P. Singh entered into alliance with BJP in 1989 elections and gave new respectability to it forgetting the lessons of 1977 Janta Party experiment. This adjustment enabled the BJP to increase its Parliamentary share from 2 to 89 seats in 1989 parliamentary seats. The BJP then never saw back until the Parliamentary elections of 2004 in which it lost power. The BJP again repeated its performance in Janta Party Government by withdrawing support to the V.P. Singh Government on the question of Ramjanambhoomi and toppling it.

Also, the BJP had projected itself as the 'party with a difference, and quite a disciplined and non-corrupt party. As long as it was in opposition this myth could wash but once it came to power it proved to be as corrupt as the Congress whom it never tired of accusing of corruption and as indisciplined as any other party in power. Groupism emerged and now we see how it is faction-ridden in the states where it is in power like Gujarat, Madhya Pradesh and Rajasthan. However, in late eighties and nineties the upper caste Hindu middle classes swallowed the BJP propaganda uncritically and a section of them still continues to accept it without questioning.

The BJP while claiming it is most principled party, never displayed respect for any principle throughout its existence of 25 years (or 55 years if we add its Jan Sangh days?) of existence. It displayed grossest opportunism whenever it suited its politics. Mr. Atal Bihari Vajpayee, its most respected leader, had given solemn assurance in the National Integration Council in 1992 that *kar seva* on 6th December 1992 will not mean harming Babri Masjid but it will be confined to *bhajan-kirtan* (singing devotional songs) but it is now history that what happened in Ayodhya on 6th December 1992 plunging whole nation into dance of destruction and communal mayhem. Now the CBI has also exposed that Mr. Vajpayee himself was involved in this conspiracy. He had delivered a speech in Lucknow on 5th December 1992, which clearly indicates his involvement in the conspiracy.

The BJP which had talked of being secular in its new *avtar* ended up adopting the Hindutva agenda again to win more and more seats by playing up communal sentiments. It adopted rapidly anti-minority postures time and again to increase its vote-share. However, when it formed alliance with other 'secular' parties to form the ruling alliance (National Democratic Alliance) it again pretended to push its Hindutva agenda to the background. Again it was nothing more than a political stratagem.

It was once again exposed in Gujarat when it fully backed up Narendra Modi in his massacre of Muslim minority. It is said that Mr. Vajpayee wanted to remove Narendra Modi but gave in to younger militant leadership led by persons like Arun Jaitly and backed him up instead by condemning Muslim role in Godhra in the Party session in Goa. Again Mr. Vajpayee patted Narendra Modi on the back when he won two-third majority in the Gujarat elections of December 2002 by organising massacre of Muslims and said, "I am your advocate".

The BJP not only described Gujarat as the 'Hindutva laboratory' but also its younger leadership boasted that they would repeat the Gujarat model in other states. It is different story that it badly lost the Himachal Pradesh elections soon after and Narendra Modi had to be withdrawn from election campaign there. It is great tribute to Indian democracy and diversity. In fact the Gujarat massacre instead of increasing the BJP popularity as it expected it was beginning of its decline. Mr. Vajpayee himself admitted that we lost 2004 Parliamentary elections because of Gujarat. The people of India rejected BJP's politics of anti-minorityism and reposed its faith in religious pluralism.

Thus it will be seen from above account that the BJP's history of last 25 years has been quite chequered and there is hardly anything to celebrate silver jubilee of its coming into existence. It is historically not correct to say that a new party came into existence in 1980 but an old party changed its colour temporarily to suit its convenience. The fact is that the Jan Sangh (BJP from 1980) did not show consistency even in following its communal ideology and lost confidence of its traditional constituency too.

Contemporary Challenges to Secularism and Democracy–Religious Response

India is a secular democracy constitutionally though there are several problems in practice. On the whole India has given not so bad account of itself. Despite onslaught from communalist and fundamentalist forces India has not swerved from its secular democratic course in terms of its legal and political structure. Though India has been witnessing communal violence ever since early sixties communal situation far more worsened when the

BJP launched Ram Mandir drive and polarised the country along communal lines as on the eve of partition, even worse.

Towards the end of last century demolition of Babri Masjid was a major blow to Indian secularism. Babri Masjid became, as if, the symbol and taste of Indian secularism. Secularism in India is nothing if not pluralism. India has been religiously, culturally and linguistically pluralist for several thousands of years. This religious and cultural pluralism survived thanks to tolerance of our people. It is remarkable that we do not have communal conflict throughout medieval period. Communalism and communal violence is a modern phenomenon, which is product of colonial period. Feudal polity was basically –non-competitive and communal phenomenon is product of modern competitive politics.

The colonial period saw competition for power between the elites of two communities and they invoked religion for mobilising masses from respective communities. Religious identity thus became a powerful tool for political elites of the two communities to exploit and exploit they did with maximum intensity possible. Thus though communal strife is not religious strife, it does appear to be one.

The leaders of Hindu Mahasabha and Muslim League in pre-independence India used religious rhetoric and created sharp perceptions of 'religious strife' among people of their respective communities. Jinnah was modern liberal constitutionalist but when he failed to arrive at a 'satisfactory' political arrangement with the Indian National Congress he began to use religious rhetoric to mobilise Indian Muslims behind him.

After independence the Jansangh (formed in 1951), which as later on renamed as the BJP in 1980 used Hindu religious rhetoric to grab Hindu votes in state and parliamentary elections. When ordinary religious rhetoric did not help much it discovered the utility of Ram Mandir for sharper political appeal to Hindus of all castes. Mr. L.K. Advani led the Ramjanmabhoomi movement with great verve and intensity in late eighties of last century. It paid rich political dividends and he rode to power in the Toyota-built Ramrath.

Ramjanmabhoomi movement resulted in sharp polarisation of Hindus and Muslims in late twentieth century, which continues until today. It was basically the communal rhetoric of the BJP which resulted in Gujarat carnage of 2002 in which more than 2000 innocent citizens lost their lives and hundreds of women were raped and killed most barbarically. The Hindutva in Gujarat was transformed into 'Moditva' as Narendra Modi was mainly responsible for the carnage.

Here in this article we are not mainly concerned with politics of BJP, which is well known to any student of Indian politics. We are more concerned here with response or otherwise by the religious people in India in general, and in Gujarat, in particular. It is because of dubious role played by religious leaders that religion appears to be main culprit in the eyes of many people. These politicians deliberately provoke religious fanaticism to make political gains.

This impression easily gains ground because either many religious leaders actively cooperate with communalists or keep silent about the gross misuse of religion for political ends. Thus in the eyes of people religion, not politicians, come to be blamed. Religion *per se*, cannot be responsible for the communal malaise. It is like a tool which can be used either way.

Basically religion is for spiritual guidance of the people and hence can be a major resource for peace and social justice. It can become, as liberation theology indicates, a powerful option for the weaker sections of society. Instead religion has more often been used by powerful vested interests of which religious functionaries become a part. Worse, religious functionaries and priests themselves create powerful establishments and join hands with politicians to protect their establishments.

A truly religious person should always be anti-establishment. Buddha, Christ, Muhammad, Guru Nanak, Kabir and others all fought against establishments in their own times and transcended their period. Their followers, on the other hand, created huge establishments in their names and became cause of conflict rather than resource for peace. To create true religious spirit one has to shed all vested interests. One should shun all temptations of power and pelf.

It was very painful to note that during most of the communal riots those belonging to various religious traditions became either active collaborators or kept silent. During the Gujarat carnage too it was nothing different. With a few honourable exceptions all other religious leaders kept quiet and politicians like Narendra Modi and his henchmen cynically exploited Hindu religious sentiments for their political ends. In fact Narendra Modi came back to power by getting thousands massacred.

India, as pointed out, is a multi-religious and multi-cultural country and modern secular democratic polity can survive only if religious people are determined to promote religious and spiritual values. This globalised world cannot escape being religiously plural, secular and democratic. Globalisation is creating pressures of its own which disrupt our religious values and culture. In this period of globalisation we have to be firmly rooted in our religious values.

Indian plurality alone can be our valuable asset and religious response has to be based on tolerance, respect and compassion for others. Religious leaders of India must come together and resolve to promote common religious values. If we reflect sincerely there are many values, which are common to our respective religious traditions. One can easily identify eight values which are central to all religious traditions. These values are as under: (1) justice; (2) peace; (3) equality; (4) love; (5) compassion; (6) non-violence, (7) truth and (8) human dignity.

Also, we have had glorious tradition of living together and made rich contribution to Indian culture and hence Indian culture is essentially a composite culture. We have to further strengthen and enrich this composite culture and our religious traditions, seen in the light of values mentioned above, do not come in our way in doing so. We have shared much in common for centuries and people of religion should not allow few politicians to undo all our shared values and traditions and promote intolerance and hatred.

The people of religion should make it clear to their followers that those who promote hatred and intolerance cannot champion the cause of religious community but their own. All religious people, particularly religious leaders who do not have narrow sectarian interests at heart should come forward and boldly take stand against violence and untruth being promoted in the name of religion by politicians and their cohorts who might pretend to be religious leaders.

There is inspiring example of religious leaders of Albania who recently came together and issued a statement of what they called "Shared moral commitment". The statement issued says among other things: "We, the traditional religious communities in Albania: the Muslim community, the Orthodox Autocephalous Church of Albania (Orthodox Church), the Catholic Church, and the Bektash Community, feel called upon to point the way to the future and we recognise and accept that our religious communities differ from each other, and that each of us feels called to observe their own faith." "At the same time", the statement says, "we recognise that our religious and spiritual traditions hold many values in common, and that these shared values can serve as an authentic basis for mutual esteem, cooperation, and free common living throughout the territory of Albania."

The statement also further proceeds: "We, the Muslim Community, the Orthodox Church, the Catholic Church, and the Bektash Community are proud of our history of multi-religious co-existence... We proclaim that the dignity of the human person and human value is a gift of God. Our faiths, each in their own way, call us to respect each person's fundamental human rights. Discrimination and violence against persons or the violation of their basic rights, for us, breaks not only man-made laws, but also God's law."

I have quoted only a few excerpts from this statement, which was issued by religious leaders of the communities mentioned therein on 18th March, 2005 from Tirana, the capital of Albania. This statement greatly applies to our Indian situation too and it is high time our Indian religious leaders too should come forward and take similar bold step. India, in fact, is more pluralistic than Albania and our plurality and shared values can be traced to much longer period. Also, we are facing acute crisis today on communal front. It is therefore, high time that our religious leaders should morally intervene in this strife-torn situation and see to it that Gujarat-like situation does not repeat and our multi-religiosity remains our asset and does not become a liability. We can meet challenges to secularism and democracy and steer clear of fascistic politics only if our religious leaders intervene firmly to cut unscrupulous politicians to size.

Communal Riots–2004

Like the year 2003, 2004 also did not witness any major riot. In fact the Gujarat carnage of 2002 was so traumatic that it may take sometime for the country to see communal violence on such scale. It is well known fact that major communal riot cannot take place without planning and organised efforts. The Gujarat carnage would not have been possible without BJPs and Gujarat Government's involvement. Of course it cost the BJP dearly and one of the reasons of loosing the Lok Sabha elections in 2004 was the Gujarat carnage as admitted by no less a person than A.B.Vajpayee, the BJP Prime Minister. Thus, for the time being the BJP dare not involve in organising rioting on such major scale.

It is for this reason that both in 2003 and 2004 we do not find any major sustained communal violence except for riots in which couple of lives were lost. It is interesting to note that for last few years Western zone of the country, i.e., Gujarat and Maharashtra have mostly witnessed communal violence. Gujarat still remains communally sensitive and without major de-communalising campaigns. Though there is Congress-NCP secular alliance in Maharashtra, there are no serious efforts to ideologically fight the Shiv Sena-BJP combine. Shiv Sena-BJP though it failed to come to power in the last state assembly election, it continues to wield ideological influence.

In M.P. state elections had taken place in December 2003 and the BJP had won. The BJP is trying to Hinduise tribals in Jhabua and other tribal belts of M.P. in order to win their political support. It had campaigned in a major way in Jhabua district, which is adjacent to Gujarat state. Thus Jhabua became communally quite sensitive. Thus communal clashes took place in Jhabua district between Bhils and Christians on 17th January.

Actually Bhils attacked Christian Missionaries and killed one person.

Communal tension was on the rise for last few months, following the decision of the RSS-VHP cadres to prevent religious conversions by Christian missionaries. Backers of the latter, belonging to the ferocious Bhil tribe, struck back on Friday night with bows and arrows in the Alirajpur area killing one person (unofficially three), injuring over a dozen, and setting a few vehicles and buildings ablaze. It was alleged that the most serious incident had occurred when a religious procession of Sadhvis attached to a Hindu Saint Asaram Bapu at Amkhunt village was attacked and the women manhandled. The Sadhvis were distributing religious literature when the surprise attack occurred.

Earlier a 9-year-old girl was raped and murdered and her body found in a toilet inside a missionary school it had raised communal temperature as some Christians were suspected to have done that. But it was a false rumour and Chief Minister Uma Bharti herself confirmed that the culprit arrested had no connection with the church.

Vadodra in Gujarat again witnessed communal violence on 27th February in which three persons were killed and 13 others were injured. The violence erupted after the Tazia procession was stoned in Bavamanpura area. One person was beaten to death. Paresh Pushwani when he was travelling on scooter was attacked by a mob of 200 persons. He succumbed to his injuries in the hospital. One another person was hit by the police bullet and one person was stabbed to death. Thirteen persons injured included four police personnel in stone pelting. Nagin Parmar and Chotalal Borsi were attacked by sharp weapons by a mob in Panigate area of which Borsi succumbed to his injuries. On 29th February one person was stabbed to death again in Panigate area. But police refused to accept it as a communal incident and ascribed it to personal quarrel.

On the eve of Moharram small incidents took place in several towns on 2nd March in India. Moradabad in U.P. witnessed stone throwing, one person was stabbed in Baroda, Gujarat, ships were closed in Ajmer in Rajasthan. In Pratapgarh one laundry was set on fire.

Ahmadnagar in Maharashtra experienced communal violence on 7th March when a Shiv Sena MLA was arrested for provoking violence on 3rd March. Ahmadnagar had witnessed communal violence on 10th of Moharram (3rd March) and next day, i.e., on 4th March Chitre Road, Sarjepura, Tillikot, Milindnagar and Delegate areas Muslim shops were attacked, burnt and looted.

One person was killed in Chirli village of Gwalior in M.P. on 7th March on the occasion of Holi and 23 were injured of whom many were critical. The clashes between Hindus and Muslims started when Holi revellers threw colour on some Muslims. Knives and other weapons were freely used during the clashes.

Next rioting broke out again in Gujarat in Savarkundla Town of Amreli district on 14th May. A police head constable Abdul Sattar Baloch stabbed one Sukhabhai from the Koli community. He later succumbed to his injuries and people returning from his funeral procession began to stone Muslim houses and set a truck ablaze.

Meerut, a communally sensitive city in U.P. witnessed communal flare up on June 19 in which two persons were killed. The communal flare up took place after one Babi Gujar was killed on 18th June and people returning from his funeral began to stone near an Eidgah. Communal violence intensified thereafter and one person was stabbed and one was killed by firing. Curfew was imposed in the Sardhana area of Meerut where disturbances broke out. The police sources said three persons were killed. Many were arrested. Curfew continued next day also and in all 48 persons were arrested.

Next Sanghavli village in Muzaffarnagar district in U.P. came under spell of communal violence on 21st July in which one woman was killed and 20 persons were injured. One Dalit girl two and half years old Shivani was knocked down by a car belonging to a Muslim. Thereupon Dalits attacked the Muslim locality and began to fire.

Gujarat continues to take cake in communal violence. Verawal in Gujarat witnessed communal frenzy on 26th July in which 2 persons were killed and 8 were injured. The violence between the two communities broke out on the question of eve teasing. A young Hussain Zair was killed in Taj Society when police opened fire to disperse rampaging mobs that resorted to heavy stone pelting and setting ablaze nearly 40 shops and as many vehicles, police said. Another person was stabbed to death in Jalaramnagar area and was brought dead to civil hospital.

On 16th August Akola came to experience communal violence in which one person was killed and one was severely injured. During the celebration of independence day there was some quarrel between two groups and violence broke out. The person who died was identified as Rau. Six persons were arrested. This led to communal tension in the area.

On 7th August there were serious clashes between Hindus and Muslims in Akot of Akola district in Maharashtra in which 3 persons were injured. It started with a man being wounded by a scooter of another community. Stone throwing started after arguments between them.

Then on 29th August in Dekhar Gaon of Anjha Taluka in Mehsana district of Gujarat witnessed clashes between two communities in which more than 15 persons were injured of which two persons were in critical condition. The police reached the spot on time and brought the situation under control. According to the police a son of a retired police officer had gone to the village for Puja and clashed with persons of minority community and others got involved from both communities.

Jalna and Purna in Marathwada district of Parbhani in Maharashtra witnessed bomb blasts near a mosque after the Friday prayer on 27th August in which 23 persons praying in the mosque were seriously injured. The persons who threw bombs came on motorcycles and their faces were masked. Their identity could not be established immediately. Since it was on the eve of state elections it was suspected that communal forces tried to ignite communal violence to polarise Hindus and Muslims. The department declared security alert throughout the State in view of these bomb attacks. Mr. Sharad Pawar, the NCP chief also warned in a press conference in Marathwada that communal mischief will not be tolerated.

Moradabad in U.P. another communally sensitive place, saw communal disturbances on 15th September in which one person died. The problem began with dispute about the construction of a wall in the courtyard of a mosque. Stoning and firing took place between Hindus and Muslims and one person was killed and 18 persons were injured including two policemen. The members of two communities fought despite the presence of the police personnel.

Bhadohi in U.P. known for carpet weaving experienced communal violence on 24th October when idols of Goddess Durga were being taken out. It took violent turn when some slogans were raised during the procession of idols. The mob set afire several shops including an electronic shop on Chauri and Gyanpur Roads. About 24 persons were injured. Rapid Action Force and additional police forces had to be deployed to control the situation. The mob also damaged buses and obstructed movement of trains on Bhadohi-Varanasi-Janghai route. 10 persons were arrested for rioting and violence.

Bhopal in M.P. saw communal clashes in the Shahjahanabad Police Thana area on 26th October in which one person died and one was critically injured. Curfew was clamped and judicial inquiry ordered. Deceased was identified as Jaiprakash. Two children quarrelled and their elders intervened leading to communal clash.

Silchar town in Assam also was rocked by communal violence on November 7 in which 50 shops belonging to minority community were burnt and looted and they sustained loss amounting to crores of rupees. It all started when police refused to give permission to take out a funeral procession of an employee who was murdered through minority locality. The mob went on rampage and curfew had to be imposed.

All the riots we have described above started with small incident which are quite common place but did not assume serious proportion and could be controlled easily as there was no intention by any communal party to exploit these incidents for engineering communal violence for political purposes. No major communal riot can take place without previous planning and providing infrastructure for the same. Any of these incidents could have assumed serious proportions if any communal party had intended to exploit it for their interests.

The major riots also start with small triggering incidents. In that case police is also under pressure not to act and let the violence spread. In post-Gujarat situation, the communal forces did not want to engineer any major riot and hence both in 2003 and 2004 we see only small communal incidents but no major and widespread communal violence. In all these instances the police could effectively control communal violence as they could act independently without any political pressure. If the police is under strict instruction not to allow communal incidents and politicians do not interfere no riot can continue beyond few hours. Widespread communal violence takes place not only by the connivance of unscrupulous politicians but by their complete involvement.

The following is the summary of various small riots that took place in different states:

Date	*Place*	*Injured*	*Arrested*
6/01/2004	Sajaynagar, Vadodara, Gujarat	NA	NA
8/01/2004	Buldana,Maharashtra	07	NA
18/02/2004	Godhra, Gujarat	06	35
22/02/2004	Ujjain, MP	10	57
04/03/2004	Yugutpura, Baroda, Gujarat	05	NA
04/03/2004	Bhavnagar, Gujarat	06	NA
07/03/2004	Yeotmal, Maharashtra	16	NA
04/05/2004	Chabuksawar, Baroda	05	02
7/05/2004	Cheta Camp, Mumbai Maharashtra	18	NA
15/05/2004	Gomtipur, Ahmedabad, Gujarat	08	16
02/08/2004	Belgaum, Karnataka	50	NA
15/09/2004	Anand, Gujarat	01	NA
11/09/2004	Bhandara, Maharashtra	20	60
19/09/2004	Baroda, Gujarat	06	NA
24/10/2004	Kushinagar, UP	25	38
01/11/2004	Zakaria Bander, Mumbai, Maharashtra	07	NA

India Shining, Communal Darkness

The media blitzkrieg launched by the NDA Government showing India Shining may not be illegal, as the Prime Minister maintains. But certainly is immoral as crores of rupees of public money is being spent on it and it is certainly not merely to inform the public for the 'achievements' of the NDA Government but to win forthcoming elections. The NDA Government is trying to convince Indian public that India is shining under its rule (or misrule?)

Is India Shining? Well it all depends on how one looks at it. Even from economic perspective such claim is totally untenable. In a country where millions are unemployed, hundreds are committing suicide because of poverty and hunger to the extent of even killing their families and millions of children drop out from school before reaching even 5th standard how can one claim India is shining? Just because few members of middle class are making it good under globalisation? Just because few millionaires have become billionaires? Just because some politicians of ruling NDA are able to amass enviable wealth unscrupulously?

But we are more concerned here with communal situation under NDA than economic situation. India despite its bewildering diversity has remained united thanks to our commitment to secular polity. Secularism in India means that state remain neutral to all religions and see that religious majority does not reduce our democracy to majoritarianism and minorities are protected and are free to follow their religion without any let and hindrance.

However India has suffered very badly on this score under NDA. India can politically shine only if its secular polity is not tempered with. Can India shine politically when its main ruling party remains tied to organisations like RSS, VHP and Bajrang Dal, which are avowedly anti-minorities? No less a person than the Prime Minister of India said in the crowd of RSS and BJP supporters in Straten Island in USA that 'RSS is my soul'. Can there be any doubt about BJP's active connection with the RSS? Mr. L.K. Advani personally attends the RSS rally in Khaki *chaddi* and gives salute to RSS flag. And he does so when he is Home Minister of India. What message will it send to the police force?

Will police force then be able to control communal violence impartially?

The Congress regime did not have any brilliant record of communal peace in the 45 years of its rule. No one disputes this. But its leaders did not have allegiance to the RSS, much less VHP and Bajrang Dal. They did not stuff premier research bodies like the ICHR and ICSSR (Indian Council of Historical Research and Indian Council of Social Science Research) with those who openly deride secularism. These two premiere research bodies were controlled during the Congress rule by those academics whose secular credentials were never in doubt.

But after the NDA came to power under over all control of the BJP these premiere organisations were captured by the RSS and VHP supporters. It is a great tragedy that such research bodies in social sciences be controlled by those who are avowed opponents of secularism. Even moderate BJP person like the late Prof. M.L. Sondhi was not tolerated and the Human Resources Ministry removed him from chairmanship of the ICSSR. If these organisations are controlled by avowed opponents of secularism what direction social sciences would take? Social sciences are the very basis of intellectual life of the country. It cannot be allowed to be controlled by those who are opponent of our constitutional values. They are making all efforts to undermine the secular values of the Indian Constitution. How India can remain secular under such dispensation?

The British rulers distorted our history in order to divide us which, ultimately resulted in division of our country. These textbooks are being changed for the worse during the NDA dispensation. The so-called secular parties supporting the NDA, and keeping the BJP in power are also party to these serious attempts to undermine our secular values. The children are growing with a sense of hatred towards minority communities. Thus it is not only hate politics but also hate education and there is social environment of hatred and polarisation as never before during 56 years of independence.

It was the BJP leadership, which raised the controversy about secularism in early eighties describing it as western concept unsuitable for Indian culture and Indian society and then dubbed it as 'pseudo-secularism' and based on 'appeasement of minorities'. A high pitched propaganda was carried out on these grounds to cultivate Hindu vote bank thus seriously damaging inter-community relations.

It was certainly result of such high-pitched hate propaganda that communal carnage like in Gujarat could occur which put the entire country to shame in the comity of nations. The Ramjanambhoomi matter was raised by the BJP during nineties to win elections and the BJP came to power ultimately on this hate propaganda and now it has worked out a clever strategy to perpetuate the controversy. While the BJP keeps on saying that construction of Ram temple is not on NDA agenda, the RSS, VHP and Bajrang Dal keep the issue of temple construction alive and they raise this issue with much more vehemence whenever elections are due in any state or in the Centre.

This time the Prime Minister himself initiated his election campaign from Ayodhya and again promising that 'give us five more years and the temple will be constructed.' How can a 'secular' government promise people to construct a temple or a mosque? And when Shankaracharya of Puri tried to intervene and established contacts with the Muslim Personal Law Board to solve the issue through dialogue and it was about to be resolved the RSS and VHP chiefs stormed the Shakaracharya's place. They forced him to retreat so that temple issue remains alive and exploitable for votes.

Also, the issue of Uniform Civil Code, which is purely secular issue and pertaining to gender justice was communalised by the BJP by adopting as 'Hindutva Agenda'. What an irony? And do the Hindutva leaders believe in gender justice? Are they ready to give equal rights to women? All of us know that a secular issue like UCC was communalised by the BJP leaders only to create anti-minority feelings among the Hindus and to damage harmonious relations between the two communities. Earlier all women organisations were demanding UCC but once it became Hindutva agenda it was given up by all secular women's organisations.

And by the way any party which feels proud of its 'Hindutva agenda and proclaim it publicly can be elected to run a secular state? Can the secular constitution be safe in the hands of a party with the Hindutva agenda? Can India politically shines under a Hindutva party? Can there be communal peace under it. The BJP used to claim that when it comes to power there is no communal riots. What happened in Gujarat under its rule is now a history. It will make all secularists and humanists shudder forever. The Gujarat came close to fascists and Nazis of Germany.

The BJP has been in power since 1999. There was not a single year under it that did not witness communal violence. According to our research based on newspaper reports and other sources number of riots took place every year, in the year 1999, 52 riots took place in which 43 people were killed and 248 injured. In the year 2000, 24 riots occurred in which 91 people were killed and 165 injured. In the year 2001, 27 riots erupted in which 56 were killed and 158 injured. In the year 2002, 28 communal riots were recorded (including Gujarat) in which 1173 persons lost their lives and 2272 were injured (unofficially in Gujarat alone more than 2000 people were killed according to private counts). And in the year 2003, 67 riots took place in which 58 people were killed and 611 were injured.

How truthful is the claim of the BJP that no communal violence occurs when it is in power? It is true these riots took place in those states also where the BJP was not in power but it has overall responsibility in the country and in most of these riots its family organisations like the RSS/VHP/Bajrang Dal were involved. There was not a single year, which was riot free under the NDA rule led by the BJP.

Now we have reports from Madhya Pradesh that under the BJP Chief Minister Ms. Uma Bharti a RSS Pracharak has been appointed as her adviser with cabinet rank. She has also set up a Hanuman temple in the courtyard of her chief ministerial bungalow. Is secularism shining or communal darkness intensifying? Where will all this end? Can anyone ever expect that India can remain secular under the leadership of Sangh Parivar? The BJP is an ideological child of the RSS and has always refused to sever its umbilical chord from its ideological mother.

When dual membership controversy arose in 1978 (and Mr. George Fernandese, now with BJP along with Raj Narayan and

Madhu Limaye had raised it) the Jansangh members resigned from the Janata Party bringing down Morarji Desai Government rather than resigning from the RSS. And RSS has consistently refused to give up its Hindu Rashtra concept, which is in direct confrontation with the concept of secular India.

Those who think that India can politically shine only if secularism goes strong can never accept the NDA rule in which the BJP is a dominant partner, let alone if the BJP wins majority of its own. And the day BJP wins majority of its own all steps will be taken to convert India into Hindu Rashtra, even if it is not possible for them to repeat Gujarat like situation throughout the country. Then India will never shine again.

Indian Muslims and Lok Sabha Elections

The Lok Sabha elections have been declared and will be held in couple of months. In democracy elections are most important events and it must be said Indian democracy has fulfilled this condition satisfactorily and has never failed, not even in the times of emergency in mid-seventies of the last century. Very few other Asian and African countries have held elections with such regularity as India.

The numerical minorities like Muslims play an important role in deciding the fortune of political parties. For a long time the secret of Congress's success in parliamentary elections lay in Muslims and Dalits voting in its favour. But after emergency when Muslims and Dalits ceased to vote for the Congress its fortunes were in doldrums. It led Mrs. Gandhi to woo the Hindu votes by playing the Hindu card and communalism and communal violence began to spread much faster in the country. And to add fuel to the fire Rajiv Gandhi got the Supreme Court judgement in the Shah Bano case reversed by enacting the Muslim Women Act on one hand, and opening the doors of Babri Masjid, on the other. He also laid the foundation stone of Ram Mandir in Ayodhya in 1989 elections and lost the elections to an alliance formed by V.P. Singh.

Thus, it will be seen that Muslim votes often, though not always, are quite important for political parties to win elections.

It is estimated that in about 100 Lok Sabha seats, their votes are quite decisive. How important are their votes can be understood from the fact that even the BJP is trying to woo Muslims in this election. Even the RSS is trying to woo Muslims on the election eve. The RSS spokesman Ram Madhav declared that "All those Muslims who love their motherland (as if Muslims do not love their motherland) are welcome to become Swayamsevaks." The RSS has even put one *shakah* in Maharashtra under a Muslim Swayamsevak, as if to prove its point.

The RSS, however, is mounting pressure on the BJP to include ideological issues like construction of Ram temple etc. to keep its Hindutva base intact. Mr. Ram Madhav also said that the Muslims who become Swayamsevak are expected to 'respect' Hindu sentiments and that, he said, included construction of Ram Mandir and banning of cow slaughter.

It almost amounts to endorse the Hindutva agenda and Hindutva ideology. Thus, they are ready to admit Muslims in their fold only on their terms. Nevertheless it shows that even RSS thinks that the Muslims can be admitted at least to woo their votes for Lok Sabha elections. The BJP of course is making right kind of noises to attract Muslims to secure their votes. The Government has released an advertisement in Urdu papers with the main title *Hamara vada: dange aur fasad se paak Bharat* (Our promise: India free of communal riots). The ad carries a picture of Vajpayee speaking in the Shah Alam camp of Ahmedabad during the Gujarat carnage. The ad also carries certain extracts of Vajpayee's speech in which he appealed for peace in Gujarat. This ad was carried in *Inquilab*, an Urdu paper from Mumbai on 10th February.

Of course one reason among others for peace talks with Pakistan is coming Lok Sabha elections. The BJP hopes to cash in on establishing peace during coming elections and more than others, Muslims would welcome the peace moves especially from north as Northern Muslims have divided families. In Kashmir also the BJP is trying to attract Muslims. The BJP held a rally in Kashmir and Venkaiah Naidu told the people that "BJP is not anti-Muslim. This campaign is by our rivals to keep Muslims away from our party. We have so many Muslim governors in various states." But he had no answer when asked whether BJP, if it comes to power of its own will repeal Article 370. He only said that development would be the key issue.

It is interesting to note that the Muslims have matured and learnt from their experiences over the years. Gone are the days when Muslims could be swayed just by wining over leaders like the Shahi Imam or other leaders of his ilk. The reckless stand taken by their leaders during the Shah Bano movement and Babri Masjid-Ramjanambhoomi campaign has taught them a lesson.

Thus, when recently Mulayam Singh Yadav threw a bait by announcing that schools on Fridays will remain open only up to 12 noon so that Muslim children could go for Friday prayers the Muslims refused to buy it. Hardly any Muslim leader welcomed the move including the members of Muslim Personal Law Board, as these leaders knew that this will boomerang and the BJP will draw maximum benefit. Even a member of the MPLB opposed the move and some leaders even said how is it going to benefit Muslims as most of the young boys do not offer *namaz* (prayers) on Friday.

Mulayam Singh Yadav had announced this thinking Muslims would fall for it and he would benefit in the Loksabha elections. When the Muslims cold-shouldered it and the BJP opposed it he quietly withdrew the measure very next day. Now one thing is clear that neither Muslim masses nor their leaders are going to fall for such cheap tricks. They are now demanding concrete results in terms of jobs and economic well being. Emotional issues are no more fundamental to them, though they may be important.

Even in Bihar some Muslims have formed an independent front demanding more jobs for Muslims. They argue it is true Laloo Prasad Yadav has checked communal violence but has not done anything beyond that and this is not enough for Muslims. Security of life is one thing and material well being something else. He must deliver on this front also else Muslims would not vote for him.

Even the Muslims in U.P. have similar feelings towards Mulayam Singh. He too has checked communal violence but nothing beyond that. It is for this reason that Mulayam Singh has announced series of other measures as well. He has created 3000 posts for Urdu teachers, has made provision in recent budget for modernisation of madrasas and has also announced creation of Persian and Arabic University in Rampur to protect Islamic heritage in these languages. These are encouraging signs. Muslims should not fall for emotional issues any more and demand concrete measures for their economic well being and better education facilities.

There is one more factor, which must be taken into account: the regionalisation of politics and importance of alliances for forming the government at the Centre. Thus there is no longer the all India pattern of voting, like others Muslims too now vote on regional basis. In U.P. now Muslims prefer to vote either for SP or BSP and in Bihar for RJD and in West Bengal for the Left Front or the Congress. In Andhra Pradesh they vote for TDP or the Congress and in Tamil Nadu for DMK or AIDMK while in Kerala they may prefer to vote for Left Democratic Front or the Congress.

This is an important development or more in keeping with the regional diversity among Muslims themselves. Muslims have never been a homogenous mass as many political leaders reduced them to for their own vote bank politics. The Muslims in India are as diverse as Hindus and others. Now this diversity is getting reflected in their voting pattern too. Their development pattern differs from state to state. For example, the Muslims in Kerala and Tamil Nadu are better off both in educational as well as economic field compared to Muslims in U.P. The Muslims in Gujarat though generally poor have three trading communities, i.e., Bohras, Khojas and Memons which are quite well off compared to Muslims in Bihar and U.P. However, the Gujarat carnage under Narendra Modi led BJP government tried to greatly harm these trading communities.

Thus, Muslims will certainly vote in coming Lok Sabha elections on regional pattern keeping their regional interests in mind. It is interesting to note that in Andhra Pradesh, particularly in Hyderabad many Muslims are favourably inclined towards TDP although it has alliance with the BJP.

Since voting takes place now on regional basis there is no Muslim leader with all India appeal. It is more democratic. The regional diversity among the Muslims in a huge country like India, should be reflected fully in their political behaviour also. Until now the Muslim leadership both religious as well as political, was from North India. It is no more so as there is hardly any all India leadership. Regional leadership is emerging among Muslims too.

However, since the Sangh Parivar has deeply penetrated in the South also, one thing will remain of common concern for all Muslims in India that is secularism and communal harmony. Any regional party which, is committed to secularism would attract Muslim votes. Security of life is still most important consideration for Muslims in India whatever region they belong to.

Thus, in coming Lok Sabha election too secularism will remain prime consideration for the Muslims throughout India. Whatever Vajpayee says, it is hardly going to influence them because they know that BJP is controlled in final reckoning by the RSS and Vajpayee also has the RSS soul in him and he is *atal* (firm) on that whatever moderation he displays for his acceptability as the NDA leader. This is the gut feeling of any Muslim anywhere in India.

They have experienced it that the BJP has neither the party of any difference nor it has fulfilled its promise of maintaining communal peace in the country. Gujarat can never be effaced from Muslim memory.

Minorities and Lok Sabha Election

Coming days will assume greater and greater importance as election battle comes closer. The coming Lok Sabha elections are assuming increasing importance as for both the alliances, i.e., the BJP alliance – NDA – on one hand, and the Congress alliance, on the other. The Congress, which was shunning alliances until recently, in fact as recently as the elections in the four states in last December, has already entered into alliance with 16 parties and is negotiating with some more, particularly in U.P.

Despite the bravado, and India shining campaign or feel good factor, the BJP is far from sure about its decisive victory. If I am not wrong, it is even scared as the Congress has entered into alliance with so many regional parties. No party, the Congress or the BJP, can win elections on its own image. The NDA elections could win Lok Sabha elections in 1999 for variety of reasons, chief among them was that it had no inhibition to enter into alliance with any party, even if it happened to be ideologically its opposite. It was determined to come to power whatever apparently its ideological cost. It was the Congress, which had all reservations about entering into alliances with other parties and hence was defeated.

Now the Congress had shed all its complexes about alliances and is working hard to woe regional parties and sending shivers down the BJP spine. BJP has not only succeeded in wooing more parties, it has also lost some of its old allies like the DMK, Paswan`s Lok Shakti etc. The two biggest Hindi belt states like Bihar and U.P. are far from its grip. How can its fortune shine? In Maharashtra also, the Congress-NCP alliance and likely alliance with other smaller parties, is not going to help the Shiv Sena-BJP alliance in Maharashtra. In Tamil Nadu after alliance with DMK the Congress fortunes have improved and so is the case in Andhra Pradesh after Congress's alliance with TRS.

In West Bengal, BJP's alliance with Mamta Banarjee can hardly help NDA. The Left Front Fortress is quite impregnable. North East does not have many parliamentary seats and except Meghalaya BJP hardly has any toehold in that region. Yes, Gujarat, M.P., Rajasthan and Chattisgarh are its stronghold and BJP's position would improve slightly in these states but it would not help much. As against this it is likely to loose some seats in Maharashtra, Andhra Pradesh and Tamil Nadu. Thus the sum total may not prove.

It is for this reason that BJP which had maintained in 1999 that we could win elections without support of the Muslims and now is out to woo Muslim minority. No less a person than Mr. Vajpayee had said that our victory has shown that we can win without Muslim support. Problem is Atalji is not so *atal* (firm) after all. He keeps on changing his views like other politicians.

Today he is in desperate need of Muslim minority votes to win coming elections.

They have brought Arif Mohammad Khan and Najma Heptullah into BJP. Najma Heptullah had never contested any election so far. She remained confined to Rajya Sabha. She has no following among Muslim masses whatsoever at all. Arif Khan did have an image of a progressive Muslim who could stand for principles. He too was not a mass leader but had acquired great deal of popularity by resigning from BSP when it entered into alliance with the BJP for forming Government in U.P. All secularists thought he is really man of principle. He resigned from Rajiv Gandhi cabinet on principle and again resigned from BSP from principle. But he slurred his image by joining BJP. He cannot convince anyone whatever reasons he gives for joining BJP. He talked of building bridges with Hindus. Who knows better than Arif Khan that the BJP is ideologically controlled by RSS and it is not only party of Vajpayee but of Narendra Modis and Uma Bhartis and when crucial time comes Vajpayee also throws his lot with them rather than they throwing their lot with Vajpayee.

Anyway Arif Khan has lost the image he had built for himself by joining the BJP and Arif Khan may certainly personally gain but BJP can hardly gain anything by inducting few such Muslim faces. Muslim feel double threat from Sangh Parivar – of their very existence and of their religio-cultural identity.

Whatever the BJP leadership says today on the eve of Lok Sabha elections about the Gujarat riots (Shri L.K. Advani even called it a blot on the 'fair rule' of the BJP). But they all stood by Narendra Modi when his Government was involved in butchery of helpless Muslims in Gujarat in 2002. Then the Muslim carnage helped the BJP in Gujarat to win elections and now wooing Muslims is likely to help them. Thus their only principle is to win elections rather than respect human life or secular values.

The Muslims are feeling intensely threatened by the Sangh Parivar on both levels, i.e., on physical as well as on the level of their identity and even if few more Muslim leaders join BJP the Muslim masses are not going to support it in the elections. As we have already pointed out in an earlier article Muslim masses have stopped reacting emotionally and even the leader like Mulayam Singh Yadav had to hurriedly withdraw Friday prayer concession he offered to Muslim students.

Muslim masses no longer listen to leaders who want to manipulate their votes for their own political purposes. All those leaders who mattered during the eighties have been totally marginalised today. No new influential leader with all India image has emerged thereafter. And with regionalisation of politics this may not happen. The Muslim masses are not only going to vote according to their regional interests but also on the basis of defeating communal candidates.

The BJP has included in its vision document not only Ram temple but also uniform civil code and deletion of Article 370 from Constitution. How can then any Muslim be convinced that the BJP has given up its Hindutva agenda. On the contrary there is always a lurking fear in the minds of Muslims that if ever the BJP emerges with greater strength the NDA partners will be further subdued. On issues like Gujarat none of them could protest, not even symbolically and if BJP is further strengthened in the Lok Sabha, the NDA partners would be further emasculated.

Thus, no Muslim would run the risk of voting the BJP to power. And not only Muslims now the Christians are also under attack and the Church has also sent out a clear signal to its followers that they should vote on the basis of values and merit of the candidate. According to the Catholic Bishops Conference of India Catholics should vote for a person who "stands for values to promote human dignity, social equality, religious harmony and national integrity."

In fact the Muslim intelligentsia could ask for no better conditions for voting. Of course as far as Muslims are concerned there is no church or central religious or secular authority to guide them. But some organisations floated by Muslim intelligentsia are performing similar role and asking Muslims to vote for those candidates who are known for their commitment to secularism and well being of minorities. Two leaders of a Muslim political organisation All parties Muslim Political Conference have stated in a press conference in Delhi that a political conference of Muslims would be held in Delhi on 15th March in Gandhi Peace Foundation. This conference is going to prepare an agenda for removing educational and economic backwardness of Indian Muslims and place it before various political parties.

The Muslims in India today also feel that for Vajpayee and Advani it is not enough to express regret over what happened in Gujarat in 2002 but they should also see to it and commit themselves to get justice to the victims of Gujarat. Narendra Modi Government is determined to deny them any justice. He is going ahead with his agenda. He also intends to delete Good Friday from the list of public holidays in Gujarat. Is central leadership of the BJP doing anything to stop Narendra Modi from enacting his anti-minorities agenda?

Now we have also Uma Bharti in M.P. determined to pursue her Hindutva agenda under the active guidance of the RSS? If it is a fact that the ideological strings of the BJP are in the hands of the RSS and BJP is unable to sever its relation from it, is RSS prepared to shed its anti-minority bias? Is it ready to give up its serious reservations against minorities like Muslims and Christians? There is no sign of it anywhere in the air.

While the RSS is strongly committed to its ideology it is highly regrettable that the only well-organised Dalit Party the BSP is committed only to gaining power, even if it has to make serious compromises with the Sangh Parivar. It is very weak ideologically. Had it not been so the Dalit-minority alliance would have created a serious challenge for the Sangh Parivar.

Ms. Mayawati has repeatedly betrayed the cause of minorities and secularism in her insatiable desire for power. It has complicated the scene and weakened secular cause in the country. It is most unfortunate. Weaker sections are hopelessly divided and their leaders are more interested in power and have no hesitation in betraying the cause of their own people for that purpose.

The Lok Sabha election results could be very different if Mayawati throws her lot with people that with power.

India Under BJP

Many people had earnestly thought that BJP is the party, which will deliver and would provide a clean governance. In mid-eighties the Bofors scandal was in the air and was being discussed most widely throughout India. It had greatly tarnished the Congress image. Earlier in early seventies Mr. Jayprakash Narayan also had launched anti-corruption movement and Congress's name was sullied. The BJP was in the forefront of anti-corruption movements and was projecting its clean image. It used to project itself as 'a party with a difference' and this slogan attracted many, especially from upper caste, upper class intelligentsia towards BJP.

The BJP in opposition succeeded in creating an image for itself of its desire and could entice people to vote for it. But these upper caste upper class who fell for the BJP propaganda did not realise that any party in opposition can talk of corruption-free governance but real test is when the party comes to power. Then one has to see whether it really delivers what it promises. The BJP, anybody will vouch for it, has badly failed in providing corruption-free governance. In fact, it proved far worse than the Congress.

It has number of scandals to its credit. Serious allegations were made against son-in-law of Prime Minister himself. Also, an officer from PMO Shri Brijesh Mishra close to Prime Minister came under shadow. Even the RSS wanted him to resign. And who does not know the corruption scandals known as Tehelka.com. All these officers and many more were involved. The BJP Party president Bangaru Lakshman was caught on the tehelka.com camera accepting Rs.100,000 from a supposed representative of a defence supply company.

Then came the petrol pump allotment scandal and the *Indian Express* carried a series of articles exposing the Sangh Parivar and its allotment of petrol pumps to members of Sangh Parivar and called Sangh Parivar as *Pump Parivar*. This was not enough. Number of scandals were exposed in the defence establishment by the Chief Vigilance Commissioner. There was corruption even in buying coffins for our soldiers who laid down their lives for our country in Kargil war.

Mr. Fernandese, the trouble shooter for the BJP had to resign due to scandals exposed by tehelka.com and he had vowed not to join the ministry until cleared by the inquiry commission appointed by the Central Government to probe into tehelka.com allegations. However, he put pressure on Vajpayee and joined the cabinet again without being cleared by the inquiry commission. In no other country this could have been allowed. The entire opposition refused to recognise him as defence minister and would not even ask him questions relating to defence department. Still Mr. Fernandese continued without feeling any prick in his conscience.

There were other scandals too. Premier plots of land were allotted to RSS and other members of the Sangh Parivar at prices lower compared to those of market. No satisfactory explanations were forthcoming for these allotments. All this shows that the BJP was attacking the Congress for corrupt practices not because it was honest itself but only to woo the voters towards itself. It had absolutely no scruples of its own.

Corruption is only one aspect. But much more dangerous aspect is its intensifying communal divide in the country. BJP is basically a communal party. It invariably projects itself as ultra patriotic, as more patriotic than any other party in India. But it has done maximum damage to secular fabric of India. No communalist or a communal party can ever be patriotic whatever its rhetoric.

India cannot survive without harmony between religious communities and harmony is possible only when one thinks of interests of all communities, not of any one community. The BJP has always advocated cause of 'Hindus' and doubted patriotism of other communities. Such an approach brings about polarisation of communities in the country. The BJP was not even as much concerned with the security of the country as with construction of Ram temple in Ayodhya. And it went on increasing the gap between Hindus and Muslims in order to win Hindu votes.

It is not wrong to say that the BJP is trying to destroy the very idea of India. Our freedom fighters led by great visionaries like Mahatma Gandhi, Jawaharlal Nehru and Maulana Azad had based their idea of India on harmonious living of all religious communities and the basic *mantra* for this harmonious living was secularism. Secularism, as defined by the Constitution of India, not only meant freedom of religion for all its citizens but also priority of citizenship over religious affiliation.

The BJP completely destroyed this vision. It came to power by polarising the communities, by demolishing Babri mosque. It was not, as pointed out by many, demolition of mosque, but demolishing the idea of India. It created the myth of 'Hindu culture' as against the reality of composite culture. It tried to destroy Indian diversity – immortalised by our leaders in the slogan 'unity in diversity' and created the myth of 'cultural nationalism'. It considers cultural nationalism as its hallmark.

It saw in Narendra Modi as a 'Hindu hero', one who is responsible for carnage of Muslims in Gujarat. Even the Prime Minister Shri Vajpayee patted him on the back when he won elections in Gujarat after massacring more than 1000 people. He was seen not only as hero but a model of Hindutva and *moolmantra* for BJP to win elections in other states. Can such party whose very politics is based on murder and mayhem of minorities can govern the country? Can it keep India united? Can it strengthen its security? Can it end terrorism? It is for people to judge.

The noted writer and literature Khushwant Singh also has written in his recent book that intensifying communal feelings means, "end of India". The BJP singles out Muslims and Christians as foreigners and that these foreigners can never be loyal to this country. How can a party like BJP, which comes into power by dividing and polarising communities can ever promote unity and integrity of the community.

Fortunately India is so diverse – in fact bewilderingly diverse – that parties like the BJP cannot go on wooing Hindus on the slogan of cultural nationalism. Each religious community in India is highly diverse including Muslims. M.A. Jinnah also failed completely to unite Indian Muslims behind him precisely for the same reason. There were highly diverse cultural, linguistic religious and political trends among Muslims that no single party, let alone single leader could claim to be their sole representative. The Hindu community is supposed to be even more diverse.

How such a community can ever be represented by a single party like the BJP. It thus had to align with 22 other parties to form a government at the Centre. It is doubtful whether such a desperate coalition as NDA can be re-elected specially with such poor performance and several corruption scandals behind it. It is desperate coalition as it includes regionally diverse, ideologically at loggerheads and faction-ridden parties washing dirty linen publicly. It stuck together so far not because it is coherent group but for lack of worthwhile alternative.

Unfortunately the Congress so far thought it does not need to enter into coalition with other like-minded parties and can come to power of its own. Now India's socio-cultural, caste and religious diversity is translating itself into political diversity. Only coalitions worked out on the basis of divergent interests of these communities can hope to govern the country and deliver. The Congress has to take this newly emerged reality into account and enter into coalition of social, cultural and religious forces and work towards fulfilling their political aspirations.

Even in many developed democracies of the West, several countries like Germany, Italy and similar other countries have to enter into coalitions to provide stable governments. It is high time for the Congress leaders to reflect on the emerging realities in India and change its political strategies, if it has to defeat communal forces, which are striking at the very roots of Indian unity and integrity.

It is also responsibility of other secular parties, if they are really secular and care for idea of India, they must not align with any communal outfit. It is really unfortunate that many so-called secular parties have aligned themselves with a rank communal party like the BJP just to enjoy pleasures of power. A party like the TDP has in particular to re-think its strategy of supporting the BJP. In fact the BJP is in power mainly because of its crucial support. It is true TDP has to face the Congress in Andhra Pradesh. But it can certainly win elections in A.P. of its own if it provides clean governance.

On the other hand its continued support to the BJP coalition can cost it dearly by alienating the minorities. It is not enough that TDP is trying to keep communal peace in A.P. its support to NDA headed by BJP is providing much needed fuel to communal fire in other states. If the Chandrababu had not provided much needed support to the NDA Gujarat carnage would not have taken place. Thus the TDP also cannot escape the responsibility for what happened in Gujarat. Thus TDP is also contributing to what Khushwant Singh calls "End of India".

What India is undergoing today is highly agonising for any sensitive soul committed to Indian unity and integrity. The politicians are playing their games to come to power by dividing India. The committed citizens should not shirk their role in such a situation and dedicate themselves to ushering in an era of communal peace, harmony, unity and integrity.

Where Nanavati, Incorrect

Justice G.T. Nanavati who has been investigating Godhra incident and the Gujarat riot that followed recently said that he has so far found no evidence that the state machinery and police were involved in Gujarat communal violence. Justice Nanavati has given this statement to the press and also spoke to a T.V. channel on these lines. He was quoted by a news agency as saying, "Evidence recorded so far did not indicate any serious lapse on the part of the police or administration in controlling the communal clashes. When there was outcry against his statement he gave a clarification on phone to *Indian Express* that "I had said that so far no serious allegation had come on record against police and the administration during the district level hearings." He further explained that "This does not include the hearings conducted with regard to Godhra incident and affidavits which have been filed before the Commission."

The Commission was appointed on March 6, 2001 and the Commission has received so far over 3000 affidavits from riot victims. According to newspaper reports Nanavati said that some of these affidavits included allegations against a few police officers from some districts."

Such a statement from the inquiring judge at an unfinished stage is quite improper. It can give wrong impression and the accused can even treat it as a 'clean chit' in their favour. The legal community of Gujarat was also of the opinion that this was improper on the part of Justice Nanavati. Former chief justice of the Gujarat High Court B.J. Diwan maintained, Nanavati should not have made the statement.

As a retired judge of the Supreme Court Justice Nanavati should know better that before completing an inquiry and without thorough inquiry no such comments could be made. It can vitiate even further findings, as victims may not come forward to record their evidence. The victims are already under tremendous pressure not to name anyone and if head of the Commission gives such statement it may further put them under pressure.

The case of Best Bakery in Baroda is quite illustrative in this regard. The main eye-witness has gone back on her earlier statement obviously under intense pressure and threats. According to *The Indian Express* (dated 20th May, 2005) "Till last Saturday everybody knew Zahira Sheikh as the key witness in the Best Bakery case. It was Vadodra's most gruesome incident in last year's communal violence. Twelve people were burnt alive. Zahira, an eye witness, had cried, had made loud representations and demanded justice on several occasions. Including when the then national Human Rights Commission Chairman Justice J.S.Verma and Chief Election Commissioner J.M. Lyngdoh came visiting."

After turning hostile Zahira has disappeared. She and her family refuse to have interaction with those around them. Even her elder sister refused to divulge where her sister is and also refuse to give her own name. Zahira was seen with BJP MLA Madhu Shrivastav in the court premises and this led to several eyebrows being raised. One can well understand what was cooking and how witnesses are being pressured, lured or threatened to weaken the cases against the accused in burning, looting and murdering cases. In such atmosphere of fear and threat justice Nanavati's kind of statement can further discourage key witnesses from appearing before the commission.

It is not unknown in ordinary murder cases how criminals exercise intense pressure on eye-witnesses not to give witness. In this case the whole might of state is involved and how they can threaten and pressurise is not beyond imagination. Not that witnesses can not be found for involvement of police and state machinery in Gujarat carnage but people in many cases are unwilling to talk for fear of consequences.

Justice Nanavati should know as an experienced Supreme Court judge how things work in India. He should have also known the over all situation in Gujarat before rushing to the press making such statement. Much has appeared in media as to what happened in Gujarat after Godhra incident. Not one but several retired High Court and Supreme Court judges had visited Gujarat and had known first hand about the happenings there. An expert panel of judges from Supreme Court and high courts headed by Justice V.R. Krishna Iyer has even prepared a comprehensive report entitled *Crime against Humanity* detailing involvement of police and state machinery and the ruling party.

Justice J.S. Verma, the Chairman, National Human Rights Commission, himself had passed severe strictures against the State machinery and the way it handled communal violence in Gujarat. Besides these eminent judges hundreds of eminent citizens and concerned people had visited and prepared reports of Gujarat carnage and complicity of state machinery. The former direct general of police, Maharashtra and Governor of Punjab, Julio Ribeiro had strongly castigated the Gujarat police and its role in controlling communal violence.

Mr. Ribeiro in an interview to the *Times of India* dated 10/9/2002 had said, in a reply to a question "What in your opinion was the reason for the failure of the Police in Gujarat" had said, "The top brass must take the blame. I did not sense a whiff of leadership from top police officers. Senior officers have been reduced to mute spectators as they have little control over the force. Generally, senior police officers discipline errant subordinates by transferring them to insignificant wings. But in Gujarat, officers from the subordinate ranks manipulate all the transfers and postings at the police station level, which is the cutting edge of the force." This speaks volumes about the role of police in Gujarat and is quite damning for top police leadership.

He also commented in the same interview that many people told him that the police were recording absolutely incorrect FIRs. "I (Ribeiro) met a respectable Hindu gentleman who said that the police did not take down the names of the rioters he had seen and wrote that it was a group of unidentified people. If people who have seen their mothers and sisters raped and burnt before their eyes have no hope of getting justice, they will all turn into terrorists and why are we talking about ISI and Pakistan when we are doing their job for them by creating terrorists?"

This damning evidence of police inaction and involvement in Gujarat carnage should have been taken notice of by the honourable judge before he made his pre-mature comments in the public.

Even if it is true that Justice Nanavati had not received complaints about police behaviour during hearings in the districts other than Ahmedabad and Baroda, it was improper for him to comment of the role of police and administration in a hurry. It is overall situation, which matters, not piecemeal evidence. A investigator, much more a judicial officer of highest rank, has to keep overall situation in mind before commenting. It is also not true that there are no complaints against police in the areas covered so far by Justice Nanavati Commission, i.e., Panchmahal district and other districts except Ahmedabad and Vadodra where worst incidents took place.

There are serious complaints, particularly against police in Panchmahal and other districts also. I have myself visited these areas and heard heart-rending stories from victims themselves and their bitter complaints against police inaction or complicity. In the Eral village of Panchmahal district a woman called Madina told inconsolably how they hid in the nearby fields for two/three days and then tried to escape from there but were caught by the mob and her daughter and niece Shabana and Suhana were raped and killed and police was nowhere to be seen. They made desperate calls to the police to rescue them. In fact her entire statement is on camera with us.

There is another heart-rending story from Randhikpur village in Dohad district. A woman called Bilqis aged 19 and her family sensed danger and phoned police and got usual reply they can do nothing about it. The family kept on hiding here and there and at least was caught by the mob on 2nd March. Bilqis – three month pregnant was raped by three men and taken to be dead, regained her consciousness after sometime and survived. However, 14 members of her family were massacred and her 3 year-old child was among them.

She asked police to record her statement but police, after dilly-dallying recorded wrong statement and took her thumb impression. She was suspicious and when collector visited her refugee camp she drew his attention. Collector repromanded police and asked them to record proper FIR and file case on the basis of second FIR. However, meanwhile the Collector was transferred (as all good, conscientious officers were transferred by Narendra Modi) and police filed the case on the basis of first FIR and destroyed the case. This too is on record on camera with us.

How then justice Nanavati drew his conclusion? *The Asian Age* also has produced in its edition of 22nd May 2003 has reproduced under the caption "What's Nanavati talking about? Here is proof." in original Gujarati an affidavit filed before the Commission about the police complicity and inaction when the mob cut off two hands of a Muslim woman. Such an attitude on the part of inquiry commission can vitiate the whole inquiry and discourage people from appearing before it.

The head or members of inquiry commission should not make any public comment before the inquiry is finally over. It is unfortunate that Justice Nanavati chose to speak pre-mature on the subject of his inquiry thus lowering the dignity of the commission and making people loose confidence in his impartial nature of inquiry.

Bomb Blast, Communal Violence and Secular India

The recent bomb blast in Mumbai on 25th August 2003 is a wake up call, if we care. It should shake us up into deep reflection as to what is happening to our country which gave birth to doctrine of non-violence hundreds of years before Christ and also during our freedom struggle in last century. Why so much violence in contemporary India whether it is communal violence or such retaliatory violence in the form of bomb blast. Such sectarian and arbitrary violence seriously compromises with our doctrines of non-violence and secularism. We cannot build modern India without these doctrines.

First we would like to throw some light on the recent bomb blast. The police maintains that one Sayyad Mohammad, his wife and daughter were involved in these bomb blasts in Mumbai on black Monday, i.e., on 25th August. The police also says that this was organised by an organisation called the Gujrat Muslim Revenge Force backed by Jaish-e-Muhammad and Lashkar-i-Tayyaba of Pakistan. Also we read news about suicide bombing regularly in Kashmir as well as in Palestine and other places.

Let me say here with all the emphasis at my command that any form of violence, much less in revenge, can be justified in the name of Islam. The names like Lashkar-i-Tayyaba, Jaish-e-Muhammad (the army of Muhammad the Prophet) are highly misleading. Such names are adopted only to provide religious gloss over heinous acts of violence. Muslims should not be misled by such pious sounding names. Muhammad has been described in the Qur'an as "Mercy to the nations". Can anyone kill ruthlessly in his name?

Suicide bombing promoted by these Pak-based organisations, to say the least, is totally prohibited by Islam. The Imam of Al-Azhar Mosque, Cairo, also said in his lecture in Malaysia that suicide is *haram* (prohibited) in Islam. And suicide bombing is doubly prohibited as it takes lives of innocent people and often they happen to be children, women and old persons. There is no way that such acts can at all be justified.

The Qur'an says that killing one person without justification amounts to killing whole humanity and saving one life amounts to saving whole humanity (5:32). Thus the Qur'an has very rigorous standards about respecting the right to live and no one has right to deprive others of this right to take revenge or otherwise except through due process of law. Also, no one has right to kill non-combatants even if one has waging jihad. Shari'ah law strictly prohibits killing non-combatants, children, women and old people. And in such bomb blasts or suicide bombing only such people get killed.

Jaish-e-Muhammad, Lashkar-i-Tayyaba etc. are working against the express rules of Shari'ah. Their high sounding and pious names should not deceive anyone. The bomb blasts in Mumbai on 25th August killed more than 50 persons all of whom were totally innocent. So many children were orphaned and many women were widowed. Can it be called an Islamic act even remotely? It is so shocking that two Muslim women were involved in this brutal act. It should really deeply concern all of us that all communal organisations are using women for their selfish ends. Women who give birth to life should never be involved in any act, which leads to extinguishing life. And one who is truly religious can never indulge in revenge killing in the name of Islam. The Qur'an requires Muslims to suppress their anger rather than kill in retaliation. Thus we find in the Qur'an among virtues of the believers "Those who spend in ease as well as in adversity and those *who restrain (their); anger and pardon men. And Allah loves the doers of good." (3:133).*

In view of this verse there should be no doubt that acts of retaliation has absolutely no place as far as the Qur'an is concerned. A true believer has to restrain his/her anger and should pardon rather than kill in revenge and should be doer of good. Thus all these religious sounding armies should wind themselves up if they at all believe in Islam and should devote themselves to promote peace and security for innocent people. This bloodshed is most irreligious act. Mohammad Sayyad, his wife Fahmida and daughter Farhin are not the real culprits. It is these organisations like Jaish-i-Mohammad and Lashkar-e-Tayyaba who are brainwashing these semi-literate people. They are Muslims but have no knowledge of Islam.

Indian Secular Democracy

As there is no place for violence and revenge killing in Islam there is no place for it in a secular democracy. Had there been no Gujarat carnage in post-Godhra phase there would have been no attack on Akshardham temple in Gandhinagar and these five bomb blasts in Mumbai since December 2002 in which many innocent lives were lost. There is no doubt that violence breeds violence.

The private armies like Lashkar-i-Tayyaba are no responsible to anyone and no one has elected them. For violence they perpetrate, howsoever strongly condemnable it may be, they are not responsible to anyone. But this cannot be said of Gujarat Government which was directly responsible for horrible violence perpetrated against innocent Muslim citizens of Gujarat after Godhra incident, which is equally condemnable. One must say the Godhra incident was perpetrated by some Muslims but what happened thereafter in Gujarat the Narendra Modi led government was directly responsible for it.

Can a government elected by people of a secular democratic country be pardoned for what it did to those innocent citizens who lost their lives, homes and other properties? Certainly not. Even the Central government, which is equally responsible for maintaining secular democratic values, did nothing to stop such violence in a state which put whole country to shame in the eyes of the world.

If organisations like Lashkar-e-Tayyaba are a blot on the fair name of Islam government led by Narendra Modi in Gujarat is a blot on the fair name of secular democracy like India. We rejected the idea and ideology of Pakistan as it was against our commitment to secular democracy. It is thus our collective duty to keep secular democracy going in our country. Those who use religion for appealing for votes cannot be friends of this country, as those who invoke Islam for acts of retaliation cannot be believers in Islam.

Fifty-five years after our independence won on the basis of ideals of secular democracy we see more and more communal violence and still minorities are feeling insecure on one hand and deprived of their right to honourable and dignified existence. In fact our leaders of freedom struggle like Gandhi, Nehru and Abul Kalam Azad had expected that with the passage of time communal rancour will be forgotten and all citizens, as propounded in our Constitution, will be able to lead an honourable secure life enjoying all fundamental rights. But not only that this goal has not been realised it is receding ever further.

It is for all of us to reflect seriously why are we continuously receding from our goal. Is democracy a means for best form of governance or clever means to realise ambitions of some unscrupulous politicians by manoeuvring religious sentiments of innocent people? Can a democratic country afford blatantly communal organisations promoting hatred against minorities and branding them as enemies of the country?

Can we provide security even to the majority community if such hate politics is blatantly resorted to by these rank communal organisations? When these bomb blasts take place innocent citizens belonging to majority community get killed. Is government not then responsible for these deaths? Can we prevent this severe danger to our internal security only through policing? Our police force is also corrupt, communal and inefficient with a few honourable exceptions. How can we rely on such police force to protect innocent citizens?

And can even best kind of policing guarantee full security? It cannot if hate-politics is not kept under cheque. Today America is also chasing terrorists all over the world with no success. Terror attacks, if one goes by what is happening in Iraq and where America had gone to put and end to terror, are increasing and America is totally helpless. You cannot solve such problems by employing mighty armies and efficient policing but by providing people justice and living with dignity.

Today it is a fact that Indian Muslims are feeling alienated and insecure and are facing a ballast of communal propaganda. In such a situation it will not be wise to believe that every Muslim will keep his/her cool and will not be fragile enough to be brainwashed and misled by terrorist organisations operating from across the border. Unless we give a sense of security and dignity to Indian Muslims it will be very difficult to guarantee internal security.

Today we face much greater danger in the form of terrorist attacks as number of terrorist organisations have come into existence after 1990 when the Kashmiri youth took to violence. Earlier during the eighties and before number of major communal riots had taken place but no such bomb explosions took place right up to the period Babri Masjid was demolished by the Sangh Parivar activists by inciting some Hindus to grab their votes to come to power. It is since then that Sangh Parivar intensified its hate campaign beyond all limits and we are experiencing such bomb explosions in various parts of India.

We must learn a lesson and leave behind communal hatred and instil true patriotism in the minds of our youth. Patriotism does not lie in loving only territory but all the people of the country as well and respecting their right to dignified existence. If we want to be proud of our past let us be proud of philosophy of Upanishads, compassion of Buddha, love from the Bible and justice and benevolence from the Qur'an. Let us bury the hatchet of Mandir-Masjid conflicts forever.

Ayodhya's Voice

I visited Ayodhya recently along with the Magasaysay awardee Mr. Sandeep Panday who has been working here for quite sometime to bring peace to this strife torn town. It is so interesting to talk to people of this place. I had to hold a workshop on communal harmony for Ayodhya and Faizabad towns and Sandeep was helping us in this connection. We met a cross section of people to hear their voice.

The country hears only the voice of Sangh Parivar and their most aggressive members like Singhal and Togadia. The media also has no time to project the voice of people of Ayodhya. Perhaps it does not sell. What sells is the powerful voice of Sangh Parivar and this Parivar has convinced the world that it is most authentic voice of 800 million Hindus of this country.

The communal forces always tend to homogenise the whole community as if millions of people belonging to a community speak one voice and surrender their minds and bodies to one individual or one party or one clique of persons. It is this one individual or party or group which takes all decisions and others simply endorse it. No dissent is ever tolerated. It is violently suppressed if it ever raises its voice. Before partition Jinnah also projected himself as the sole representative of Indian Muslims. All others had to endorse his decisions.

The Sangh Parivar always maintains that all Hindus want to build the Ram temple at Ayodhya and that it is historical fact that a temple stood there and Babar demolished it and build a mosque in its place. It is a 'proven fact' and no one can question it. And the one who does, is an 'enemy of Hinduism'. The communalists have sole right to understand and interpret history.

It is miracle of modern day propaganda through media that has converted a non-existent problem into the most potent problem. What did not exist has not only become a powerful problem but has also become the cause of killing of thousands of innocent people across India. It was on account of Ramjanambhoomi-Babri Masjid problem that 59 people were set afire in Sabarmati Express in Godhra on 27 February 2002 and more than one thousand people killed most cruelly in retaliatory act in Gujarat from 28th February onwards and continued for more than six months.

And it was on account of this non-existent problem that BJP rode to power though it had repeatedly failed to do so before. Shri L.K. Advani's *rath yatra* in 1990 failed to lead to Ayodhya as planned but did lead to Delhi as intended. The rath may not reach Ayodhya in near future but it does help retaining Delhi. The raths in medieval period helped win wars so the modern Toyota rath led the BJP to power in Delhi.

The people of Ayodhya know this better than anyone else. They have paid heavy price for it and still continue to pay. And they have been as helpless so far as other people of India have been. They have silently borne the brunt of Sangh Parivar's aggression for years. They are, it seems, no longer prepared to do so. Every time the VHP leaders announce their programme of '*kar seva*' or *sant yatra* or Ram Lalla *darshan* the people of Ayodhya have to shut their shops. Lakhs invade the town disturbing their normalcy and often inviting prolonged curfews. Every citizen of Ayodhya shudders to think of VHP programmes in their town.

Now again the VHP has announced its programme in Ayodhya on 17th October. Lakhs of 'Rambhakts' once again will march to that town for 'Ram Lalla Darshan'. Everyone I met in Ayodhya told me that every time election is announced the VHP tries to organise its show in Ayodhya as if this is the only way for BJP to win elections. It is people of Ayodhya who pay price for the election anywhere in India. The BJP perhaps knows no other way of winning the election.

We met Mahant Gyandas who is chief Mahant of Hanuman Garhi temple which is one of the most significant shrines of Ayodhya. The Mahant was sitting surrounded by his followers. It is important to note that the land for Hanuman Garhi temple was donated by the Nawab of Avadh and the temple was built by one of his Nawab's Hindu courtier.

I asked the Mahant whether he would like Ramjanambhoomi temple to be built at the site of Babri Masjid. Gyandas told me the temple can be built only when Hindus and Muslims come together to build the temple. Hindu-Muslim unity is more important than the temple. If they cannot agree to build the temple let us wait for court's verdict. It cannot be built by shedding human blood.

When Gyandasji was saying this I was reminded of Maulana Azad's presidential address at the Ramgarh session of AICC. Maulana had said in his presidential address that even if an angel descended from heaven and declared that I have brought the gift of India's freedom from heaven, I would refuse to accept it until Hindu-Muslim unity is achieved. For, if India does not get freedom it is India's loss but if Hindu-Muslim unity is not achieved, it is humanity's loss.

The Hanuman Garhi's Mahant was also making almost similar point. If the temple is to built it is Sangh Parivar's loss but if Hindu-Muslim unity is disturbed it is entire country's loss as well as loss for whole humanity. But who cares if humanity suffers as long as the Sangh Parivar can come to power. Mahant Gyandasji is against VHP and considers it as anti-Hindu. VHP, he tells me, has no right to talk in the name of Hindus. Hindus have not elected them to represent them or to build Ramjanambhoomi temple in their name. He also said that those who tore open the stomach of a pregnant woman and threw the foetus into the fire cannot even qualify as Hindus, let alone building a temple in the sacred city of Ayodhya in their name.

Sandeep had also convened the meeting of many other Mahants and some citizens of Ayodhya who have constituted an organisation called Ayodhya ki Awaz (Voice of Ayodhya). The Mahants and other people of Ayodhya have floated this organisation in order to fight the VHP plan to convert Ayodhya into a battle ground for their war for power. They have suffered silently so far but can bear it no longer and have decided to fight it out peacefully and democratically. Ayodhya ki Awaz has now become voice of all peace loving people of Ayodhya.

The meeting was attended by some important Mahants of Ayodhya like Mahant Bhawnath Das who was also Sarpanch of Hanuman Garhi and is president of Samajwadi Sant Sabha. He presided over the meeting. Jugal Kishore Shashtri also took part in the meeting who is convenor of Ayodhya ki Awaz and also edits the weekly paper *Ramjanambhoomi.* He counters the VHP propaganda through his paper. Shri Shashtri is quite vocal and committed to maintaining peace in Ayodhya.

Another Mahant Madhuwan Das, a Mahant associated with Hanuman Garhi and who is also a corporator from Ramjanambhoomi ward was also present in the meeting. Mahant Girish Tripathi who has done his M.A. in political science from JNU also took part in the meeting. Badal Acharya who is son of Chief Mahant of Dant Dhawan Kund and is preparing to take over as Mahant himself and Rangesh Achari son of Rajsabha Mandir too came for the meeting. One Sadiq Ali, an activist who repeatedly suffered in Ayodhya is also actively associated with this organisation and was present in the meeting.

In his introductory remarks Bhawnath Das said that it was high time that we fought against those who go to the extent of setting fire to the Sabarmati compartment killing scores of innocent Hindus in order to organise carnage of Muslims so that they can win the elections in Gujarat. They would like to convert whole India into Gujarat, if they could. Now we must show courage and fight the VHP menace.

A concrete programme was chalked out for facing the situation on 17th October when the VHP is again trying to bring lakhs of its supporters to Ayodhya. All Mahants present in the meeting felt that since elections have been announced in the four states the VHP is again staging this drama and it should not get away with it every time. Everyone present felt that this committee should demand ban on the entry of outsiders like Singhal and Togadia and a memorandum to be submitted to the chief minister of U.P. to this effect. There was some difference of opinion whether they should demand ban on entry of so-called Rambhaktas. It was suggested that those who want to come for genuine Ram Lalla darshan should come in groups of four or five. However, Jugalkishore Shashtri was of the opinion that those brought by VHP should not be allowed to enter Ayodhya at all on 17th October.

It was also decided to stage a peaceful *dharna* at the Gandhi statue in Ayodhya on 2nd October to highlight these demands. The members of working committee and some others should take part in this *dharna*. It was also decided that citizens of Ayodhya should resist entry of VHP supporters on 17th October and one person from every house in Ayodhya should take part in it. Suitable pamphlets and stickers would be published for mobilising the people of Ayodhya.

It is indeed heartening that many Mahants and other people of Ayodhya are girding up their lions to fight the VHP campaign, which has nothing to do with building Ramjanambhoomi temple but only to keep alive this controversy for political purposes. The voiceless people of Ayodhya who have suffered for so long are now giving themselves an effective voice. The Mahants have also decided not to sit it out silently. They are preparing to throw gauntlet to the VHP at last.

State Election Results–Victory of BJP or Communalism

The election results in three states of Madhya Pradesh, Rajasthan and Chattisgarh were quite unexpected, even stunning in a sense. No one, least of all the Congress expected to loose in all three states in Hindi heartland. It has, naturally, boosted the morale of the BJP tremendously. Many are expecting that the dates for the Lok Sabha elections may be advanced by the Prime Minister, to cash on this victory.

The BJP itself never expected such victory. The Prime Minister himself admitted he was expecting to win in two states and the other two the Congress was expected to win. Though the Congress win in M.P. was within the realm of doubt everyone thought Rajasthan will fall in the lap of the Congress. However, even Rajasthan went to the fold of BJP with comfortable margin.

There is need for deep reflection. The BJP, it is interesting to note did not employ communal card and did not speak the language of Hindutva throughout its election campaign in all the four states and only employed the discourse of development. In fact in case of M.P. it was Digvijay Singh, the then Chief Minister of M.P. who tried to employ what was construed as 'soft Hindutva'.

Is it genuine change of heart in case of BJP? Can we say the BJP leaders have come out of clutches of RSS-VHP? Will the BJP now fight all elections on the basis of developmental issues? Or is it only temporary tactics on the part of the BJP. If it is genuine change of heart every secularist will welcome it and it will rid India of hate and divisive politics being employed by the BJP. But all available evidences shows it is quite unlikely to happen.

The BJP's only obsession is power, even if it is at the cost of unity and integrity of the country and even if it is through shedding blood of innocent people. The BJP when it came into existence in 1980 after the break up of the Janata Party, had declared that it had adopted secularism and Gandhian socialism as its policy and it took pledge not to resort to communal politics anymore.

What was the result? Did BJP really renounce communal politics? It did but only temporarily. On the secular plank it lost the parliamentary elections very badly. It got only two seats in the 1984 Lok Sabha elections. It was shaken to the core. And it did not hesitate for a moment to renounce its secular and socialist plank. The party, which had taken oath never to resort to communalism began to question the very philosophy of communalism and dubbed it as an alien western concept. It also began to denounce Nehruvian secularism as 'pseudo secularism' and amounting to 'minority appeasement'.

So much for the change of heart on the part of BJP. In fact it was only after formation of the BJP in 1980 and its 'renunciation' of communalism that the BJP became most aggressively communal in mid-eighties. It was after this oath for secularism that BJP raised the question of Ram Mandir and changed the whole direction of Indian politics. Now in view of Mandir politics, communalism has been institutionalised. Indian politics was, until then, nothing, if not secular. And now we heave a sigh of relief, if Hindutva issues are not raised by the BJP in its election campaign.

The reason for the BJP not using Hindutva issues in M.P., Rajasthan and Chattisgarh elections are obvious. Firstly, when Digvijay Singh raised 'soft Hindutva' issues in M.P. in anticipation of the BJP raiding the hard Hindutva issues and particularly so as the BJP had nominated Sadhvi Uma Bharti as the chief ministerial candidate, the BJP vowed not to raise Hindutva issues and raise only developmental issues.

Uma Bharti had played crucial role in Mandir politics and had aroused feelings of hatred among Hindus using her sharply communal rhetoric and everyone was expecting that she would fight M.P. elections employing Hindutva rhetoric aggressively. But in a way Digvijay Singh, himself a shrewd player in election game thwarted this possibility by raising issues of cow slaughter etc. The BJP thus changed its tactics and decided to take Digvijay Singh on another turf.

M.P. was known for its bad roads and shortage of electricity and drinking water. The BJP realised that these issues will be far more important for people of M.P. than Hindutva plank. It realised this particularly after Uma Bharti failed to raise Hindu emotions on the question of Bhojshala in Dhar. Digvijay Singh government frustrated her attempts to turn Bhojshala-Kamal Maula Masjid issue as another Rammandir-Babri Masjid issue by throwing open Bhojshala to Hindus on every Tuesday.

Also, people of India are tired of such emotional issues and no longer respond to them as vigorously as they did during eighties and nineties. This is precisely why the BJP is in a bad shape in U.P., the very epic centre of mandir politics and it had to strike alliance with otherwise its arch enemy BSP and that too broke, fragile relationship as it was. The Bhojshala-Kamal Maula Masjid issue also did not evoke any warmth in Hindu hearts in M.P. and hence BJP shrewdly raised the issue of electricity, roads and water.

Today the BJP is indeed facing a great dilemma, i.e., Hindutva versus development issues. After winning Gujarat elections using Gujarat carnage as winning formula and discovering in Narendra Modi as a Hindutva icon giving the BJP a new hope. The BJP leaders then made statements that we would use Gujarat model to win elections all over India. However, immediately after that the BJP lost elections to Congress in Himachal Pradesh and Narendra Modi, the Hindutva icon, had to be withdrawn from campaign. Thus the BJP came to conclusion that India is too diverse to apply the Gujarat model in other parts of India. It was forced to change its strategy once again.

The RSS and Vishwa Hindu Parishad want to keep their iron grip over BJP and dictate terms to it. The BJP, unable to come to power of its own due to this bewildering diversity of India, has to depend on coalition politics (also often described as 'coalition *dharma*' by BJP leaders) and moderate its Hindutva rhetoric. But it also has to face pressures from RSS-VHP as their volunteers do great deal of work during elections. It cannot win elections without the support of these volunteers.

The BJP thus uses development discourse from public platform but clandestinely uses Hindutva propaganda to exploit hard Hindutva votes. There is clear evidence that the Hindutva volunteers were doing door to door campaigns swaying voters' sentiments on hard Hindutva issues like construction of Ram temple on one hand, and converting India into Hindu Rashtra, on the other. These RSS-VHP volunteers were distributing Hindutva leaflets along with election cards from door to door.

It is also interesting to note that all the tribal areas which used to vote for the Congress in M.P. heavily voted for the BJP this time and the RSS leaders claimed that it was because of work done by Vanwasi Ashrams (i.e., forest dwelling religious centres) in tribal areas. The RSS is concentrating on tribal areas and making these tribals proud of their 'Hindu' identity though in fact tribals are not Hindus. They do not worship Hindu gods and goddesses. Thus the RSS has greatly succeeded in Hiduising the tribals and turning them into Hindutva vote-bank.

In Gujarat too in post-Godhra carnage tribals and dalits were used on a large scale to massacre Muslims. Most horrible carnage took place in tribal areas of Baroda and Panchmahal districts. On the other hand, the Congress does hardly any work among tribals. It has taken these tribal votes for granted. In Chattisgarh too, which is primarily a tribal state and the Congress used to win elections in these areas, it lost heavily and BJP was main beneficiary of tribal votes. Jharkhand state is also primarily tribal and BJP won elections there too and formed Government after it separated from Bihar.

The Congress has to do lot of introspection if it wants to come to power in the states as well as at the Centre. It has to won back tribal areas, which is no easy task for it as the RSS is working very hard among tribals to convert them into Hindu vote bank. Secondly it will have to give up its arrogance that it can win elections or its own and there is no need to enter into coalition with other like-minded secular parties. The Congress still lives in the past and wants to bask into past glory. It is not going to help it any more.

Though it had passed a resolution at Simla to enter into coalition with other like-minded parties but in practice it never did and suffered heavily for it both in Gujarat last year and in these three states. In Gujarat too, if it had entered into coalition with parties like the NCP, the BJP would have lost many seats and would not have won elections by two-third majority. Also, if in these three states it had entered into coalition with the BSP, CPI and other smaller parties it would certainly have won elections if one goes by vote percentages.

The Congress should also realise that masses in India are no more mesmerised by the Nehru family. There is need for more dynamic leadership rather than a leader from only Nehru family. Sycophancy would no more help the party. What is needed is vision and ability to alter the terms of politics once again. Nehru attracted Indian masses mainly because of his futuristic vision of India. Indira Gandhi also sustained this vision and continued to exercise great influence on the minds of Indian voters. The Congress will have to think on these suggestions sincerely to win back the Indian electorates.

5

Secularism and Riots

2002—Riots in Maharashtra

The Maharashtra has been witnessing riot after riot both major and minor. Among major riots were in Malegaon in October 2001 and now in Sholapur. Malegaon riot was not only a major riot but had shaken the whole state. More than 13 persons were killed in that riot. In last few days two riots in Sholapur and in Badlapur shook the state. In Sholapur more than 9 persons were killed while in Badlapur there was no loss of life but resulted in large destruction of property.

Several other riots also took place like in Jalgaon, Pune, Buldana and other places. Ironically it is Shiv Sena which has been alleging that more than 44 riots have taken place in Maharashtra under the Vilasrao Deshmukh Government. It also alleged that properties worth 31 crore was lost in these riots. It is therefore, important to examine who is responsible for these riots.

The riots in Sholapur are quite disturbing. Sholapur is no doubt communally sensitive place. It had witnessed riots in early eighties. But it was peaceful since that time. Sholapur is a major city in Maharashtra and is well known for its textile industry. It is known for its working class character. Most of its population consists of working class. But like in other places in India there is severe crisis in textile industry and people are suffering economically.

Muslims form a substantial part of the Sholapur population.

There are about 20 per cent Muslims in the population of 10 lakhs. These Muslims, it is interesting to note, mostly belong to the lower castes like Baghbans and others. There are also those who are in weaving industry. There is also the *bidi* rolling industry which employs large number of workers, mostly women. Then there are many low caste Hindus from Andhra Pradesh most of whom also work in looms. Thus Sholapur has unique character of its own.

Politically speaking it has been traditionally a Congress stronghold. The Sharad Pawar Congress also has its influence. The Shiv Sena -BJP does not have much influence in this industrial city. It is also important to note that low caste Muslims like Baghbans are quite assertive there. It is from this city that backward caste Muslim movement arose and also the Muslim Marathi writers' movement which was led by Prof. F.H. Bennur, a retired professor of political science in the local college. The Muslim Marathi writers movement has acquired credibility of its own and holds its sessions regularly.

The rioting in Sholapur started on 11th October on Friday on the question of insulting remarks against the Prophet of Islam by an American Baptist priest Jerry Falwell. A protest rally was taken out by the Muslims in Sholapur. The Muslims had also given call for observing *bandh* on that day. The police fired in the air to disperse the crowds as some Muslim boys tried to force Hindus who had not closed their shops. When they refused these boys tried to forcefully close their shops and trouble began.

The police responded by declaring curfew in Tilak Chowk and other affected areas. The protest march had started after the Friday prayers and there was no leader worth the name to restrain the protesters. The protestors also attacked the nearby Navratri Mandap. The local mandal members retaliated and the riots broke out. Later the house of former BJP MLA Narsingh Lengji was also attacked. However, the MLA was not at home at the time of attack.

The violence then spread to various parts of the city and as usual it is poorest and weakest sections of society who suffered. Shashtrinagar is an area where poor people, rickshaw drivers, bidi workers and others stay. And there are mostly qassab (butchers) in the Tashqand Chowk area.

Once riots broke out areas like Tilak Chowk, Begumpeth Vijapurbees and suburban areas of Neelamnagar, MIDC and Saharanagar were affected and mostly Muslims suffered in these areas. In these areas shops, factories and houses belonging to Minority community were set afire. In many cases the rioters broke open the shops, looted the goods and then set them to fire. Some 10 rickshaws were burnt near Begumpeth rickshaw stand. The Gujarat sari shop belonging to Abdul Qadir Khatri was looted and burnt and he sustained a loss of Rs. 10 lakhs and other sari shop belonging to Abdur Rahim Khatri sustained a loss of Rs. 5 lakhs. In all 7 sari shops were set afire. Many factories were also totally destroyed in this area.

The former BJP MLA's house was set on fire in Sideshwarpeth by the Muslim miscreants. Though Mr. Lengji, the former MLA was not at home at the time his family members were there. They were saved by his Muslim neighbour Ismail Wurud. This was a good gesture of humanity and friendship on his part. The senior police inspector of the area was suspended for negligence of duty.

The showroom of optics Dr. Abu Sufyan and his house were attacked near employment exchange on next day (Saturday) in the morning and whole establishment was destroyed. But Abu Sufyan and his doctor wife Yasmin were persuaded by their Hindu neighbours to leave the place and migrate to a safer area. That saved their lives.

It should also be mentioned here that the role played by Maulana Shahabuddin Salafi was very laudable. He restrained the Muslim youth in Saharnagar area and Asranagar area otherwise the Muslims would have suffered far more damage. The Muslim youth were quite violent in their behaviour. It was restraint and wisdom exercised by the Maulana and also Police Commissioner Mr. More that saved the situation. The Maulana also protected many Hindu lives in these areas.

Maulana Shahabuddin Salafi was very critical of the violent Muslim youth. He felt they were not at all guided as to how to behave during the *bandh*. These youth attacked the Durgadevi puja pandal and this news spread like wild fire in the city and resulted in this disaster. It was outrageous on their part to have attacked the pandal. The Deputy Chief Minister Shri Chagan Bhujbal blamed the communal forces for the planned manner in which they tried to wreak havoc in Sholapur. He alleged that these forces wanted to repeat Gujarat in Maharashtra but the riot was brought under control.

Badlapur village in Thane district went up in flames on 20th October. It has population of about 10,000 of which Muslims are in majority. This was the fourth riot in Thane district in last eight months. Earlier three other places in Thane district Kalyan, Bhivandi and Murbad saw communal violence. In this village most of the Muslims are from Kokan area and are generally well to do. They have rice mills, shops and other business establishments. The percentage of education among Muslims in Badlapur is quite satisfactory.

Several shops and factories like saw mills belonging to minority community were set ablaze by the Shiv Sena and BJP activists. The clashes started between Hindu and Muslim youth on the question of teasing a Muslim girl who had come to Badlapur for pursuing her education. Though no one was killed in these riots 10 persons were injured two of whom are said to be serious. All the injured have been admitted to hospitals in Mumbai. The main loss was economic.

According to Minister of State for Home, Shri Kripashankar Singh, 40 persons have been arrested in connection with these communal disturbances. Among those arrested are two Bhartiya Janta Party Corporators (Badlapur is in Corporation area), Sharad Mhatre and Sanjay Bhoir – and a former corporator Maood Kohari, an official said. However, Mr. Singh refused to confirm. Mr. Singh said he was unhappy with the police commissioner of Thane as number of communal incidents have occurred in this district.

Inquiries on the spot revealed some rivalry between Shiv Sena and BJP in this area and one of the reasons of this communal incident is the race to capture more Hindu votes in the area. The incident of eve teasing was mere spark. Communal situation was simmering in Badlapur for some time, members of both the communities said. Bajrang Dal has been quite active in this area for past eight months. The Muslims of Badlapur said that they had voted for the BJP corporator Mr. Bhuir and why should they be subjected to such violence.

Amravti district - Shendurjana Ghat in Vidarbha area of Maharashtra also witnessed communal incidents at the time of immersion of Durga images on 21st October. There was stoning on the procession when it was passing through a mosque area. More than 90 persons were arrested. The police had to resort to firing in the air to control the mob. However, there was no loss of life.

Though number of riots (more than 44) have taken place in Maharashtra during the PDA regime the entire blame cannot be pinned on the government. The Hindutva forces are keen to capture power in the state and are busy polarising Hindus and Muslims. In Jalgaon and other places repeated attempts have been made to engineer communal violence for this purpose. It is not basically fight between Hindus and Muslims who want to live in peace. The VHP and Bajrang Dal, motivated by their political agenda are spewing poison and provoking violence. All these disturbances in Maharashtra should be seen in this perspective. It seems that the present Government in Maharashtra is trying to control communal violence but major and minor incidents are taking place from time to time. Mr. Bal Thakckaray of Shiv Sena tried to provoke Hindus through his utterances on his Dasehra eve speech instigating the Hindu youth to form suicide squad. Such utterances keep the communal situation on boil and an small incident becomes spark for minor and or major communal riots. The Hindutva forces are determined to keep India polarised on communal lines. At the hands of these forces India is going the Pakistan way where the *jihadi* groups keep Pakistan in a state of turmoil.

As these riots are occurring quite frequently in Maharashtra the State Government has now decided to revive the Maharashtra Prevention of Communal, Anti-Social, and other Dangerous Activities Act. It was allowed to lapse in eighties with enactment of NASA. But it is sought to be revived in view of frequent communal incidents. The accused or the potential offender can be detained for a period of six months under this Act. There is no doubt if the government acts promptly and takes proper measures occurrence of such incidents can be prevented. Riots take place only either with government collusion or negligence.

Defeat of NDA, Victory of Secularism

Crushing defeat of NDA led by the BJP in the recent general elections is certainly victory of secular forces. The BJP-led NDA had won in 1999 not so much as for its ability to deliver and provide better governance but because the BJP understood the significance of coalition politics and the Congress did not. When the Congress realised the importance of coalition it entered into electoral arrangement with different secular parties in different regions and inflicted crushing defeat on NDA. The NDA defeat was so massive that its leaders were totally stunned by it.

One can say that this was liberation of the country from communal forces who had bared their fascist fangs in Gujarat in 2002. It would be wrong to say that only Narendra Modi was guilty of the Gujarat carnage of 2002; the BJP-led NDA at the Centre was equally responsible for it. Despite hue and cry from all over the country the central leadership of the BJP and NDA not only kept quiet but extended full support to Narendra Modi in his fascist-like pogrom of Muslims in Gujarat. Mr. Fernandese even said in Parliament debate on women being raped and their wombs split that there is nothing new in this and that it has happened in this country for years.

The TDP leaders may not have lent active support like Mr. Fernandese but kept silent and never insisted on removal of Narendra Modi. Mr. Chandrababu Naidu allegedly settled for few hundred crores for his state and continued to support the NDA Government despite blood bath in Gujarat. His conscience was also not shaken. He also paid heavily and was swept out of power in Andhra Pradesh as Muslims refused to vote for him. Though this was not the only reason, it was one of the important factors for his being voted out.

The BJP leaders of course less said the better. They supported Narendra Modi to the hilt. When the BJP won Gujarat elections after the carnage with two-third majority all BJP leaders not only praised Narendra Modi but maintained that we would repeat the Gujarat model throughout the country i.e. that we would like to win elections in other states by organising blood bath of innocent members of minorities. What a shame? These were public statements made in full glare of T.V. cameras. Even Mr. Vajpayee when asked whether BJP would repeat the Gujarat Model averred "Will you repeat Godhra?" rather than firmly discounting such possibility. "Can then Mr.Vajpayee be described as statesman?" Will a statesman ever lend moral and political support to such carnage? He would rather resign than lead such a party which thrives on blood bath of innocents.

There is no doubt that BJP is a Hindu nationalist party and is firmly aligned to the RSS ideology. Mr. Vajpayee himself said at Straiten Island in USA among his VHP supporters that he has RSS soul. Who does not know that in 1978 also the Bharatiya Jan Sangh preferred to resign from the Janata Party rather than severe its relations with the RSS when Raj Narain, Madhu Limaye and George Fernandese raised dual membership controversy. Thus its loyalty to the RSS is unquestionable and its commitment to what Vajpayee used to call 'coalition dharma' was very superficial. It is nothing but a political arm of RSS.

One must not forget that in these five years it never tired of implementing the RSS agenda. In this respect its so-called 'coalition dharma' never came in its way. And its coalition partners who styled themselves as secular also became party in implementing this RSS agenda. The whole education system was communalised. That is the first priority of all communal and fascist forces to control education. Mr. Murli Manohar Joshi was a hardcore RSS man and he was put at the helm of Human Resources Ministry. He successfully implemented RSS agenda by communalising our education system. The RSS schools teach textbooks openly preaching hatred against minorities, especially in Sishu Vihars. Thousands of students study in these schools.

The premier social and historical research organisations like the Indian Social Science Research Organisation and Indian

Historical Research Organisation were handed over to hardcore RSS and VHP persons. All this will have to be wrested back from their control. It was a systematic conspiracy. Similarly key personnel were appointed from RSS supporters in premier educational research body like the NCERT which prepares textbooks which form the minds of lakhs of students every year. Mr. Joshi got these textbooks changed in keeping with his RSS commitment. Many eminent historians protested but to no avail. The damage was done and Mr. Joshi was to prepared to undo his RSS agenda. It was to implement this agenda that he was given this ministry.

Now the new coalition government led by the Congress and supported by the left (or may be the Left also joins the government) will take over and it should be its top priority to undo the damage done to the education system. As pointed out before education system plays very crucial role in shaping the minds of its future citizens particularly in a multi-religious, multilingual and multi-cultural country like India who, of necessity, should have a secular polity to build a integrated healthy nation. The RSS tried to lay the foundation of Hindu Rashtra dividing and polarising the country on religious lines.

The secular coalition will have to give top priority to this agenda of secular education and an education system, which would inculcate equal respect for all religions and eliminate the traces of hatred from our textbooks. The earlier Congress Governments also never sowed firm commitment to promote secular education. The history textbooks in particular, have never been seriously overhauled. It was because of this that it became very easy for the BJP to consolidate its position on issue like Babri Masjid-Ramjanambhoomi controversy. Those who had read these text-books during fifties and sixties grew up to be full citizens of this country and uncritically swallowed the Sangh Parivar propaganda about Ramjanambhoomi and captured power easily.

The secularity of the country is most essential ideological asset of our nation. The Sangh Parivar has seriously damaged it already and all efforts should be made to restore its secular character. The Human Resource Ministry should be headed by someone strongly committed to secularism and his/her priority should be to restore secular character of our education and necessary changes in history text-books. Nothing can be of greater importance than this. Also, ICSSR and ICHR should be liberated from the clutches of communal forces. These are premiere social and historical research organisations.

It should also be remembered that the BJP would like to revert to its original communal agenda. In order to win secular and minority votes it was trying to project itself as non-communal organisation. In the last days of campaigning the BJP also tried to convince the Muslims that it is not against them and Mr. Vajpayee even promised Muslims in Kishanganj, Bihar that if elected to power again NDA Government would like to appoint 2 crore (perhaps it was slip of tongue and meant two lakhs) Urdu teachers. But Muslims refused to be persuaded as how could they forget Gujarat after all and vote for a party that idolised Narendra Modi as Hindutva hero.

The Muslims voted very cleverly to defeat BJP candidates all over India and particularly in U.P. where BJP had maximum stake. Therefore, there is every chance that the BJP might go back to its communal agenda to win back a section of upper caste Hindu votes and since it is already being reprimanded by its ideological masters like the RSS and VHP that it lost because it diluted the Hindutva agenda. Thus the new secular government will have to be very cautious in its approach towards communal problem.

The Home Ministry also has been stuffed with those closed to the RSS ideology in various positions. Mr. Advani too is known to be RSS man and it is not imaginable that he would defy it in placing people in key positions. Also, there is great need to strengthen the intelligence machinery. Intelligence failure is very common phenomenon in any major communal violence. Also, communalisation of police particularly during last twenty five years of communal hype by the Sangh Parivar, is something to be taken very seriously. I have conducted more than 150 police workshops and have seen raw prejudices among the police personnel. It is highly necessary to have re-orientation courses for the police.

These things should not be taken lightly. All our developmental efforts will succeed only if there is peace and harmony in the country. And for this the secular government should do everything possible to restore secular values and confidence of the minorities. It would also raise the status of India in the comity of nations. Gujarat has considerably damaged it. Muslims and Christians have greatly suffered under the BJP-led NDA rule.

The Congress should also reflect seriously on its past mistakes. It often allowed free play to communal forces. Now it should not repeat those mistakes. Since the Left will be supporting or joining the government it is hoped that it would continue to put pressure on the Congress to contain communal forces with great determination. It is not easy to cleanse the whole system but it is highly necessary to restore sanity and integrity.

The minorities should also have full faith in the Indian democratic system. It was free and fair elections, which could bring about complete change in the situation. Many Muslims had despaired that no change is possible. Some even joined BJP out of this desperation. All of them have been belied. Indian democracy has great resilience. Long live Indian democracy. And the masses also defy all caste and communal barriers on such crucial junctions and vote to restore social and national health.

New Secular Government and its Secular Tasks

The new United Progressive Alliance Government (earlier called United Secular Alliance which was more meaningful) has been welcomed by all progressive and secular forces in the country. The victory of this alliance has proved to be liberative for the minorities and the oppressed people of India. The NDA Government led by the BJP was not only communal and anti-minorities but also pro-rich and anti-poor to the extreme. Even the Amnesty International Report made public on 26th May has lambasted the Indian Government for its poor human rights records particularly in Gujarat. Now even the BJP and Shiv Sena leaders have admitted that they lost because of Gujarat carnage.

It is for this reason that the minorities in particular have welcomed the new government, particularly so as it is backed by the left forces whose secular credentials are unimpeachable. Thus this government certainly inspires confidence among minorities and the poor. However, this initial confidence has not only to be sustained but strengthened through proper action. The Congress has always been ideologically secular but lost its secular orientation during the last days of Mrs. Indira Gandhi and began to be dubbed as the 'B-team' of Hindutva Party BJP. The minorities began to be alienated from the Congress until they deserted it after demolition of the Babri Masjid during the Prime Ministership of Shri Narasimha Rao.

Once it lost the confidence of minorities, particularly the Muslims, it lost power at the Centre and could not regain it until it could win the Muslim confidence again. The Congress had to work hard to convince Muslims again to regain their confidence. Now let us hope the Congress will not go off the course. Not only this it will have to take steps to inspire confidence among them. It should be seen as a party sympathetic to the problems of minorities. For that number of steps will have to be taken, some of which are suggested here.

It would greatly inspire confidence among minorities if a ministry of minority affairs is created and some minority leader of integrity is put in charge of it. In fact one of the Congress leaders from Maharashtra Mr. Gurudas Kamat also has made this suggestion. All minorities like the Muslims, Christians, Sikhs, Buddhists and Jains should be included under it. All put together these minorities constitute more than 20 per cent of Indian population. Indian Muslims alone are around 150 million.

The ministry can study many of the problems facing these minorities, which are of huge proportions. Today no government ministry even monitors data and indices pertaining to these minorities. The Gopal Singh High Commission Report prepared during the eighties, which had painfully collected data on minorities was also put in cold storage and its recommendations were never implemented. The data was collected during early eighties and hence has become totally outdated. The Report prepared after lot of hard labour was not even tabled in the Parliament. When I spoke to the then Prime Minister Shri V.P. Singh about it in 1990 he was not even aware about its existence.

Had there been a full-fledged ministry such reports would not have been wasted like this. It is true there is a minorities commission but it hardly has any powers. It has often been described as toothless tiger. It functions under Welfare Ministry and its budget is also controlled by this ministry. Thus the Commission is totally at the mercy of the welfare minister. It has hardly any priority for the ministry. Since I was on one of its sub-committees I know its plight very well. And the NDA Government appointed a BJP man as its chairman. What sympathy such a person would ever have for minorities. The very psychological orientation of BJP members is anti-minority. This was very much demonstrated when Mr. Trilochan Singh, the Chairman of National Minorities Commission gave certificate to Narendra Modi Government in Gujarat when Muslim carnage was taking place in 2002 and when the National Human Rights Commission was lambasting Mr. Narendra Modi. So much for the credentials of the NMC.

However, it may take time to take decision for setting up a ministry for the minority affairs, which is also bound to generate political controversy with the BJP in opposition. Meanwhile it is suggested that the National Minorities Commission should be strengthened and should be made statutory. Today it has no statutory powers at all and its recommendations are not binding on the government. Often its reports are not even tabled in the Parliament. The NMC must be given statutory powers and its recommendations should be made binding on the government. This should be done as early as possible as it is long standing demand.

The NMC should also be asked to gather fresh data on the pattern of the Gopal Singh High Commission and suitable recommendations should be formulated on its pattern and these recommendations should be implemented to uplift the economic and educational status of minorities. This should be given top priority. In fact reliable data on all India pattern about minorities is not available and in the absence of such data no suitable policies can be made.

The other suggestions relate to communalisation of education. Even during earlier Congress and other regimes no serious efforts were made to de-communalise our school textbooks, particularly relating to history. The BJP campaign for Ramjanambhoomi would not have succeeded to such an extent if our history text-books had not been what they are today. The British rulers had designed our history textbooks to divide us and rule over us. These text-books were never seriously revised and made genuinely secular so as to de-communalise our education system.

It is for this reason that you find educated middle class people who avail of these faulty text-books much more communal than the poor illiterate masses. Our education system really makes them communal and injects communal ideas into their minds. Thus one can hardly fight communal forces if our education system is not thoroughly reformed. Our education system should be devised to inculcate secular rational outlook, on one hand, and, respect for all religions, on the other. But unfortunately our education system is producing communal bigots instead.

Thus text-book reform is an urgent need and should be attended to on priority basis. The Human Resources Ministry under the leadership of Arjun Singh should pay attention to this task. This will really strengthen our secular polity and would permanently checkmate communal forces from capturing power. The BJP rode to power on the basis of Ramjanambhoomi issue and this issue in turn became so powerful because of the mind-set created by our text-books. It is difficult task but first step must be taken by appointing a suitable commission, which can thoroughly examine all text-books taught throughout India and then suggest steps to reform them. Education is a concurrent subject and, therefore, should not be difficult to devise them for whole of India. Of course regional considerations would be there and guidelines could be given for states to prepare these text - books suitably.

There is another important area, which needs to be attended to with similar sense of urgency. It is the textbooks taught in the RSS run Shishu Vihars some 32 thousand in numbers. These schools do not take grant from government but that does not mean they should be free to teach what is totally contrary to our constitutional values. The textbooks taught in these schools are highly objectionable and inject poison against minorities. We have examined these textbooks and what is written there in will never be permitted by any secular government.

Similarly, if one finds any objectionable material being taught in madrasas too, steps should be taken to remove such objectionable material from madrasa text-books also. So far I have not found any objectionable material but our study may not be thorough and madrasa text-books should also be thoroughly examined. No institution, public or private, should be allowed to violate the spirit of the Constitution. Thousands of students study in these private schools who grow with hatred towards other religions because of such textbooks and thus it becomes very easy to communalise polity.

Such a step to de-communalise our textbooks will strengthen our secular foundations. Unfortunately it has remained highly neglected area and as a result we have witnessed thousands of small and big riots throughout the post-independence era culminating of course in the Gujarat genocide. Much of this could have been avoided if we had courage to reform our textbooks right after independence. Now at least, after having paid heavy price, we should not hesitate to take this much needed step on top priority.

Another important area of reform is functioning of the police. Since police is also educated through these very institutions they also get easily communalised. I have seen that in the police training colleges there are no orientation lectures on secularism. The policemen handle communal riots with such communalised mind-set and as a result they tend to be anti-minority in their behaviour. Various inquiry commission reports, particularly the Madon Commission and Srikrishna Commission Reports on Bhivandi-Jalgaon and of 1970 and of Bombay riots of 1992-93 have severely castigated the role of the police in these riots. In Gujarat carnage of 2002 it was even worse and yet no steps are being taken to effectively de-communalise the police. The Congress-led UPA Government should pay urgent attention to this problem as well. We have much to learn in this respect from the Left-Front Government in West Bengal.

BJP Back on Aggressive Hindutva

The BJP was so sure of its victory in the last Lok Sabha election that it feigned to have given up its Hindutva card and even tried to appeal ('appease') to minorities for votes. In Bihar the then Prime Minister Shri Atal Bihari Vajpayee even promised in his speech at Kishenganj that he will appoint 200,000 Urdu teachers, if elected to power. However, the Indian electorate inflicted crushing defeat on the BJP-led NDA and elected the UPA Government instead.

However, the Sangh Parivar overconfident of BJP's victory could not accept the defeat in true democratic spirit and is feeling highly frustrated. The NDA members, particularly those of BJP are even refusing to behave as a responsible opposition in the Parliament. They have been obstructing the procedure and refusing to allow the Parliament to function on one pretext or the other. They raised the issue of 'tainted ministers' and stalled Parliament for days. They did not even allow debate on budget and it has to be passed without any discussion. They thus made history of sorts. Thus the NDA leaders are responsible for waste of public money and answerable to the electorate. If they do not follow the norms of democratic behaviour they do not deserve to be elected.

What is worse is that they are now adopting quite aggressively their old Hindutva course which, they had assured Indian people, they had abandoned. In 1980 also they had assured people of India that they have adopted 'secularism and Gandhian socialism' but abandoned it in favour of aggressive communalism the moment they faced crushing defeat in Parliamentary elections of 1984 when they got only two seats.

Again facing defeat in Lok Sabha elections of 2004 they have gone back to Hindutva politics with vengeance. Thus communal forces can hardly be relied. While in power and sure of their continued hold on it they feign to be secular and adopt aggressive communalism the moment they loose power. They have played the same game this time around. Now they are going back to aggressive Hindutva in view of state elections in Maharashtra and in Bihar after a few months.

One such issue is of Veer Savarkar. Mani Shankar Aiyer ordered removal of poems of Veer Savarkar from the cellular jail of Andaman. The BJP is raising hue and cry over the issue. In Maharashtra of course they have left it to Shiv Sena as Savarkar's issue is highly emotive in Maharashtra. Thus the BJP who is part of alliance with Shiv Sena wants the Sena to provoke electorate on this issue while it would take up another issues. This itself shows that the BJP is not genuinely concerned with Savarkar issue but wants to exploit it for election purposes through Shiv Sena.

Veer Savarkar's grand niece Uttara Sahasrabuddhe who teaches political science in the Bombay University, has alleged that both the Congress and BJP-Shiv Sena are trying to turn Veer Savarkar into an election issue. According to her this was hardly a good reason for the Sena and the BJP to boycott Parliament when the budget was being passed, she maintained.

She also said that if the Sangh Parivar was sincere in its protest against what the Congress had done, it should ask the lieutenant governor of the Andamans to put the plaque back. The lieutenant governor Mr. Ram Kapse, was a BJP appointee and belongs to that party. She also said in her statement to the *Asian Age* that Savarkar was a rationalist. He never thought cow was so sacred and not be killed. He specifically wrote in one of the articles, she noted that "the cow was a useful animal once upon a time when we were dependent on agriculture. But don't make it a sacred animal. If you believe that God resides in a cow it's foolish."

Savarkar also maintained, according to her that if you want to differentiate between Western civilisation and Indian civilisation, then you must know that after the Renaissance movement the West took to rationalism as its basis and made tremendous progress. We still stick to what is written in Vedas and Puranas, and because of this tendency we are stuck in the past.

Of course she rightly points out that "The Sangh Parivar cannot eschew or digest these essays. The Sangh Parivar considers cow as sacred and VHP and Bajrang Dal harass even those who take old oxen or buffaloes for slaughter. One of the main agendas of the BJP is to ban cow slaughter throughout India. The BJP even justified killing of Dalits in Haryana who were skinning dead cows a few years ago?

Thus it is clear that the BJP wants to exploit Veer Savarkar's issue for its own political purposes while totally rejecting Savarkar's rational thoughts. It would hardly convince anyone of its sincerity.

Another issue BJP is preoccupied with is that of arrest of Uma Bharati, former Chief Minister of M.P. In fact there are indications that the BJP wanted to get rid of Uma Bharati as Chief Minister of M.P. and her arrest warrant came as a relief to the BJP central leadership. She may be an aggressive agitator but she was a failure as a chief minister and had created complex problems for the Party.

However, now the BJP is making her arrest as a national issue and flying tricolour is being projected as a national mission. Of course tricolour is our national flag and we are all proud of that but one cannot take pride by making it as a anti-Muslim measure. Uma Bharati went to hoist tricolour on an Idgah, which is a disputed site. The Sangh Parivar had planned to convert the Hubli Idgah issue as a Babri Masjid of the South at that time though the matter was resolved amicably by persuading the Hubli Muslims to hoist the national flag on the Idgah.

Now the Sangh Parivar is thinking of taking out her *Yatra* flying tricolour. It is an old trick, which the Parivar plays repeatedly. In fact the RSS refuses to fly tricolour in its own *Shakhas* and flies *Bhagwa* flag. Let Uma Bharati fly tricolour on the RSS offices if she is so enthusiastic about flying tricolour. Let her fly it on temples as well. She is trying to earn electoral advantage in coming elections by raising these controversies. But now there is news that the Government of Karnataka may petition the Court to withdraw all cases against her thus depriving her the opportunity to be a martyr. The Congress is trying to defeat her game. The BJP has never been comfortable with secular issues or issues of development. It adopted *Sadak-Bijli-Pani* issue in M.P. election as it was agitating the minds of electorate in the state then. But as it was not sure whether this will click Uma

Bharati was repeatedly raising the issue of Saraswati temple and Kamal Maula Masjid in Dhar, M.P. The other members of Sangh Parivar were playing up this issue to entice the voters for Sangh Parivar.

And now since the BJP is not in power at the Centre it has no compulsions or restraints of being in power and can try to go whole hog with Hindutva politics. BJP can never be secularised as long as it is tied firmly to the communal apron of the RSS. The RSS keeps on pressurising it to adopt aggressive Hindutva. And the BJP has to repeatedly assure the RSS that it will never offload the ideology of Hindutva without which it cannot get help of dedicated RSS cadre in the elections.

When the Jan Sangh had merged with the Janata Party and had taken pledge for secularism at the Gandhi Samadhi under the leadership of Jai Prakash Narain in 1977, it had refused to resign from the RSS membership though the dual membership controversy (both membership of the Janta Party and the RSS) had brought down the Morarji Desai Government in 1979. Thus it will be seen that it is firmly tied to the apron strings of RSS and its strident anti-minorities stance will never be diluted. Those so called NDA secular partners are deceiving themselves or fooling the people, if they pretend that the BJP will ever give up its Hindutva plank.

Also, in view of the upcoming elections in Maharashtra in October the Shiv Sena-BJP are trying to stir communal passions. The bombs thrown by unknown motor cycle riders at the mosques during Friday prayers in Prabhani and Jalna is an obvious attempt in that direction. The winning of election in Maharashtra by the Sangh Parivar is of great significance. It thinks it is an opportunity to shake the UPA Government at the Centre. Defeat of the Congress-NCP alliance in Maharashtra can have long-term consequences. If the BJP-Shiv Sena combination can win in Maharashtra they can try to win over Sharad Pawar and persuade him to join NDA. Sharad Pawar is known to have soft corner for the BJP-Shiv Sena alliance. Also, the Mumbai Municipal Corporation under Shiv Sena has passed a resolution making singing *Vande Mataram* compulsory in municipal schools. They remember *Vande Mataram* at the time of elections only.

The Sena is also very eager to come back to power and will go to any extent in playing up Hindutva card. It is very unfortunate that the Election Commission is satisfied with these parties signing pledge of secularism although their propaganda machinery aggressively works to propagate communal issues during the elections. What a contradiction. How can a party taking pledge for secularism as required by the Election Commission openly and aggressively propagate Hindutva? Can they not be disqualified on grounds of breaking their secular pledge? Is it not against the Constitution to propagate Hindutva during the election campaign? It is for the authorities to decide.

It seems secularism is becoming a distant dream in view of increasing communalisation of our politics. Forget about Nehruvian secularism even Gandhian concept of religious harmony is becoming a dream rather than reality. Every religious group, every religious community, wants to bring in sectarian issues in political arena. Those who strive for inter-religious harmony will have to face increasing challenges in coming days. And yet inter-religious harmony is so vital for our multi-religious society.

Census Figures and BJP's Anti-Minorityism

The Government of India has at last made public the population figures of 2001 census after delay of several years. Now we know that this was delayed by the BJP-led government on account of Lok Sabha elections. Whatever the reason the population figures and particularly the growth of Muslim population has caused great deal of controversy as expected.

The census commissioner Mr. Banthya either deliberately or otherwise caused sensation by not disclosing that the Muslim population figures do not take into account the fact that there was no census in Assam in 1981 and in Kashmir in 1991 due to ethnic turmoil. Had this been disclosed the Sangh Parivar would not have had another chance at Muslim bashing. Since the BJP does not want to miss any chance to bash Indian Muslims and moreover there are elections in Maharashtra, it jumped at this 'opportunity' to create anti-Muslim feelings. The BJP has yet to overcome the shock of its defeat in Lok Sabha elections.

Mr. Venkaiah Naidu, the BJP president immediately issued a statement condemning an usual growth of Muslim population. He said that differential growth rates for Hindu and Muslim populations in India are a matter of grave concern for those bothered about India`s unity and integrity. The "imbalance", he suggested, raises "serious questions of a long-term nature" when seen in connection with the phenomenon of Bangladeshi infiltrators.

BJP's anti-Muslim feelings are so strong that they had no patience even to wait for a day to find out the truth of population figures and the goof up by the census commissioner. Also without any verification whatsoever, he invoked their another pet issue of Bangladeshi infiltrators. The fact was that both the growth of Hindu and Muslim population has slowed down which is a welcome sign. Apart from other reasons the reason for differential rate of growth is that several of the communities like Kabirpanthis, Prannathis, Ramkrishna Mission followers etc. who refuse to enlist themselves as Hindus in the census report but otherwise perceived as Hindus. This can make quite a difference as far as differential growth of population is concerned.

It is also not generally known that in some states, according to 1988 data the family planning rate among Muslims is higher than that of Hindus as the literacy rate among Muslim women and their economic status is better than their Hindu counterpart. Thus in 15 states the family planning among Muslims is higher than that of Hindus in U.P. In U.P. the family planning figures among Hindus was, according to statistics compiled in 1988, lesser than those of Muslims in 15 states.

In U.P. the acceptors of family planning among Hindus in Bihar and Rajasthan are 29.4, 32.6 and 30.9 per cent respectively. Among Muslims, on the other hand, acceptors of family planning were Kerala (64.4 per cent), Andhra Pradesh (51.1 per cent), Chandigarh (35.8 per cent), Delhi (53.8 per cent), Goa (46.1 per cent), Gujarat (49 per cent), Jammu and Kashmir (35 per cent), Karnataka (34.4 per cent), Madhya Pradesh (39.6 per cent), Maharashtra (45.8 per cent), N. E. States (33 per cent), Orissa (44 per cent), Pondichery (77 per cent), Tamil Nadu (56.6 per cent) and West Bengal 42.2 per cent). Of course in U.P. and Bihar the family planning acceptance among Muslims is as low as 18.1 and 14 per cent respectively.

Thus it can be seen that religion is not the only criterion as the Sangh Parivar thinks. There are several other factors which impinge on acceptance or otherwise of family planning. Had religion been the only factor than Muslims in the 15 states as mentioned above, would not have accepted family planning in larger proportion than that of Hindus.

Also Bangladesh and Iran which are Muslim countries would not have taken lead in making family planning much greater success than that of India. In Bangladesh the rate of growth of population has come down from 6.1 in 1980 to 2.9 per cent. India's fertility rate declines in the same period from 5.0 to 2.9 per cent. Thus Bangladesh Muslims have reduced fertility much faster than that of Hindus in India. In Iran the fertility rate is just two per woman amounting to zero population growth.

It is not correct to say that Islam comes in the way of family planning. There is no clear injunction in the Qur'an against family planning. The Holy Prophet himself permitted what is called *'azl* i.e. *coitus interruptus* which was the only method then known for prevention of conception. Imam Ghazzali, a great Islamic thinker of 12th century has even permitted abortion up to third month (before life begins in the foetus according to the Qur'an) in case if mother's health or life is in danger.

Similarly Maulana Abdulaziz, an Islamic scholar of 18th century India and son of celebrated Islamic thinker Shah Waliyullah also permitted *'azl* and abortion on similar grounds. The grand Mufti of al-Azhar in Egypt Shaltut bin Shaltut also approved of family planning. Imam Shafi'i while commenting on the verse 4:3 of the Qur'an recommends small family as large family is likely to become burden on man. And now even Muslim Personal Law Board has declared its intention to promote family planning among Muslims on the pattern of Iran which has reached the goal of zero growth in population.

In view of all this evidence it is difficult to maintain that Islam categorically opposes family planning. It is true that there are different opinions and some 'ulama oppose family planning, particularly those rooted in old tradition and closer to poorer and illiterate Muslims. This should also be noted that religious teaching, even if opposed to family planning, is not the only consideration in human behaviour. Human behaviour is too complex to be reduced only to religious teachings.

In fact religious teaching may be only one among many other considerations, particularly of socio-economic nature. Economic and educational factors play an important role in fertility behaviour, among others. That is why in states like Pondichery and Kerala where female literacy rate among Muslims is higher and women are more independent, family planning acceptance is much higher compared to other states where female literacy rate is comparatively low among Muslims.

There are other factors as well like widow re-marriage. This has been acknowledged by demographers. Also, male-female ratio among Muslims is comparatively higher, i.e., there are 936 female per thousand compared to 931 female per thousand male among Hindus. And among children up to 6 this ratio is 950 girls per thousand boys among Muslims and only 925 for Hindus. Mr. Swaminathan S. Anklesaria Aiyar explains it thus: "Female infanticide and foeticide reduces population indirectly as well as directly. Even after contraception lowers the total fertility rate (lifetime births per woman), population growth can be rapid for two decades because of what demographers call population momentum: future mothers have already been born. But female infanticide and foeticide ensure that future mothers are not born, and so reduce population momentum." (See *TOI* of 12/9/04). According to Mr. Aiyar this is part of the reason for falling Hindu population growth, but not something the Hindus should boast about.

Thus there are several factors to be taken into account for understanding the dynamics of population growth in any community and for devising remedial measures. Communalists, more often than not, always bring religion into focus ignoring very vital factors as their primary obsession is with denunciation of a religious community. The BJP better take these factors into account if they really care for the country rather than the narrow interests of a section of the majority community.

The literacy rate among the Muslims according to the census figures is lowest on all India level i.e. around 59.1 per cent whereas among Hindus it is 65.1 per cent for those above 7 years of age. The gap of course is only of 6 per cent, not too wide. In fact matter is more complex than it appears. As in case of family planning the rate of literacy among Muslims in 15 states and Union Territories is more than 70 per cent. It is also to be noted that in Jharkhand, Orissa, Chandigarh, Madhya Pradesh, Gujarat, Maharashtra, Andhra Pradesh, Karnataka, Daman and Diu, Dadra and Nagar Haveli, Tamil Nadu, Pondichery and Andaman and Nicobar Islands, Muslims are doing better than Hindus. In Chattisgarh, the Muslims are ahead by 17 percentage points.

All these fact have to be taken into account. Like that of family planning this myth also needs to be shattered that Muslims do not take to modern secular education *per se*. There is increasing trend among Muslims both for family planning and for modern secular education. One should not take static view of situation as many scholars do and particularly those who are inclined to the Sangh Parivar. In secular India Muslims, despite many difficulties, also have greater opportunities as there are lesser constraints and more freedom from orthodox point of view.

Post-Babri demolition riots Muslim outlook has changed greatly and they have realised that emotional issues and confrontationist politics will take them nowhere and it is only modern education and economic progress which will ensure better future for them. Whatever figures are available point to the fact that trend for modern education is progressively increasing. What lacks are economic means rather than any traditional obstacle for modern education. One has to work hard to provide such opportunities to poor Muslims. Partly it is for the government and partly for Muslim leadership to create opportunities for education and economic uplift of Muslims.

And the RSS propaganda that Muslims will overtake Hindus by 2050 should be dismissed with the contempt it deserves. No serious demographer will buy it.

BJP and Politics of Religious Extremism

The BJP's propaganda plank in the late eighties was 'a party with a difference' and 'a most disciplined and non-corrupt party'. The Hindu middle classes swallowed this propaganda for a number of reasons. There was anti-Congress atmosphere in the country in general and V.P. Singh had launched a powerful anticorruption movement against Rajiv Gandhi Government on the Bofors gun scandal. The AASU, Khalistan and Shah Bano movements had shaken faith in the capacity of the Congress to govern the country. The Shah Bano movement by the Muslim leadership and Rajiv Gandhi's reversal of the Supreme Court Judgement by enacting the Muslim Women's (Protection on Divorce) Act also convinced the Hindus that Congress indulges in the 'Muslim appeasement' policy.

It was in such a charged atmosphere that the Hindu middle classes fell for the BJP propaganda and its ascendence began. It was seen as the only viable alternative to the Congress and 'truly nationalistic' party, which believed in 'justice for all and discrimination against none'. This was accepted as 'positive secularism as against the pseudo secularism of the Congress which appeased Muslims for their votes. These sounded as sweet words to the ears of middle class Hindus.

The communalists, of whatever variety, always resort to half -truths and downright lie to attract people of their faith community. The Muslim League before partition and the Jan Sangh and Bhartiya Janata Party (after it was re-christened) had absolutely no qualms to indulge in such propaganda to achieve their political objective of achieving power at any cost. The BJP which had got only two seats and 7 per cent votes in 1984 got 88 seats and 11.4 per cent votes in 1989 in alliance with the Janta Dal. It was a big leap for the BJP.

Then L.K. Advani rode to power with Rath Yatra to construct Ram temple with the emotionally charged slogan '*mandir wahin banaenge*' (we will construct temple there only) and he received tremendous applause and finally succeeded creating the Hindu vote bank while accusing the Congress of creating 'Muslim vote-bank'. And in 1991 election BJP won 120 seats with 20 per cent votes, something never had happened in the electoral history of the right wing Hindu party. In 1996 the number of seats went up to 161 even though the vote share remained stagnant.

Finally it formed the Government in 1999 with the help of some so-called secular parties on mixed bag of promises. However, its core issues remained what came to be known as the Hindutva issues, i.e., construction of Ram temple, abolition of Article 370 of the Constitution (pertaining to special status of Kashmir) and enforcing uniform civil code. These issues however, did not attract the rural voters much and its vote share in rural areas remained poor.

Once it came to power with the help of 'secular allies' it had to moderate its image somewhat by pretending that these core Hindutva agenda was its own and not of the National Democratic Alliance (NDA). But it did not wash with its militant organisations like the RSS, VHP and Bajrang Dal. It tried to buy off some of the members of these militant outfits by giving them Parliament tickets or even making them ministers like Uma Bharati, Adityanath and others. Persons like Vinay Katiyar were also sought to be co-opted by making them office bearers in the Party.

And as long as the BJP remained in power with the help of the allies, they could silence the militants with various baits though dissenting voices continued to be raised. But once power was lost these voices became quite shrill and at last unmanageable. Mr. Venkiah Naidu could no longer manage to contain the dissenting voices, was seen as weak and finally made to resign.

Mr. Advani who was the hero of the late eighties and who managed to bring the BJP close to power with his Ram temple campaign was thought to be capable of making the BJP power-fit once again and entrusted with its leadership. But 2004 is not 1989 and the BJP has totally lost its sheen and no longer seen to be 'party with a difference' and one with discipline and clean image.

Once it came to power its leaders proved to be more corrupt than the Congress leaders and many skeletons fell off from its cupboards. Corruption and communalism became its hall marks. The illusions were totally shattered. Carnage in Gujarat alienated the peace loving Hindus. Once it had boasted that there are no communal riots when the BJP is in power. Even this turned out to be totally untrue. The independent India had never witnessed such communal carnage as in Gujarat in 2002.

Then what remained of this 'party with a difference'? Nothing except a wreckage of its former self. Advani has no magic wand as he had in 1989-90 to rebuild the party. Ramjanambhoomi no longer evokes the kind of emotions it did in the late eighties of the last century. It is at best looked upon a political ploy. Mr. Advani did try to use this ploy on becoming the president of the party again but drew complete blank. He could not convince even his own party people. He is facing million mutinies today in his own party. He is being mocked at by RSS and VHP people.

It has been observed again and again that once you create a monster for short-term gains, it controls the master rather than the other way round. The BJP created the Ramjanambhoomi issue to win the elections and now it is this issue, which is destroying the cohesiveness and discipline in the party. The RSS and VHP militants are up in arms accusing the BJP leaders of deserting the issue of Ram temple to enjoy comforts of power. It is true that the BJP leadership had used Ramjanambhoomi issue only to capture power.

Once they had aroused the anguish among the Hindus that they cannot build temple in their own country. Little did they realise at that time that it was only a ruse to build their power base. Thus Advani's magic word 'Ayodhya' has lost all its sheen and he lost his credibility further by uttering it again. You cannot arouse religious frenzy among people and then take them for granted.

One should also remember that any misuse of religious issues for political purposes leads to religious extremism in a section of the people and no one can control it. We also have example of Zia-ul-Haq of Pakistan. He used slogan of Islamisation in eighties in Pakistan and created religious extremism and Jihadi militants who the present government of Pakistan finds extremely difficult to control. The moderate elements in Pakistan in late eighties when Zia was in control, were extremely worried about such gross misuse of Islam for political purpose and they rightly felt that this would lead to uncontrollable extremism in years to come and their prediction came true.

Only those who have no respect for religion use it cynically for political purposes. The entire Sangh Parivar has used Hindu religion for political ends. With globalisation it is becoming easier for politicians to misuse religious and cultural issues. One cannot expect even otherwise quite educated people to behave rationally and thoughtfully. This has been proved by re-election of Bush for the second term in USA. More than half the people of America bought the false propaganda of Bush that America needs rightwing Christian politics to enhance its security and hegemony in the world.

Bush mainly relied on issues like danger of terrorism on one hand, and, Christian values and family values, on the other. The hard issues like health care, outsourcing of jobs, increased unemployment etc. did not bother them. Bush has also misused Christian religion for his political purpose. The born-again Christians are dominating his administration and he increasingly relies on think tanks dominated by such rightwing Christians. The Christian revival is a fact of political life today in USA. Modern education and scientific progress has made hardly any difference to them.

Countries like India with so much illiteracy and high rates of unemployment can easily be ignited (as Gujarat has proved beyond any ken of doubt). It is thus extremely dangerous to play with religious sentiments in politics. It is highly unfortunate that BJP leaders openly associate themselves with Hindu extremist leaders of RSS and VHP and look towards them for political support and seek to pacify them.

What is most unfortunate is that these very leaders take oath of secularism and swear by Constitution while contesting election. It is true that Election Commission by enforcing its code has brought down misuse of religion in election campaign to some extent. But much more needs to be done to curb such misuse further. In fact mere declaration of secularism in election affidavits should not be enough. Any party, which raises religious issues in direct contravention of the Constitutional provisions should be de-recognised by the Election Commission. Any party, which associates itself with extremist organisations should not be allowed to contest elections.

Strict enforcement of Constitutional provisions is the only way out. The Narsimha Rao Government totally ignored the blatantly communal propaganda by Sadhvi Rithambara, Uma Bharti and others in late eighties and early nineties and the country had to pay dearly for that with demolition of Babri Masjid and following Bombay riots. The BJP Government enacted carnage in Gujarat. These are strong danger signals for ideals of our Constitution. Let us not underrate this danger any more. The extremists in the BJP do pose such danger again.

Is Secularism Dead in India?

Secularism had evoked certain controversies in India from very beginning but nevertheless it was accepted by all baring few exceptions. Since the concept of secularism did not exist in India its equivalent was also not found in Indian languages. It had to be translated. In Hindi it was translated as *dharm nirpekshta* and in Urdu it was rendered as *la diniyyatI.* Both these translations were not correct as they implied neutrality towards religion and being non-religious respectively.

Even in the west it did not mean being non-religious. It implied neutrality of state towards religion. West had ushered in democracy much before India did and secularism is quite important for democratic functioning and particularly if society as in India happens to be multi-religious. A multi-religious society cannot function democratically without secularism.

In democracy citizenship and citizens' rights are most central. While in a non-secular state religion becomes central and citizenship becomes secondary. India was from very beginning of its known history a multi-religious and multi-cultural society. Democracy in such a society cannot function without secularism as in democracy citizenship has priority over religion. In democracy all are equal citizens though they may not follow same religion or may not follow any religion at all.

Thus when the Britishers left and India chose to be democracy it had no recourse but to opt for secularism as well. Only a secular democracy can ensure equal rights for all citizens. The argument that since Pakistan chose to be Islamic nation India too has right to become a Hindu Rashtra is not valid one. Pakistan was based on two-nation theory and was primarily a Muslim nation it could choose to be Islamic nation (though a modern nation-state and a religious state are anomalous) but this course was certainly not available for India, it being a multi-religious, multi-cultural and multi-lingual country.

Thus India rightly chose to be a secular country in the sense that Indian state shall not privilege any religion and that followers of majority religion shall not have more privileges than the followers of minority religions in terms of citizenship. Also that state shall protect all religions equally without any distinction.

This came to be known as Nehruvian model of secularism and a broad consensus was evolved around it. Only the Jansangh, which had very narrow political base until then rejected any concept of secularism and stood for Hindu Rashtra. However, even Jansangh while merging into the Janta Party in post-emergency period in 1977 accepted secularism and Gandhian socialism and took pledge to this effect on Gandhiji's samadhi in Delhi. However, for Jansangh it was more a tactical move than a principled stand.

Though in its new *avtar* as BJP it continued to swear by secularism but began to promote most militant Hindu nationalism in mid-eighties. One of the members of Sangh Parivar the Vishwa Hindu Parishad adopted Hindu militancy without any restraint. In the post-Minakshipuram conversion period the Vishwa Hindu Parishad came to the forefront and got involved in most militant propaganda of Hindutva. There were open assaults on Nehruvian model of secularism and even secularism as such was dubbed as a western concept quite alien to Indian culture.

But for the BJP there were certain restraints and it could not reject secularism openly without drawing criticism. So it adopted a new tactics; it began to talk of positive secularism and denounced Nehruvian secularism as 'pseudo-secularism'. According to the BJP Nehruvian secularism was based on what it called 'appeasement of minorities' and it defined appeasement as allowing minorities to follow their personal law and allowing their men to take four wives.

This assault on Nehruvian secularism, which ultimately meant assault on constitutional secularism, became sharper and sharper with passage of time. The BJP ultimately adopted what it called the 'Hindutva agenda' and this agenda, as is well known, included abolition of personal laws (enforcing common civil code), Article 370 (special status for Kashmir) and building Ram Temple at Ayodhya.

Obviously a secular state cannot undertake construction of temples and mosques and BJP's Hindutva agenda was a direct blow to the Constitutional concept of secularism in India. The BJP government and its other Parivar members are openly attacking a concept of secularism around, for which there was a broad consensus, as pointed out above.

The BJP was somewhat restrained at the Centre as it is a coalition government but it had no such restraint in Gujarat where it was in power of its own. And it was in Gujarat that one could understand to what extent it would go if it ever came to power at the Centre. Gujarat was often described as a 'laboratory of Hindutva' and it became a mini-Hindu Rashtra. And after the horrible Gujarat riots, which shamed the country and winning the elections with two-third majority the BJP leaders began to say that we will repeat the Gujarat model in other states of India.

Thus it has become more than obvious that the BJP in principle rejects secularism and only adopts it tactically while in power as part of NDA alliance. Not only this it has been systematically carrying out campaign for Hindutva politics. Even the Prime Minister Shri Vajpayee is on record to have said in USA that RSS is 'my soul' and RSS, as everyone knows stands for Hindu Rashtra.

It is unfortunate that this aggressive propaganda has affected even the principal opposition party the Congress. It has also wilted under pressure and has adopted what is being described as softer variety of Hindutva. Even in late eighties and early nineties some of the Congress members had begun to talk of secularism being unsuitable for India and under pressure from aggressive BJP propaganda sought to redefine secularism. Mr. Narasimha Rao, the then Prime Minister also adopted policy of soft Hindutva and even refused to take any action while the Babri Masjid was being demolished. He was almost under awe of the BJP propaganda.

In fact the Congress commitment to secularism began to weaken in the last phase of Mrs. Indira Gandhi when she tried to utilise VHP for her survival and to compensate for loss of Muslim votes. Mr. Rajiv Gandhi too did not show any strong commitment to secularism and his notorious reversal of the Shah Bano judgement and laying the foundation of Ramjanambhumi and call for Ramrajya on the eve of 1989 parliamentary elections also delivered a great blow to Nehruvian concept of secularism.

The Gujarat carnage in February-March last year further struck fear in the minds of Congress politicians and except for few exceptions the Congress leaders are adopting soft variety of Hindutva. Though the 'Gujarat model' did not work in Himachal Pradesh and the BJP lost elections there the fear of alienation from Hindu voters is very much there in the minds of the Congress leaders.

Even during the Gujarat election campaign in post-Gujarat carnage the Congress leaders, particularly Mr. Kamalnath who was in charge of elections in Gujarat, did not allow any Muslim Congress leaders like Mohsina Kidwai or Ahmed Patel to campaign for the Congress. Not only this he did not allow even leaders like Arjun Singh to campaign for election as Arjun Singh has pro-Muslim image.

The Congress openly played pro-soft Hindutva card by making Waghela as the Congress chief of Gujarat as he was an ex-RSS man and it was thought that he will be better able to attract the Hindu votes in Gujarat. However, the soft Hindutva did not work in favour of the Congress and BJP won with two-third majority in Gujarat elections.

But instead of learning any lesson from the Gujarat defeat the Congress leaders want to play the soft Hindutva card in other states like the Madhya Pradesh. Even a person like Digvijay Singh who has been known for his commitment to secularism is now playing this card and is demanding ban on cow slaughter throughout India. He did this to embarrass the BJP and to woo the upper caste Hindu voters.

The ban on cow slaughter should be discussed on its own merit as Gandhiji also maintained. Gandhiji even refused to take up cow slaughter issue to win over the Hindu support for Khilafat movement. He maintained that both Khilafat movement and ban on cow slaughter should be taken up on their own merits and not to trade one with the other. Even our Constitution in Article 48 says that "State shall endeavour to organise agriculture and animal husbandry on modern and scientific lines and shall, in particular, take steps for preserving the breeds, and prohibiting the slaughter, of cows and calves and other milch and draught cattle."

Thus it will be seen that the Constitution also does not talk of banning cow slaughter on religious grounds but on modern scientific lines. It is regrettable that leaders of Nehru's Congress are indulging in such sensitive issues just to win elections. It is certainly weakening commitment to secularism. It can be said without fear of contradiction that Nehruvian concept of secularism is as good as dead and we are left with cheap tactics to win elections. It has serious implications for future of our democracy in a pluralist society like India. There is great need to revive Nehruvian concept of secularism, which is based on cultural and political wisdom. It can perhaps be done only by a leader of Nehru's stature as it requires courage of conviction and not simply lust for power.

The Politics of Attack on Bhandarkar Institute

The recent attack on Bhandarkar Institute in Pune by the Sambhaji Brigade is highly condemnable. In fact no words are enough to condemn such vandalism. Such attacks were highly condemnable even in medieval ages. How can then such acts be justified in 21st century? But yet we see such vandalism, taking place in our own times and under our very nose and we feel helpless. The government does not seem to be interested in taking action for its own political reasons particularly in this election year.

Howsoever condemnable the act might be it is necessary to understand politics behind it, especially the caste politics. It is also important to note denunciation or silence about it and its nuances. Also important is to note communal overtones or undertones of its condemnation. The modern India is undergoing turmoil along caste and communal lines and such events needs to be placed in proper perspective for this reason.

Such vandalism whether it took place in the past or in the present cannot be ascribed, as we often do, to mere religious or caste fanaticism. It always has a political message behind it. Some universities were vandalised in the past by Muslim invaders. We often ascribe it to mere Islamic fanaticism. It is far from true. It is strange that some scholars including some 'progressive scholars' are unearthing these past events and comparing the attack in Pune to those past vandalism. It clearly shows we are still unable to overcome our conscious or unconscious caste and communal attitudes.

An editorial in a Marathi daily from Mumbai condemned his act invoking Mughal rule. The caption of the editorial was "*Punyatil Mughlai*" i.e. Mughal vandalism in Pune. This betrays the attitude of editors of the daily. They think such vandalism was indulged into by Mughal rulers and this has been repeated in Pune. In fact such vandalism, as pointed out above, did take place in the past but by outside invaders in 11th and 12th centuries and not during the Mughal period. In fact the Mughals have contributed richly to our composite culture. There is hardly any field be it architecture, painting, music, literature, food, dresses in which they have not contributed. Our culture will be poorer without this contribution. Why then compare the acts like the one in Pune with 'Mughal vandalism'. Even Mughals would be ashamed of such an act.

Some other 'progressive scholars' invoked another mythical act to compare with Pune vandalism with. It was said that the 2nd Caliph, Umar destroyed the Alexandria library by saying that if the Qur'an contains all knowledge these books are useless and if these books contain knowledge other than that of Qur'an they are of no use. This myth was systematically spread by those hostile to Islam and Islamic power. The fact is that the library in

Alexandria was destroyed much before it was conquered by Muslims during the Umar's time. This points out widespread communal attitude among Indian intelligentsia even of the progressive variety.

Another thing we would like to emphasise here is that there is always a political message behind such acts. Those who know understand this message. The Pune act was also not without this political message. Either the conqueror or the invader displays his power and leaves the message that his conquest is complete and no one dare stop him from doing this or he destroys it because the institution was controlled by the ruler and was considered as most prestigious. Its destruction showed helplessness of the defeated ruler. One can say this of many temples destroyed by the Muslim invaders also. Destruction was not an act of religious fanaticism but an act to show that the ruler was unable to protect the temple of his own deity and so lost all legitimacy to rule.

The act of vandalism in Pune with the slogan that this is just the beginning and that Shaniwarwada (a stronghold of Brahmins) still remains is indicative of the caste war in Maharashtra. Shivaji is a symbol and remarks in James Laines book only an excuse for the destructive action. Pune is the cultural centre of Maharashtra and culture and knowledge is considered as a monopoly of Brahmins. Bhandarker was a liberal progressive Brahmin and the Institute named after him is storehouse of knowledge of which any scholar could be and should be justly proud.

It is quite significant to note that the alleged remarks against Shivaji and his mother were made by James Laine, not by anyone associated with the Bhandarkar Oriental Institute and yet this Institute was ransacked. If the leaders of the Sambhaji Brigade really wanted to show their love for Shivaji they should have demanded ban on the books instead of ransacking of the famous Institute. But they chose to vandalise Bhandarkar Institute instead.

Thus the purpose was not so much as to protest against Bhandarkar Institute but to attack the institute considered to be the storehouse of Brahmanical knowledge and controlled by the Brahmins. And that is why they raised the slogan "*yeh to ek jhanki hai, abhi Shaniwarwada baqi hai*", i.e., it is just the beginning and Shaniwarwada is yet to be attacked. The attack was not so much on the books as on the Brahminism and Brahminical culture.

There is acute struggle for political, social and cultural supremacy between various castes in India and in Maharashtra particularly between the Brahmins and Marathas. It is said that three M's (i.e. Marathas, Muslims and Mahars, i.e., dalits) always vote for the Congress and the BJP, the Party supposedly of the Brahmins is trying to capture Maharashtra along with the Shiv Sena. The Marathas would not like to loose their political hegemony in Maharashtra at any cost.

It is also important to note that the attack came after the NCP of Sharad Pawar failed to negotiate political alliance with the Shiv Sena-BJP in Maharashtra. The message is loud and clear: do not try to seize political power from Marathas. It would not be acceptable. And of course Shivaji is the symbol of Maratha power as he fought against the Mughals to retain his sovereignty. The Bhandarkar Institute provided facilities to James Laine to write the book on Shivaji with a purpose to defame him. Thus it was Brahminical "conspiracy" to de-legitimise the Maratha power. This cannot be tolerated in any case.

The NCP of Sharad Pawar is in alliance with the Congress in Maharashtra and for this reason the Government of Maharashtra is not acting strongly enough against the leader of the Shambhaji Brigade. The police did arrest 72 persons but have not touched the leader who is close to NCP leaders and ministers.

The government is silent about the whole episode and Sharad Pawar, while speaking in the Marathi Writers Conference even advised the writers to be sensitive to people's sentiments. The government moved swiftly to ban the book and might take action against the publishers Oxford University Press. The Publishers had already withdrawn the copies of the book.

The Shiv Sena also faces dilemma. Earlier its men blackened the face of Sanskrit scholar Shrikant Bahulkar for helping James Laine to write biography of Shivaji in which he defamed him. It shocked the author of Shivaji's biography and a noted scholar

Gajanan Mehendale, tore off his biographical manuscript written after 30 years of research. The Shiv Sena realised the mistake and apologised. However, the Sena leadership is silent on the act of Shambhaji Brigade for obvious reasons. If it condemns, it alienates Marathas which it cannot afford to do it in this election year. If it supports it, it would alienate the BJP's Brahmanical powerful vote bank of Brahmins.

It is quite likely that the action was planned with secret approval of a political party looking forward to Maratha votes in the coming Lok Sabha elections. Each party today has its own caste basis and all calculations are made with a view to these caste or community vote banks. The BJP in the eighties had launched a powerful attack on the Congress saying that it indulges in appeasement of Muslims to sustain and strengthen its vote bank and this greatly appealed to the upper caste middle class Hindus and they began voting for the BJP. The impression was given as if the BJP does not cultivate any vote bank and only the Congress does by 'appeasing' the Muslims.

In fact caste and community vote banks are an important consideration for all political parties. And the BJP has created its own powerful vote bank among the upper castes and also has successfully wooed backward caste and class Hindus by raising the religious issue like the Ramjanambhoomi and rode to power by demolishing Babri Masjid in Ayodhya.

It is unfortunate fact of our political life even in the 21st century that such vandalism be it of Babri Masjid, or of Wali Gujrati's mausoleum in Ahmedabad or of the Bhandarkar Oriental Research Institute in Pune are resorted to for political power struggle and such acts are defended shamelessly. Such vandalism is not monopoly of any single caste or community. We must learn painfully that human interests play much greater role in power politics than values and issues.

In all such attacks politicians gain and innocent human lives or rich cultural heritage loose out. This has been the history of thousands of years and nothing has changed even in the twenty-first century.

Future of Secularism in India

The question of future of secularism in India is very important particularly at this juncture. The fundamentalist forces are raising their head in India as in other countries of the world. No religion is exception to this. There are many reasons for this. In India Hindu fundamentalism has become much more aggressive than say Muslim fundamentalism. Secularism today is in much greater danger than ever before due to Hindutva militancy.

Secularism is highly necessary if India has to survive as a nation. But apart from survival of Indian nationalism and Indian unity, secularism is necessary for modern democratic polity. And this need for secular polity becomes much greater if the country happens to be as diverse and plural as India. Secularism is a great need for democratic pluralism.

Our leaders and freedom fighters were well aware of need for secular and modern democratic polity for India. They also knew that India is highly religious country and that secularism in the sense of hostility or indifference to religion will never be acceptable to people of India. Secularism was never meant to be indifference to religion by India leaders. It is for this reason that even most orthodox among Hindus and Muslims accepted it as a viable ideology for Indian unity and integrity.

The most Orthodox Muslim 'Ulama of Deobandi school preferred secular India to Muslim homeland or theocratic Pakistan. They outright rejected the idea of Pakistan when mooted by Jinnah. They denounced two nation theory on the basis of religion. Nehru, though personally agnostic, but never imposed agnostic or atheistic secularism. He was too much of a democrat to attempt that. He said in his answer to a query by an Indian student at Oxford University in fifties that in U.K. state has a religion (Anglican Christianity) but people of England are quite indifferent to religion but in India state has no religion but people are very religious. Therefore, in Indian situation secularism means equal protection to all religions.

Nehru was greatly committed, more than anyone else in post-independence India, to the concept of secularism. He never compromised on this question. He was well aware of the fact that secularism is a great cementing force for the diverse people of India. He, as an idealist, thought that with spread of modern scientific and technological education secularism would spread and find greater and greater acceptability. However, not only it that did not happen that way but communalism and obscurantism spread with more intensity than secularism.

There are several reasons for this all of which we cannot analyse here. Some of them of course must be mentioned. Like Nehru very few people were genuinely committed to secularism in the Congress. Many eminent Congress leaders were opposed to it in their heart of heart. They tried to sabotage Nehruvian vision in his own lifetime and they became much more active after his death. Nehru could not pay much attention to educational system in his lifetime. It could not be reformed. The old textbooks with communal approach introduced during the British period were never changed. The Congress leaders themselves approved of them. Those who did not, could not show enough courage to demand essential changes in history textbooks. Thus most of the Indians grew with subtle or pronounced communal mindset.

In fact the educated were thus more affected with communal virus than the illiterate masses who never studied in schools and colleges. Similarly urban areas were more affected with communal virus than rural areas. Formation of Pakistan also greatly affected thinking of educated middle class Hindus and they looked upon Muslims as responsible for creation of Pakistan. They were never explained the complex political factors which brought about existence of Pakistan and that it was small percentage of elite Muslims who were more responsible for creation of Pakistan than the Muslim masses who did not even migrate to that country. Jinnah, in his struggle for power with the Congress leaders never cared to understand what would be the impact of creation of Pakistan on the Muslim minority, which would remain in India.

Thus the education system did not cultivate secular outlook and conservative political outlook continued to strengthen communal mindset among the educated middle classes. The Muslim leaders in independent India, after the death of Maulana

Abul Kalam Azad and Zakir Husain, could not provide moderate and wise leadership to Muslim masses. They also remained not only extremely cautious in their approach but never prepared Muslim masses for modern secular polity in India. They were more insistent on minority rights than on necessity for change.

This attitude was further strengthened among these leaders due to frequent occurrences of communal riots. The Jabalpur riot of 1961 shook Nehru as much as Indian Muslims to the core. For the first time they became greatly apprehensive of their security and began to withdraw in their shell. This further reinforced conservatism and began hurdle in developing secular outlook among Muslims. The Jabalpur riots were followed by more intense communal violence in Ahmedabad in 1969 and Bhivandi-Jalgaon in 1970.

The end of seventies and early eighties witnessed number of major communal riots in which hundreds were killed brutally. The RSS propaganda, on the other hand, was bringing more and more Hindus in the fold of Hindutva. All these developments were sure prescription for increasingly weakening secular forces in the country.

The decade of eighties saw rise of religious militancy among Hindus, Sikhs and Muslims. This decade also witnessed horrendous communal violence in North India. It was again during this decade that Khalistan movement came to the fore on one hand, and the Shah Banu and Ramjanambhoomi movement; on the other. Mandal commission was implemented by V.P. Singh towards the end of eighties, which further gave boost to Hindutva forces. The caste stratification became much more pronounced and led to Hindu militancy apprehensive of division of Hindu votes.

And in the beginning of nineties Babri Masjid was demolished which pushed Indian secularism to the brink. It was greatest disaster and was followed by Bombay riots, which shocked whole world.

Thus we see Indian secularism has followed a tortuous course all through in the post-independence period. It is not surprising in a underdeveloped country like India with its immense poverty, insurmountable levels of unemployment and widespread illiteracy. The BJP, which came to power using its Hindutva card is not likely to give it up in near future. With every election it intensifies its Hindutva agenda. The other members of the Sangh Parivar, specially the Vishva Hindu Parishad, tend to be more irresponsible as it does not have to govern. It assumes extremist postures and threatens minorities. It is this irresponsible extremism which resulted in the Gujarat carnage which again shook the world. The BJP Government tends to be buffeted between the VHP extremism and National Democratic Coalition compulsions. It thus fails to adopt consistent policies.

In the given political circumstances the future of secularism does not seem to be bright. However, one should not take short-term view based only on given context. Human beings have always struggled to transcend their given situation. A purely contextual view tends to be realistic but also restricted one. A vision, on the other hand, may not always be realistic but has a much broader sweep. And it is this broader sweep which shapes new realities and these new realities enables us to shape our future.

Though religion will never cease to be a force in human life secularism will not loose its relevance either. The modern democratic polity cannot be sustained without the state being neutral to all religions or equally protective for all religions as Nehru put it. And it is in this sense that secularism in India will become more and more relevant. It should also be noted that we should not pose secularism and religious orthodoxy as binary opposites, as some rationalists tend to do.

Faith will always remain an important component of human behaviour and there will always remain an element of orthodoxy in faith behaviour. Rational faith is certainly not an impossibility but it tends to be an elitist phenomenon. On the level of masses orthodoxy reigns rather than rationality, even in advanced societies. Also, economic advancement and reduction in levels of poverty and illiteracy will ultimately sideline communal bigotry and enhance forces of secularism. Religious orthodoxy, if not challenged by the other's threats, would not yield to communalism. There is a Laxman Rekha between religious orthodoxy and communal discourse.

India has stupendous challenges to meet due to its economic backwardness and unemployment, which sharpen communal struggle. Unemployed and frustrated youth can easily be induces to think and act communally as he thinks his unemployment is due more to his caste or community than economic backwardness. Thus chances of secularism will certainly brighten with more economic progress and reduced levels of unemployment, particularly educated unemployment.

Indian democracy, which is here to stay, is in itself a guarantee for future of secularism. A pluralist country like India needs secularism like life-blood. India has been pluralist not since post-modernism but for centuries and no one can wish away its bewildering pluralism and this pluralism can be sustained only with religiously neutral polity. India has been passing through very critical phase now but there is nothing to despair. The present communal turmoil is not here to stay. It would certainly yield to more stable secular polity.

Reservation for Muslims

The Congress Government in Andhra Pradesh announced 5 per cent reservation for Muslims in educational institutions as well as in jobs. This has been done by creating category E for Muslims as there already exists categories A, B, C and D for backward classes. The reason for creating the category E for Muslims seems to be that Muslims in A.P. are extremely backward and poor. The order for reservation cited that in A.P. about 65 per cent Muslims live below poverty line whose annual income is less than Rs.11,000/-. It also says that 16 per cent Muslims in A.P. live below double poverty line whose annual income is below Rs. 4,500/-.

Where there is poverty there is widespread illiteracy. The literacy rate in A.P. is just about 18 per cent among men and abysmally low of 4 per cent among women. Thus Muslims are worse than dalits all over India in general and in A.P. in particular. It should open the eyes of those who keep on accusing that Islam spread through sword and that Muslim rulers were busy spreading Islam and breaking Hindu idols. Large parts of Telangana were ruled by Nizam for several centuries and yet Muslims are so poor and backward precisely in that part of the state.

It is because only the poor dalits converted to Islam and not highly influential Hindus who enjoyed high status in Nizam rule. No attempt was ever made to convert them to Islam. Even in Hyderabad city, which was the Centre of Nizam rule Muslims are abysmally poor and backward. Thus the A.P. Government created category E for poor and backward Muslims to give them 5 per cent reservation.

All those who stand for reservation for the dalits, tribals and backwards have supported this measure. Ram Vilas Paswan has always supported reservation and is now demanding reservation for dalits in private industries and also fully supported the A.P. Government's move to give 5 per cent reservation for Muslims. Lalu Prasad Yadav too extended his support along with Karunanidhi of Tamil Nadu. Even a BJP ally and former chief minister of Andhra Pradesh Mr. Chandrababu Naidu has endorsed the reservation. The TDP itself had promised 3 per cent reservation for Muslims in its manifesto for Lok Sabha elections and BJP had not objected to it at all.

As expected the only party to oppose reservation with all vehemence at its command was the BJP and other members of the Sangh Parivar. The BJP while contesting elections for the Lok Sabha was wooing Muslims for votes and was promising sky to them. Mr. Vajpayee while campaigning in Bihar even promised to appoint 2 crore Urdu teachers if voted to power (yes, that is what he said in his speech and this was not appeasement of Muslims as it was being said by the BJP leader, it becomes appeasement only when the Congress leaders say so). The BJP raised hue and cry as soon as the A.P. Government announced the reservation under E category for Muslims.

The BJP described this reservation as 'anti-national' and announced that it would launch a fortnight long campaign agitation "against appeasement". Mr. Venkaiah Naidu told reporters on 18th July that "The decision to give 5 per cent reservation to Muslims in educational and jobs is dangerous, divisive and against national interest. It is a trial balloon for the entire country and part of the ongoing appeasement politics."

Not surprisingly Atal Bihari Vajpayee fully endorsed the BJP move to oppose A.P. Government's announcement for 5 per cent reservation for Muslims in jobs and educational institutions.

Addressing the BJP Parliamentary Party on 20th July, Mr. Vajpayee described Andhra Government's move as "unconstitutional" and "illegal". He also felt that the controversial decision would give "rise to religious conversion in the state". For Mr. Vajpayee reservations should always be on the basis of social and economic backwardness and not on the basis of religion."

Of course one could never expect BJP to support reservation for Muslims and also perhaps for Christians. However, whatever the BJP stand it is bound to be anti-minorities. One could not expect it to be favouring minorities on any issue. But reservation on religious grounds by itself can be a contentious issue. It has to be debated in all its consequences. Many otherwise committed secular people also have expressed doubt on the issue. Even among Muslims there is no unanimity. It is therefore, important to discuss this issue in all its complexities. It should not be debated only in terms of pro - and anti-Muslim rhetoric.

It is important to note that this issue representation of Muslims in government jobs in U.P. and Bihar had played an important role in creation of Pakistan. The upper class privileged Muslim minorities of U.P. and Bihar was quite apprehensive that they would loose their privileged positions in government jobs in united India as it would have Hindu majority and the Hindu majority would take away most important jobs leaving Muslims high and dry. This fear did play an important role in creation of Pakistan movement.

These upper caste and upper class Muslims from U.P. and Bihar migrated to Pakistan for retaining their high positions and for quick promotions. But the low caste poor Muslims had no such inspirations nor they could have got such jobs with few exceptions. These poor and illiterate Muslims who were in large numbers, therefore, remained indifferent to Pakistan movement. They had nothing to gain or loose. But today new middle class among Muslims is emerging from these backward class and low caste Muslims.

Until recently in independent India all the benefits of parliamentary seats or government jobs have gone to the so-called *ashraf* only. Mr. Ali Anwar from Bihar in his *Musawat ki Jang* (Battle for Equality) has pointed out the plight of dalit Muslims in Bihar and maintains that in all these years of independence no backward caste Muslims ever got an opportunity to become M.P. or MLA though such Muslims constitute more than 90 per cent of Muslim population. Only in the recent Lok Sabha elections some M.P.s belonging to dalit Muslims have been elected M.P.s.

Though theoretically there is no discrimination on such grounds in Islam but caste discriminations (as the words *ashraf* and *ajlaf*, i.e., noble and low point out) has always existed and short of untouchability low caste Muslims (*ajlaf*) have not been equitably treated. The implementation of Mandal Commission Report in 1990 gave new hope to these dalit Muslims and a new awareness have been born among them. Many low caste Muslims like Shabbir Ansari in Maharashtra, Aijaz Ali and Ali Anwar in Bihar and others in U.P. are trying to organise them and struggling for reservations for them under Mandal Commission categories.

These Muslims point out that general reservations for Muslims on religious grounds would benefit only the so called *Ashraf* Muslims and will hardly percolate down to poor dalit Muslims. These leaders would prefer reservation for Muslims only under Mandal Commission categories. This too is not an easy task. The concerned governments and backward caste commission has to take clear and bold stand.

Apart from this the important question is should there be reservation on religious ground? I think it is very complex question and would be difficult to answer in yes or no. It has to be examined from different angles. Firstly any reservation purely on religious grounds is bound to invite vigorous opposition particularly from Sangh Parivar. It would give an emotional issue to RSS and BJP looking for emotive issues after loosing power. Many secularists would also not support such a move unreservedly. Even there would be no unanimity among Muslims on this, as pointed out above.

This would also necessitate constitutional amendment as Constitution provides reservation only on caste grounds. One can of course argue that there are dalit Muslims and dalit Christians as there are Hindu dalits. And if the argument is that there is no caste system among Muslims and Christianity, one can argue it is only a scriptural view of religion and not anthropological view as in practice there are corresponding castes among Muslims and Christians too. Why not reservations for them? There is no caste system theoretically among Buddhists too yet reservations have been extended to neo-Buddhists?

The argument that extending reservations to Muslim and Christian dalits would encourage conversions to these religions is not constitutionally sound. One is free to convert under the Article 25 of the Constitution. Yet, one must realise that politically it is a volatile question. Muslims and Christians too should take politically wise decision. In this era of privatisation the government jobs are contracting. Though there is demand for reservation in private jobs it will not be easy for any government to bring private jobs within the ambit of reservation. Some positive discrimination or affirmative action may be possible but that too will take long time and will not be easy to achieve.

The best thing in the given complex situation would be a mixed bag solution. Muslims and Christians could be assured reservation under Mandal categories. Secondly, the governments, Central as well as state could make special arrangements for higher education for weaker sections of society and even create institutions to search for talents among them and ensure jobs for them. Thirdly, on patterns of affirmative action in US industries, private sector foundations could be created for education of such sections among dalit Muslims. Lastly leaders of Indian Muslims should convince well-to-do Muslims in India and abroad to donate generously from Zakat money to create educational endowments and foundations in India to establish educational institutions of good qualities for poor Muslims be they from upper castes or lower castes. There is immense potential for such endowments.

I hope the Indian Muslims will give thought to these suggestions and critically reflect on the complex question and would not try to beg for reservation pushing up communal temperature and handing on silver platter a much sought for issue to the Sangh Parivar.

6

Gujarat Imbroglio

Three Years After Genocide in Gujarat

It was on 28 February 2002 three years before that genocide of Muslims started in Gujarat a day after train burning incident in Godhra on 27th February 2002, a day earlier. Every sensible person had condemned what happened at Godhra though it was far from clear as to who was responsible for train burning. Now the U.C. Banerjee report indicates that it was accidental fire which started from inside the compartment.

However, Narendra Modi, the Gujarat Chief Minister, a hardcore RSS man, asserted that it was done by Muslims to massacre the Ramsevaks and justified the genocide in Gujarat on Newton's law of action-reaction. It is now well known that he had instructed top police officials in a meeting in Gandhinagar on 27th evening not to interfere with what rioters do on the streets next day. Harin Pandya, the assassinated minister of Narendra Modi Cabinet testified this before People's inquiry Commission and also told his father what Narendra Modi had instructed police officers on 27th February. Harin Pandya's father testified before the Nanavati Commission.

Thus, complicity of the Gujarat Government in supporting the genocide is hardly in doubt. By any account it was the most horrible massacre of innocent citizens belonging to minority community in Gujarat in the post-independence period. The only other parallel is anti-Sikh riots of 1984. The BJP had often boasted that no communal riots take place when it is in power. And

Gujarat saw one of the worst genocide of Muslims when it was in power with great majority in the Gujarat Assembly.

What was worse that even then Prime Minister Shri A.B.Vajpayee justified the massacre saying that had Muslims condemned Godhra incident enough, such a massacre in Gujarat would not have taken place. Though Mr. Vajpayee had reminded Modi of his 'Rajdharma' also (though without taking any action against him), he is too well-known for his flip flops. Mr. L.K.Advani, the then Home Minister, even gave clean chit to Narendra Modi that he has 'maintained' law and order in Gujarat effectively after the Godhra incident.

Thus if the top functionaries of the government of India were backing Narendra Modi why should he not have done what he did. So much for BJP's claim of maintaining communal peace when in power. What is worse, the victims of the worst massacre in Gujarat could not hope for any justice. Modi even tried to wind up all relief camps, something which had never happened before. His administration even threatened to cut off water and food grains supply if the relief camps were not wound up. He had no mercy for the victims of brutal violence. And all this in the land of Gandhi who lived and died for peace and communal harmony.

All the institutions of the state – legislative, executive, and judiciary have been communalised. Who then could come to the rescue of the poor victims? Both bureaucracy and police were deeply affected (with honourable exceptions). The Amnesty International impartial keepers of the rule of law has also recently compiled the report "India – Justice the Victim – Gujarat State fails to Protect Women from Violence." It has been compiled in 2005 and released just a month ago. Like other reports on Gujarat genocide it makes horrible reading. The genocide in Gujarat was not only failure of law and order. It would be understatement to say so. It was deliberate and planned genocide.

The Amnesty Report under the title "Police connivance in the violence" says, However, police not only withheld assistance and then quotes Concerned Citizen's Tribunal, "Worse still [than the failure to prevent violence] is the evidence of their [the police force`s] active connivance and brutality, their indulgence in vulgar and obscene conduct against women and children in full public view. It is as if, instead of impartial keepers of the rule of law, they were part of the Hindutva brigade targeting helpless Muslims."

Further the Amnesty report states, "Local inquiry reports list testimonies of police providing diesel from their official vehicles to burn down Muslim homes. Similarly witnesses told the Nanavati-Shah Commission that the Rapid Action Force had supplied petrol from their official vehicles to the mob to set ablaze houses belonging to the minority community. Another witness told the Commission in Ahmedabad that a police inspector encouraged the mob to attack the Muslims in her area. "The inspector directed that petrol be taken from his vehicle and it was used by the mob to set our society on fire."

*It should be noted that the Rapid Action Force had been specially set up by the Home Ministry at the Centre to control communal violence. It has been set up out of CRPF (Central Reserve Police Force) which generally had good reputation in controlling communal violence. And earlier it had established good name in several other riots by handling them efficiently. In Gujarat under the surcharged communal atmosphere even RAF was communalised – a matter of great shame for it. Its fair name was tainted.

The police behaviour is not surprising if we keep in mind that many officers of Gujarat police force are reportedly members of Hindu right wing organisations and in their actions may have sought to further the objectives of those organisations rather than impartially carry on their professional duties, remarks Amnesty International report. This by itself is highly objectionable that members of police force be members of such rightwing organisations but in Gujarat such things are not only permissible but even desirable and hence one finds complicity of the police in such flagrant manner. In any other civilised society police officers will be dismissed if they join any such force. Independence of police from all such political outfits is an essential requirement.

The other horrifying aspect of the Gujarat carnage was violence against and rape of women. It was as if rape of all human values. Under the title "Violence Against Women" the Amnesty report says that in all violence communal, racist or ethnic violence against women is specific one. The report says, "In one of the earlier incidents of violence in Gujarat or other parts of the country had sexual violence against girls and women, committed in public, been such a key feature."

The report says that they (women) became victims of grave abuses because their identities as both women and Muslims intersected. For right wing Hindus attacking the Muslim minority, Muslim women became the hated symbols of the community, which they sought to threaten, humiliate, hurt and destroy. The women, even if not direct victims of assault and rape suffer most emotionally and psychologically, as they have to care and nurture families torn apart by violence and mayhem.

In Gujarat, women were subjected to large scale sexual abuse, apart from physical violence. The cases of Kausar Bano and Bilquis Begum are most talked about. Kausar Bano in Naroda Patia locality of Ahmedabad worst affected by communal frenzy, was eight month pregnant. Her abdomen was split open, the foetus extracted and killed. Such brutalities were unheard of in the history of communal violence in India. Bilqis Begum is another case in point from Randhikpur village of Dahod district.

She was six months pregnant and gang raped by the VHP hooligans and nine of her relatives were killed before her eyes. She was taken as dead by the mobsters but she fortunately survived to tell her story. The police officers and doctors also became part of this abominable crime. They aided and abetted.

And these were not isolated cases. According to Amnesty report several hundred Muslim girls and women were reportedly stripped and dragged naked before their own families and thousands of violent Hindu attackers who taunted and insulted them with obscene words and threatened them with rape and murder. They were then raped, often gang-raped, beaten with sticks or *trishuls* and swords, had breast cut off and wombs slashed open by swords and rods violently pushed into their vaginas before a large number of them were cut into pieces or burned to death.

What was worse, due to state complicity in all this, the victims had no way to get justice within the state of Gujarat. The Supreme

Court had to intervene and transfer the cases out of the state and these cases are now going on in the state of Maharashtra. More than 3000 cases closed by the state police for 'want of evidence' had to be reopened as per directive of the Supreme Court. The Bilqis Bano case was one of them. The CBI was asked to take over these cases. These helpless victims had otherwise totally despaired. The lower judiciary was totally communalised and higher judiciary in Gujarat is also partly contaminated with communal ideologies. What was more shocking was that the state appointed prosecutors were members of VHP. How on earth could these victims ever get any justice?

We must remember all this not for promoting any negative feeling but so that such things are not repeated in future in India. It would keep us reminding that when communal and fascist forces come to power what happens to our country. The fight against communal forces should go on through democratic methods. They must be isolated and weakened. Intolerance and hatred can never be part of democratic culture. Democracy thrives only when culture of peace and tolerance prevails. There is great need in democracy for a vibrant and healthy civil society. Such a society can be born only out of well informed and committed citizens.

Godhra Train Burning Incident and Banerjee Report

The Sangh Parivar is understandably upset at the U.C. Banerjee Inquiry Committee Report on the Godhra train burning incident. The subsequent Gujarat carnage was justified by the Sangh Parivar solely on the basis of this incident describing it as a conspiracy by Muslims of Godhra with involvement of ISI of Pakistan. Even the BJP Prime Minister Shri A.B.Vajpayee justified the Gujarat carnage saying that the Muslims of India did not 'condemn it enough' and hence this carnage took place. Mr. L.K. Advani had similarly justified the Bombay riots of 1992-93 saying that "Hindus were anguished" by burning of few Hindus at Jogeshwari. Subsequently the Supreme Court discharged all the accused in the Jogeshwari incident. But the Sangh Parivar took law in its own hand and perpetrated communal violence in Mumbai in 1992-93.

In case of Godhra too before the truth was out within 24 hours communal carnage started in other parts of Gujarat in which more than two thousand citizens were butchered or burnt alive most brutally. Without any preliminary inquiry Narendra Modi and his cohorts drew definite conclusion and before any one could know what had happened started the butchery. Narendra Modi propounded theory of action and reaction referring to Newton's theory.

Now that Banerjee Committee appointed by Lalu Prasad Yadav as Railway Minister has come to conclusion that the fire probably started by cooking from inside, the Sangh Parivar is denouncing it as 'political act' as if their theory of conspiracy was established beyond any ken of doubt. More than hundred persons (135 persons) were accused of pre-planned terrorist attack by one community. Ten charge sheets have already been filed.

Conspiracy theory has several loopholes. How did the conspirators know that there are Karsevaks on Sabarmati Express. The train was also running more than four hours late. And as for Karsevaks being on the train inquiries show that even RAW, L.B. and Railway Police did not know anything about it. In fact Karsevaks were scheduled to return a day earlier but were delayed by a day. How could then conspirators know that Karsevaks were on the train that day? They could not know more than government intelligence agencies. Even if they did, delay of more than four hours could have upset their plans. In such matters even minutes matter, let alone hours.

Even pulling the chain, cross examination in the court clearly brings out, was not the handiwork of Muslims, the chain was pulled by Karsevaks themselves as some Karsevaks chasing the vendors on Godhra railway platform were left out when the train moved. They pulled the chain twice. The conspiracy theory maintains that the accused had pulled the chain, stopped the train to carry petrol or inflammable liquid into S-6 and set fire. The forensic report also clearly states that no traces of hydrocarbon were found on the floor of S-6 compartment. That clearly means no petrol was spread on the floor of S-6 to set fire to it. However, Modi maintained that Muslims had used 140 litres of petrol. He never said what was his source of information.

With so much petrol the whole compartment would have exploded and charred completely.

The Dy. SP, Railway also said in his statement that he did not see petrol or any other liquid being carried by anyone inside the compartment. The survivors had superficial injuries on upper part of their bodies. Had petrol been thrown on the floor and set to fire, they would have had injuries on lower parts of the body. Also, no Karsevak has admitted petrol being smuggled in and poured out on the floor.

Haribhai Joshi, an income tax officer from Ahmedabad who was travelling in S-6 with his wife said he saw only smoke and no fire. His wife died and he crawled out of the compartment. Though he crawled on the floor he had no burn injuries. If petrol had been thrown on the floor to set fire, Mr. Joshi could not have crawled on the floor. His wife was sitting near the window and did not come out in time and died of asphyxiation. In fact all those who died do not seem to have died of burns but of asphyxiation.

The post-mortem reports the less said the better. Unfortunately much has not come out in the press about it. Mr. Mukul Sinha, the defence lawyer rolled out startling information in a talk recently. His information was based on cross-examination and examination of relevant documents. There are several flaws in the report. Post-mortem was done before the inquest report. Inquest was done at 6.45 P.M. whereas post-mortem began at 4.30 P.M. Post-mortem is always followed by inquest.

What is more important is to note that post-mortem was done at railway station itself and one doctor has signed it on 14th March though it was done on 27th February. This doctor was perhaps very honest and put the date when he signed the report. Mr. Mukul Sinha concluded that perhaps post-mortem was never done as there were no signs of severe burns on the bodies of the deceased. Also very few bodies actually had been identified. Most others could not be identified at all.

The then Railway Minister Mr. Nitish Kumar obliged the BJP led Government by not holding any inquiry as long as NDA was in power. Actually inquiry should have been immediately held following the incident. It was Lalu Yadav of the UPA

Government who ordered inquiry headed by U.C. Banerjee, a retired Supreme Court Judge. Justice Banerjee has concluded that the fire was result of cooking inside the compartment as some traces of grains were found inside. It is incidental spark which fell on rubber fittings causing dense smoke which later at a higher temperature turned into fire.

It has been testified by witnesses that smoke was noticed before fire. Also, looking at the other aspect of the matter the train stopped hardly for five minutes after pulling of chain and it was physically impossible to carry out such in operation in such a short time. To carry several cans of petrol (about 60 litres as estimated by forensic experts) inside S-6 through the vestibule cutting its canvas is almost impossible. In fact they entered through S-7 and the rubber cover of that S-7 vestibule was not cut. That evidence was also sought to be destroyed. S-7 was not preserved as an evidence and was used for 7 days after the incident. In fact if the culprits had entered through S-7 cutting its canvas, how could it be used for seven days before it was grounded.

Also, the terrain was such as to make such an operation impossible. There was a deep drain between the Signal Faliah and the track and thick shrubs asking it impossible for the miscreants to cross it and enter the train. The Karsevaks were also carrying trishuls and how could they allow outsiders to enter the compartment without resistance with petrol to set fire to the compartment.

All these factors have to be taken into account if the conspiracy theory is to be substantiated. It is unfortunate that Justice Nanavati inquiring into Gujarat communal carnage and Godhra incident has hurriedly debunked Justice Banerjee report without having any concrete evidence to support conspiracy theory. It is not becoming of a Judge inquiring into these incidents to dismiss other judge's inquiry report. He should have waited for completion of his own inquiry before making such statement. Remember he had given a statement absolving the police from its role in Gujarat riots before he started the inquiry. It was only after public hue and cry that he took back his statement.

This clearly shows that Narendra Modi has appointed a Judge with careful consideration to obtain the result he wants.

For Sangh Parivar minorities are always to be blamed and for this there is no need for any judicial inquiry. It is a forgone conclusion for them that Muslims are violent and any violent incident should be blamed on them. That also gives them opportunity to seek revenge and kill them ruthlessly. Even the person of the stature of the Prime Minister also could not refrain from making provocative statement like who set fire to the train in Goa in 2002. When he said this and that Muslims did not condemn the Godhra incident enough he clearly took it for granted that Muslims from Signal Faliah were real culprits and had hatched the conspiracy to set S-6 ablaze. It is highly regretted that the Prime Minister of the country could become so blatantly partisan for his party totally forgetting his constitutional duties.

Of course Banerjee Committee's report is still not final as many police officials avoided appearing before it perhaps to conceal the real truth. It is being said that Government is thinking of giving it the status of a commission under the Inquiry Commission's Act so that justice Banerjee could summon the police officials and other witnesses. If that happens it would be possible to know the truth, which was sought to be suppressed so far by those who were waiting for an opportunity to fan fires of communal violence. It is highly necessary that truth be known, not for seeking revenge but to avoid such incidents in future and keeping the communal zealots under check.

As for the charge that Lalu Prasad Yadav is using it for election purposes let those who are making this charge against him forget that Narendra Modi had exploited the Godhra incident blatantly for his election campaign in December 2002 and he had not hesitated to carry dead bodies of unfortunate victims of Godhra incident in procession in Ahmedabad to ignite communal fires. Now the Chief Election Commissioner is objecting to such use of the Banerjee Committee Report but why the Election Commission allowed Narendra Modi to exploit the Godhra incident for is election purposes? It is for the Election Commission to clarify this issue. Of course ideally no one should exploit such issues for electoral purposes. But then who will throw the first stone?

Gujarat Carnage and Muslim Women

The Gujarat Carnage after the Godhra train burning incident in early 2002 brought disgrace to India. Such brutal communal carnage had never taken place before in the post-independent India. It attracted world-wide attention and number of countries including the European Union and United States sent its official representatives to find out what went wrong and why such carnage took place at all.

From within India also several human rights groups, women's groups and human rights activists rushed to Gujarat to express their sympathy and solidarity with the victims of Hindutva aggression against helpless minority victims. Never before so many activists had rushed to any communal violence scene in India. So many reports were prepared of the ghastly crime against humanity and still that work is going on. There are several aspects to be probed and every probe raises cries of shame.

The crimes against women were really unspeakable. The women particularly those who are working for women's rights and empowerment were greatly perturbed at what happened with them in Gujarat. Many women activists went and interviewed the victims in refugee camps. Yet so much needs to be explored. The wounds inflicted on minority women can hardly heal especially when they were subjected to such unspeakable crimes. Still they are living with sense of shame and agony.

Recently a team of women activists from different countries like France, Germany, U.K., The Netherlands, Sri Lanka and India visited Gujarat and wrote a report *Threatened Existence-A Feminist Analysis of the Genocide in Gujarat*. This report comprising 244 pages is a must for all those who want to know of festering wounds two years after the carnage. The report has been written after months of pains-taking research.

In the introduction to the report these anguished women say, "The specific targeting of women, as part of a conscious strategy to terrorise the Muslim population of Gujarat, also particularly concerned the panellists (of women). According to Rhonda (one of the panellists), sexual violence played a fundamental role and was used 'as an engine of the mobilisation of hatred and destruction. It further says, "The scale and brutality of the sexual violence unleashed upon women was new, or felt as it was new, to the panellists who could not be prepared for the testimonies they heard even though they were aware of the centrality of this method in the violence of 2002."

Meera, who lives in Gujarat and was acutely conscious of what had happened in Gujarat in February-March 2002 described it as follows:

"Many doubts arise in your mind [about the erosion of citizenship] particularly when you come face to face with women who have undergone brutal sexual attacks and mass rape. For first time married women broke their silence on the sexual attacks they suffered. A mother spoke of her two daughters but did not say that she herself was a victim....testimonies were often given with young children looking on, punctuated with long silences. None of us could sleep that night; a community was being held to ransom – accept your citizenship or....We exchanged experiences of Bosnia, Palestine, Israel but the extent, brutality and the varied methods of Gujarat were unheard of."

Thus these women panellists Sunila Abeyeskera of Sri Lanka, Rhonda Copelon of City University of New York, Anissa Helie of France, Gabriela Mischkowski of U.K., Uma Chakravarti of Delhi University and Wahida Nainar of the Netherlands, Farah Naqvi of Delhi and Meera Velaydan of India came to conclusion that sexual violence that took place in Gujarat was really unheard of and such things were not to be found even in places like Bosnia, Palestine and Israel.

On their Gujarat wide tour these women heard story after story of sexual crimes at the hands of supporters of Hindutva. Yasmin, a woman survivor from Panchmahal district told the panellists "They cut off breasts of her (neighbour's) daughter, it is difficult to forget, it still swims in my vision. I have lost my mental peace."

Another woman survivor Sabah from the same district said, What had those kids done to them? I cannot forget those girls [who were raped]. We have to try and arrest them [the rapists]. Quoting Sabah's testimony the report says, "We ran in different directions and hid in the field. But the mob found some of us and started attacking....I recognised two people from my village Gano Baria and Sunil – pulling away my daughter. She screamed, telling the men to get off her and leave her alone. The screams and cries of Ruqayya, Suhana, Shabana, begging for their *izzat* [honour] could clearly be heard. I could do nothing to help my daughter from being assaulted sexually and tortured to death."

In Tanika Sarkar's words, "The pattern of cruelty suggests three things. One, the woman's body was a site of almost inexhaustible violence, with infinitely plural and innovative forms of torture. Second, their sexual and reproductive organs were attacked with a special savagery. Third, their children, born and unborn, shared the attacks and were killed before their eyes."

And despite such sexual savagery perpetrated against Muslim women in Gujarat, the NDA Government at the Centre, not to speak of Narendra Modi Government in Gujarat not only remained silent spectator but occasionally justified it. Remember Defence Minister Mr. George Fernandese justifying this in a debate in Parliament on Gujarat said that this is nothing new, it has been happening in India for ages. Even the Prime Minister, though a poet and claiming poetic sensitivity remained silent, if not justified it *a-la* Fernandese.

The panellists in the report make one very pertinent point about Muslim women being sexually assaulted to such a degree as in Gujarat. The report says, "The women of the community suffer attacks in two ways. In the first case they are members of the collective, like any other, and are liable to be attacked. At the same time, they are the biological and cultural reproducers of the community and their bodies symbolize the body of the community and its boundaries. In the Hindutva project, the control of the Muslim other through gender and sexual domination is at the forefront of the political strategy in Gujarat and elsewhere."

Thus it would be seen that sexual assault is not simply fulfilment of ones lust; it is much more than that in such cases. By sexually violating the women of the 'other' you are destroying their honour and humiliating them as a community and treating body of women as body of the community. Woman's honour must be destroyed to destroy the honour of the community.

Thus supporting this view the report says that the sexual assault incidents were not just random or isolated incidents. They were widespread and pre-planned. For many cases – Gujarat, Rawanda, the former Yugoslavia – such wide scale violence could not have been conducted without a significant measure of complicity, if not participation, by the State. In Gujarat, it is clear that all events, including the mass use of rape and sexual assault, occurred with the knowledge of highly placed State actors, and in many instances, were carried out with full participation and support of the police.

There are many witnesses to the fact that the police often hit the stomachs of pregnant women in so called combing operations. A police officer of the rank of DCP himself entered the house and beat up small girls and women. One woman who was six month pregnant had an abortion. He said to these women "We will keep all your men and make you prostitutes." Besides this there was lot of suggestive sexual violence, hitting women on breasts, targeting private parts and targeting pregnant women.

Unfortunately RSS and VHP women themselves were participating in this violence against Muslim women. Safia, a woman from Ahmedabad testified that the daughter of a Bajrang Dal leader was pulling women by hair and throwing them in fire. Other eyewitnesses also alleged that another woman was catching Muslim women and passing them on to the VHP and Bajrang Dal men to be raped.

This writer has also visited Gujarat number of times and heard similar testimonies which, are indeed hair raising. The idea of recounting these stories is not to ignite fire of revenge but to understand what the Hindutva agenda is and what counter measures to fight this menace are required. India is a secular nation and it is duty of all of us to keep it secular and to promote peace and harmony.

The secular forces have to draw up their own strategies so that Gujarat like events do not repeat and we are able to keep violence away from our secular democracy. We will have to remember Gujarat to ward off fascism from our land. Unfortunately the communal forces are united and secular forces are divided thus giving enough opportunities to communal forces to play havoc with our secular system. It is for the secular forces to keep Gujarat violence before their eyes so that the consequences of allowing political space to communal forces remains before them.

All of us who believe in secularism and humanism should spare no efforts to unite secular forces in the country.

One Year of Gujarat's Shame

On 27th of February 2002 began the carnage in Gujarat, first in Godhra when 59 person's were burnt alive in compartment no. S-6 of Sabarmati Express coming from Ayodhya and then from 28th February began carnage of Muslims in Central and North Gujarat and some other parts. It is one year since and wounds have still far from being healed. In fact no one is talking about healing touch even.

If anything the Sangh Parivar is aggravating the situation. Election campaign in Gujarat was launched and fought on that basis and when the BJP won with 2/3rd majority they celebrated it and talked about repeating the Gujarat experiment elsewhere. The top leaders of the BJP declared this with a buoyant spirit and with glee. Even the Prime Minister Shri Vajpayee when asked will Gujarat be repeated, instead of repudiating the statement asked rhetorically "Will Godhra be repeated?" implying thereby yes, Gujarat will be repeated if Godhra is repeated. It clearly means the BJP leaders do not believe in maintaining law and order but in politics of raw revenge.

The Muslims in Gujarat had to pay very heavy price for what happened in Godhra. What happened in Godhra still shrouded in mystery one year after the event. The inquiry commission headed by Justice Nanavati has hardly made any headway. The forensic department came to conclusion after making experiments that it was an inside job. It was not possible to set fire from outside. The conspiracy theory propounded by the police has yet to be established with credibility.

The Narendra Modi Government is following flagrantly partial policies towards those "responsible" for Godhra carnage and those involved in Gujarat carnage after Godhra though he eloquently declared after getting elected in December 2002 that his government will follow the policy of 'justice for all and discrimination against none'. He has imposed POTA on the Codhra accused and has not even arrested all the culprits involved in the Gujarat carnage, let alone enforcing POTA against them.

More than 2000 people were killed in Gujarat mainly from February 2002 to May 2002 and killings continued thereafter for quite some time. Everyone agrees that it was the worst communal carnage since independence. Jawaharlal Nehru was thoroughly shaken by the Jabalpur riots on 1961 as he never expected that communal violence would breakout on such a scale in independent India. How he would have felt if he were alive when Gujarat carnage took place last year as Gujarat carnage was on far greater scale then the Jabalpur communal violence of 1961. In fact there could hardly be any comparison between the two.

In Gujarat last year 2000 persons were killed (Jabalpur not more than 55 people were killed officially – though unofficially more than 200 people were killed) whereas in Gujarat officially 1000 people were brutally massacred. Not only that about 150,000 Muslims were displaced (many of them have still not been rehabilitated and are unable to return to their home and hearth), 527 mosques and mausoleums were destroyed, hundreds of women were raped and properties worth 687 crores of rupees were destroyed.

The rapes were committed publicly. The eminent judges and citizens report *Crime Against Humanity* observe about gender crime, "The sinister aspect of these gender crimes is that they have been led and directed by elected representatives and prominent leaders of the BJP, RSS and VHP." And what is worse they are least ashamed of it.

Narendra Modi became an icon of Hindutva and was given rousing receptions by the Sangh Parivar organisations in several places. The Sangh Parivar thought it was his highest achievement. Anyone criticising this carnage enraged Modi and he considered it as an insult to 5 crore people of Gujarat as if all Gujaratis were with him in this carnage and that victims themselves (i.e., Muslims) were also proud of this carnage since Muslims are also part of 5 crore Gujaratis.

The fact is that only Sangh Parivar fanatics and their followers supported the carnage. A large number of Gujaratis deeply resented it and condemned it in various ways. Their voices were muffled initially but became loud and clear in course of time. The Sangh Parivar in Gujarat led by Narendra Modi equated itself with whole of Gujarat. All communal forces consider themselves as representatives of entire community. No religious community is homogenous, much less Hindus who are highly diverse. No one organisation, political, social or cultural, can represent entire community.

And even if religiously and culturally any community is homogenous (which is not so and even Muslims are not at all homogenous in this sense and there are all sorts of divisions among them – regional, cultural, those based on caste and biradaris as well as sectarian) one cannot expect all its members to hold same political views in democracy. It will be very negation of democracy.

Such homogeneity of political views will lead to authoritarianism and this is precisely what the Sangh Parivar wants. They have no love lost for democracy and their motto is if you are not with us you are against us. What is worse in case of communal forces if you are not with them you are against that religion itself. If you are not with Muslim League you are against Islam and if you are not with Hindutva, you are against Hinduism.

Thus the moment someone criticises Narendra Modi Government-led massacre in Gujarat it is immediately dubbed as criticism of Hinduism or insult to people of Gujarat. Recent mild criticism of law and order situation in Gujarat by industrial leaders like Rahul Bajaj and others led to outburst by Narendra Modi and now CII is threatened with split in Gujarat. It clearly shows that there are no signs of remorse for the Gujarat carnage. The Sangh Parivar, particularly the VHP is all ready to observe the anniversary of Godhra carnage and serious law and order situation is developing but no mention is made by them about the brutal killings of Gujarat following Godhra.

As pointed out above the refugees are far from settled. Those who have gone back to Naroda Patia which was the worst affected area of Ahmedabad where about 100 persons were burnt alive, are living in fear on the occasion of first anniversary of Godhra incident. Many of them have already left and gone to safer areas to live with their relatives. Even today Muslims are living in mortal fear of being attacked.

The fear seems to be genuine as those guilty of massacre are roaming freely. While police has arrested several people in case of Godhra carnage and has already enforced POTA on them, in case of Gujarat carnage the bigwigs who provoked the mob have not even been touched. Those arrested are the ones who became instrument in the hands of these leaders. Even in case of these small people the process of justice is just crawling. Most of 50,67 rioters who were arrested in Ahmedabad are now out on bail.

According to the *Times of India* reporters Sourav Mukerjee and Amit Mukerjee, "of the total 961 riot cases, in 414 enough evidence against the accused could not be gathered and so chargesheets could not be filed, while out of the rest 509 riot cases in 30 police stations of the city, trial has begun in just one case. In 38 other cases, investigations are yet to conclude." So much for Narendra Modi's "justice for all and discrimination against none."

And those arrested are the ones belonging to lower strata of the society who were provoked and used to kill Muslims. Also, it is these people who were mostly burnt in Godhra carnage as mostly dalits were taken to Ayodhya as 'Ramsevaks'. There is absolutely no move to arrest the real culprit belonging to top rungs of BJP-VHP. It should also be noted that the prosecutors appointed belong to VHP and they can hardly be trusted during the course of trial, if at all many of these cases reach trial stage.

The Gulbarga Society case in which 39 persons were done to death including Ahsan Jafri, a former Congress M. P. has hardly reached trial stage though it is one year by now. According to senior public prosecutor L. Patel, "hearing on Gulbarga Society case had to be postponed because the crime branch filed supplementary charge sheet during the trial the Court suggested that the case would continue once the supplementary charge sheet, which named more accused is also committed for trial."

Most of the accused arrested have secured bail but a large number of accused still remain at large. It is doubtful whether they will be brought to justice. It is well known that hardly anyone in riot cases are ever punished. Most of the accused in anti-Sikh riots of 1984 went scot-free and Srikrishna Commission Report is gathering dust in Mantralaya in Mumbai. The NCP leader Sharad Pawar had promised to implement it within three months of coming to power. It is more than three years since and not a single accused has been brought to justice.

As the former President Narayanan put it so aptly "We have failed the Constitution, Constitution has not failed us", we have repeatedly violated the letter and spirit of our Constitution. The basic category in the Constitution is citizenship, not religion. Our rulers still prioritise religion over citizenship. This injures the dignity of individual and dignity of difference or difference with dignity.

However, it is heartening that a large number of Indians, irrespective of their caste and creed are still sensitive to sectarian violence and have a sense of commitment to the great ideals of secular democracy. As long as these citizens are ready to stand up and be counted the struggle against communal fascism will continue and forces of fascism will find it very difficult to march ahead without strong resistance.

Justice Aborted in Gujarat

The judgment delivered by Justice H.H. Mahida about the Best Bakery case in Vadodra in which 14 persons were killed on first March 2002 in the post-Godhra carnage in Gujarat shocked the country. Justice Mahida acquitted all the 21 accused in the case. The main witnesses like Zahira Sheikh and others turned hostile and that was the main reason for acquittal of the 21 accused.

This was not altogether unexpected. The human rights activists and other concerned citizens had expressed their apprehensions much before the cases were heard by the fast track courts set up for the purpose. It was feared that justice may not be done to the victims of riots within Gujarat and that these cases may be tried outside Gujarat. As such the rate of acquittal in the communal riot cases has been notoriously high for long in India. This writer has followed such cases in many riots in post-independence India and found that the rate of acquittal is more than 90 per cent.

The Hashimpura case in Meerut riots of 1987 is quite glaring in this respect. Some 23 Muslim youth were dragged out of their houses on 23rd May 1987, loaded on trucks, taken near a canal outside the city and shot dead by the PAC and their bodies thrown into the canal. Two of them survived to tell the story of this bestiality. The PAC commandant and others who committed the heinous crime were identified but no action was taken. After many years when Mulayam Singh Yadav came to power in U.P. that these persons were served with summons and yet no case has been filed against them, much less prosecuted.

In Gujarat things are even worse. The administration was actively involved in the carnage. The chief minister Narendra Modi himself justified the carnage saying it was reaction to the action (i.e., what happened in Godhra on 27th February 2002). Also, the police played highly partisan role actively helping the rioters and some ministers of Modi Cabinet were also allegedly leading the rioting mobs.

Doubts were expressed even about the impartiality of the Commission headed by Justice Nanavati, a retired Supreme Court Judge appointed to investigate into the Godhra incident of burning S-6 coach of Sabarmati Express and the following carnage in Gujarat. The apprehensions were not quite unjustified as became evident from the pre-mature statement given by Justice Nanavati absolving the role of the police much before the inquiry was over.

The acquittal of the accused in the Best Bakery case further confirmed the doubts. Though it was supposed to be fast track court even then it took more than an year to decide the case. It gave enough time to the VHP-BJP people to work on the witnesses to turn them hostile. No security was provided to these witnesses specially to Zahira Sheikh, the main witness whose family owned the Best Bakery and whose father was killed when mob set fire to the bakery.

All press persons saw that after her turning hostile in the court she was accompanied by the local BJP MLA Madhu Shrivastava and he did not even allow media persons to talk to her. Thereafter she disappeared and was not available to anyone. MLAs cousin the Congress councilor was also allegedly involved in making Zahira Sheikh change her statement in the court though the MLA as well as the Municipal Councillor both have denied the allegation.

Though Zahira Sheikh turned hostile and said these 21 persons were not among those who killed 14 persons on 1st March she admitted later in the press conference in Mumbai that she turned hostile under duress and that she had received threats to her and her family's life and no one, not even Muslims and members of relief committee came to her rescue. What alone she could have done?

Zahira Sheikh and her mother Sehrunnisa both were main witnesses in the case. Sehrunnisa, 50, also turned hostile for the same reasons. She told the Press persons later I lied to the court "trembling with fear for her life." Those 14 persons killed in the incident most of them were her relatives.

It is obvious that both mother and daughter turned hostile for fear of their life. They must have received threats. It was feared even before the case went for trial. The Sangh Parivar is trying to sabotage justice in cases related to Gujarat carnage. Why otherwise the main complainants in the Best Bakery case should turn hostile? They had lost everything, a husband, a father and several other relatives.

The Human Rights activists are worried about other cases, i.e., Naroda Patia and Gulbarga Society cases in Ahmedabad as well as other cases of massacres in Mehsana and several other districts of Gujarat. Even National Human Rights Commission is concerned. Its Chairman Justice A.S. Anand said that he believed that the acquittal of all the 21 accused in the Best Bakery case in Vadodra by a special court was prima facie a "miscarriage of justice." And State Government must appeal against the verdict.

A team of national Human Rights Commission also visited Vadodra to examine the case papers and meet witnesses. However, for fear of life main witnesses did not appear before it except only one who himself is allegedly involved in threatening Zahira Sheikh and her mother. The team is expected to submit the report within a week's time. The Commission also requested the Acting Chief Justice of Gujarat High Court, the trial court and Government of Gujarat to cooperate with the team.

Though the Gujarat Government is apparently examining the trial court verdict the Home Minister Amit Shah did not give any assurance whether the Government will appeal against the verdict. It is interesting to note that just before the Best Bakery case the NHRC had asked the Gujarat Police Director General asking him to protect the fear-stricken victims and witnesses who were to appear before the trial courts. But obviously the Police did not nor the Gujarat Government cared for such instructions.

As the Best Bakery case was more important involving 14 lives the other case in Gandhinagar went unnoticed in the media. Same day, i.e., on 27th June the district court in Gandhinagar acquitted all 22 accused in a riot and plunder incident. The main complainant was police on behalf of the State Government.

The incident had occurred between February 28 and March in Pimplaj Village of the Dehgam Taluka last year where a mosque was destroyed and a farm house owned by a Muslim family plundered and farm implements were stolen. Exposing lapses in the investigation, the judgment noted that the investigating agency had not been able to recover the arms believed to have been brandished by the mob.

The additional session's judge Mr. Ramesh Bateriwala noted that "there was no attempt made by the investigating officers to parade the accused for identification." This is part of the more clinching evidence since the identification is carried out in the presence of magistrate.

These are the things happened in the Best Bakery case too. The Police did not carry out careful investigation nor did it frame proper charges. This was further helped by making witnesses turn hostile for fear of their lives. All this obviously is part of the game plan. Unless proper steps are taken by the Gujarat Government – and no one can be sure the Gujarat Government will ever do – other riot cases particularly those of Naroda Patia and Gulbarga Society wherein more than 1000 people were brutally killed are likely to go the Best Bakery way.

Justice Mahida of the Vadodra trial case who acquitted all the 21 accused rightly remarked that "Today when economic scams surfaced daily and abductors exhort money, it seems Churchill's words that India had passed into the hands of 'thugs' are coming true." The BJP had promised the people of India that it will provide clean governance and this is what we are experiencing at the hands of BJP Government. Its slogan of "justice for all and discrimination against none" also sounds hollow. It is discriminating between culprits involved in Godhra arresting them under POTA and refusing them bail and the culprits involved in the post-Godhra carnage allowing them to be released on bail and terrorising the victims.

The Police is also deeply infected with communal virus and is deliberately not investigating properly. The legal experts have opined that Best Bakery case and its fall out is a classic example of the shoddy and careless investigation with the sole motive to ensure acquittal of the accused in one of the most barbarous crimes in the post-independence India.

There is strong case for the Supreme Court to intervene *suo moto* and see that other cases, particularly those of Naroda Patia and Gulbarga Society which were even more ghastly and involving killing of 1000 persons do not go Best Bakery way. Many legal experts and human rights activists feel that these cases should be tried outside Gujarat to ensure safety of witnesses. One can hardly rely on partisan police of Gujarat and anti-minority attitude of the Gujarat Government displayed in practice. One can only hope that judiciary will save the situation.

Citizen's Report on Gujarat

The communal carnage in Gujarat early this year had shaken the whole world. The country had never witnessed such carnage before and after independence. Day after day for more than three months Muslims were massacred most brutally, toll unofficially mounting to more than 2000 though officially admitted deaths do not exceed one thousand. Heinous crime of rape was committed by the VHP provoked hoodlums against several women. In one case Kausar Begum from Naroda Patia, an eight month pregnant was raped, her womb split open and child extracted and thrown into fire. The Chief Minister Narendra Modi justified all this as equal and opposite reaction to an action based on Newton's law.

The Government of Gujarat later constituted a commission of inquiry under a retired Gujarat High Court Judge but was seen as partisan by the people. Justice Nanavati, a retired judge of Supreme Court was then appointed to head the inquiry commission. The official inquiry commissions usually take long time to complete the inquiry and even then they are hardly ever implemented.

The example of Srikrishna Commission appointed to inquire into Mumbai riots of 1992-93 is before us. It took several years to complete the inquiry but did a thorough job. Unfortunately when the inquiry commission report was submitted there was Shiv Sena-BJP Government, which obviously refused to implement recommendations of the Commission. Those who were accused were themselves in power. But what was worse was that the subsequent PDA Government led by the Congress which appealed to Muslims for votes on the ground that it will speedily implement the Srikrishna Commission Report, itself never bothered to implement it. Now its counsel pleaded before the Supreme Court that there is no need to revive it.

After Mumbai riots also People's Committee for Human Rights headed by Justice Krishna Iyer had constituted a People's Inquiry Committee consisting of Justice Suresh and Justice Dawood, retired judges of Bombay High Court which helped inquiry and speedily completed it. Its findings were almost same as those of Srikrishna Commission, which took several years to complete.

After the Gujarat carnage the concerned citizens took initiative to appoint an inquiry committee called Concerned Citizens Tribunal headed by Justice Krishna Iyer, retired justice Supreme Court. It consisted of several eminent justices and citizens like Justice Samant, retired Supreme Court Judge, Justice Suresh, retired Bombay High Court judge, K.G. Kannabiran, an eminent advocate and Chairman, People's Union for Civil Liberties, KS Subramanian, Ex-Director General of Police, Aruna Roy, a noted social activist and former IAS officer, Ghanshyam Shah and Tanika Sarkar, professors from JNU, Delhi.

The report has been published in three volumes, the third volume being compilation of important documents on the carnage. The whole report is tilted as *Crime Against Humanity – An Inquiry into the Carnage in Gujarat.* One does not know when the Government appointed Commission will come out with its report but this Concerned Citizen's Tribunal has already completed its inquiry and put it before the people's court. The VHP has dubbed it as mere slander and has even threatened to sue the tribunal for defamation, which it may never do. The evidence against VHP is so strong that this report will stand in any court of law.

The tribunal collected 2,094 oral and written testimonials, both individual and collective, from victim-survivors and also independent human rights groups, women's groups, NGOs and academics. The tribunal says, "After recording evidence, visiting sites, placing on record statements and collecting other material, the Tribunal arrived at some *prima facie* conclusions."

The Tribunal does not entirely dismiss the surmise that the Narendra Modi Government was panicky for its continuously loosing ground in election after election despite its Hindutva hyperbole and it is likely that to retrieve the lost ground it might have tried to polarise the Gujarat people along religious lines by organising such a carnage.

Thus the Tribunal report says, "Given the continuous downslide of the BJP in the state since 98, the question has been raised by many as to whether there were any electoral political calculations and machinations behind what subsequently happened in the state from February 28 onwards. While this remains in the realm of speculation, the fact is that the Modi government prematurely dissolved the state assembly and pushed very hard for early election even though the situation in the state was far from normal. For this he was widely criticised and the BJP was charged for trying to cash in on the carnage."

What a way to run democracy in the 2nd greatest democracy in the world if there is in truth in this charge. The Sangh Parivar is trying to convert our pluralism into a nightmare for the country and for its peace loving citizens. The statements of top VHP leaders are clear proof of this, if any proof is needed. The Gujarat carnage leaves no one in doubt about intentions of the Sangh Parivar. It can go to any extent or realising its objectives.

How well planned the Gujarat carnage was is evident from the fact that the Sangh Parivar hordes attacked several areas and towns in Ahmedabad simultaneously on 28th February itself. More than 100 persons were killed on the very first day of the carnage. On 28th February in the morning a mob consisting of 20-22,000 holds the whole of Gulbarga Society to ransom for over seven hours and this mob in over seven hours hacked more than 70 persons to death and burnt them alive (10-12 women and girls were raped). The former Congress M.P. Ahsan Jafri was killed in this operation and despite desperate phone calls the Police Commissioner Pande did not save these helpless people.

And at the very time mobs of 15,000 or 10,000 were killing, burning and looting in Naroda fruit market, Naroda Gam and Naroda Patiya which was worst affected by violence where more than 100 people were brutally done to death or burnt alive. And simultaneously similar operations of killings, lootings and burnings were going on in Odhav, Gomtipur, Amrawadi, Paldi, Kabadi Market Vatwa and several other places. The Tribunal Report lists all these areas. How this could be possible without meticulous planning. And the mobs everywhere were well equipped with gas cylinders, trishuls, swords and other sharp weapons.

All this started after the burning of coach S-6 in Godhra in which 58 persons perished. The assumption was that the Ghanchi Muslims of Signal Falia set fire to the coach. But this has come under doubt and it is very difficult to say who did it. The Forensic experts say it was inside job and 60 litres of petrol or some highly combustible substance was used to set fire from inside. The Tribunal report also raises several questions and throws light on the character and behaviour of the *kar sevaks* right from the time they boarded the train. It was certainly not a peaceful lot and were misbehaving with people on every station. All this has to be taken into account.

The Report gives detailed account of all major incidents not only in Ahmedabad, which was worst affected but also in various towns and villages. It is an important document for all those interested in studying the carnage in detail. It also provides extremely valuable material for future researchers and scholars.

The Report throws light on various aspects of carnage – the state and central government complicity, role of police and bureaucracy and opposition parties and communalisation of public space like hospitals and other institutions. About the Police system the Tribunal observes that "Evidence before the Tribunal establishes the absolute failure of large sections of the Gujarat police to fulfil their constitutional duty and prevent mass massacre, rape and arson – in short to maintain law and order." Continuing further it says, "Worse still is the evidence of their active connivance and brutality, their indulgence in vulgar and obscene conduct against women and children in full public view. It is, as if, instead of being impartial keepers of the rule of law, they were a part of the *Hindutva* brigade targeting helpless Muslims."

The Report also says that, "To begin with, the Godhra incident would not have taken place; had the police taken due precautions right from the beginning. Given Godhra's history and communal background, the police should have maintained a strict vigil as the *kar sevaks* crossed Godhra, on their way to Ayodhya and their return journey, more so because the climate in the country was already tense because of the VHP's Ayodhya plan. On their way to Ayodhya, the *kar sevaks* had indulged in provocative acts at Godhra station."

The Godhra and post-Godhra carnage was a grim tragedy for democratic and secular India and for which the entire responsibility goes to the Sangh Parivar. It has been creating climate of intolerance and abuse of Hindu religion for political ends which clearly defeats the very ideal of secularism in our country. One can say that Gujarat carnage is a direct result of Mr. L.K. Advani riding *rath yatra* in 1990 and subsequent demolition of Babri Masjid in December 1992. The BJP used only Hindutva plank for coming to power. Since then it has been systematically destroying the secular and democratic values in the country. One can say and the Tribunal Report also supports this idea that Gujarat carnage was possible only because there was BJP-led Government at the Centre.

BJP Sweep in Gujarats Reflections

The results of Gujarat election were surprise for everyone including of course the BJP. No one expected more than two-third majority for the BJP. All surveys except that of *India Today* (which predicted two-third majority for BJP) had predicted marginal victory for BJP and some even gave the Congress a chance. The exit poles also proved to be quite deceptive.

This sweeping victory for the BJP in Gujarat has lessons for all including the secularists and above all for the Congress. In fact it is the moment of truth for the Congress. The Congress must deeply reflect on the causes of its defeat. Let it learn the lesson that hard Hindutva cannot be fought with soft Hindutva. One should not follow – even to a limited extent – the agenda set by extremists. The Congress decided not to raise the question of communal carnage in Gujarat fearing strong reaction from the Hindu electorate. They decided to talk only about development and governance issues.

This also did not help the Congress. If it had to loose it could have lost by fighting for principles. It could have denounced the Hindutva extremism and killing of more than two thousand innocent Muslims. How can one talk of development and governance when such massacre is taking place in the state? It should have strongly taken up the case of such unparalleled violence against minority. It would have greatly enthused those committed to secularism. Not that there are no more secularists in Gujarat. But the Congress certainly betrayed them.

The Muslims of course had no alternative but to vote for the Congress as a lesser evil. The Congress again gave the Muslims only three seats to contest again for fear of reaction from the Hindu extremists. A national party, which projects itself as inheritor of the Gandhi, Nehru and Maulana Azad cant be seen to be so weak on secular ideology. It is such weakness, which has brought the nation to such a plight today.

Gandhi, Nehru and Azad were stalwarts of secular nationalism. After Nehru, Patel and Azad secularism began to be sidelined by other leaders of the Congress. Mrs. Gandhi who devised the slogan of 'quit poverty' and was seen as champion of downtrodden for the time being in late sixties, was not emphasising secularism like her father Nehru. Nehru clearly and unambiguously championed both the causes, i.e., of socialism and secularism. Nehru had courage to publicly attack communalists and their ideology. He always called spade a spade.

However, Mrs. Gandhi proved to be more power-oriented than ideologically-oriented. After emergency she almost bade good bye to her ideological commitments. She even tried to take advantage of VHP campaign against the conversion of some dalit families in Meenakshipuram to Islam in early eighties. It is on record that she encouraged VHP to launch a campaign against Meenakshipuram conversions. The VHP came on political scene with a bang due to this subtle encouragement from top Congress leadership. Mrs. Gandhi perceived loss of Muslim votes due to excesses committed against Muslims during emergency and wanted to compensate for it by winning over Hindus on her side. This had far reaching consequences. She also pampered Bhindranwale and gave rise to Khalistan movement of which she ultimately became victim.

When she was assassinated by her Sikh bodyguard a reprisal against Sikhs followed and more than 4000 Sikhs were killed. The Congress exploited it to the hilt for winning 1984 parliamentary elections and won with two-third majority. All such victories won by targeting another community prove quite fragile. There is a lesson for the BJP also here. The Congress was soon faced with serious challenges and ignominiously lost next general elections held in 1989.

It should be born in mind that in a composite nation like India with its proud record of pluralism for centuries nothing can work better than secularism as far as modern democracy is concerned. The politicians eager to come to power without doing anything concrete for the masses often resort to communal short cuts and incite hatred in one caste or community against the other to capture power thus seriously destabilising very social and political foundations of the country.

The extremists of Sangh Parivar like the VHP and the Bajrang Dal may not realise it that they are doing great harm to the unity and integrity of the country and pushing it to the brink of civil war but the senior leaders of the BJP should understand it. It is interesting to note that as the hard Hindutva of Sangh parivar marginalises the soft Hindutva of the Congress, the extremists of the Sangh Parivar marginalises the moderates of that parivar. It is Narendra Modi and Togadia who are emerging heroes today and are calling the shots. Likes of Vajpayee are getting marginalised.

The success in Gujarat is giving more impetus to likes of Modis and Togadias. But let us not forget it is temporary success. The BJP will not at all gain in long terms. But in politics who cares for long term effects. What is valued is temporary success. It immediately goes to the head. The BJP may be under pressure to adopt hard Hindutva as a strategy to win coming elections next year but it is likely to do great deal of harm not only to the country as a whole but also to the BJP interests itself.

One must keep the plight of the Congress in view. After 1984 elections in which it won two third majority it soon suffered such set back that it has not been able to recover from it. Still its chances of winning power at the Centre are not very bright unless it makes amends for its acts of commissions and omissions sincerely and rediscovers its own ideology of secularism and creates much needed balance of forces among various communities.

The NDA partners who apparently swear by 'secularism' also have to learn a lot and have to reflect seriously on their alliance with BJP. When the hot heads like Modis and Togadias are marginalising moderates like Vajpayee what of leaders like Chandrababu Naidu, Nitish Kumar and others. All such leaders will be thrown out after their utility is over. These leaders are doing nothing but strengthening the hands of BJP and extremists in its fold. Their loosening grip over the issues of governance will push the BJP leaders towards extremism to retain their hold over power. Shri L.K. Advani fuelled this extremism through his *rath yatra* in 1990. When the BJP could not come to power with its narrow political base among the upper caste Hindus in urban areas it invoked highly emotional issue of Ram mandir and ultimately captured power in alliance with some so called secular parties in 1999 elections. The *rath yatra* was first major step towards extremism. The Narasimha Rao Government showed its calculated inaction and allowed extremist elements in the BJP to grow for its own short term interest of survival in power and ultimately lost out to BJP.

There is also a lesson to learn for socialists of the Janata Dal variety. They, in their hatred of the Congress always preferred to support the BJP rather than any secular formation. The Janta Dal consisted more of leaders than followers and went on fighting among themselves. Their government thus could not last for more than a couple of years. Neither they had any ideology to bind them together nor did they have interest of governance over their own selfish interests. They did not allow Devegowda or Gujaral to rule for respectable length of time.

It is also important for all secularists to note that it is easier for unemployed dalits and tirbals to be won over by extremists and hard Hindutvawadis than by those talking of developmental issues without really delivering. In highly emotional campaigns like the one in Gujarat developmental issues or issues of governance are ignored by the people. Hatred, if worked to its extreme as the Modi did in his election campaign, can prove, temporarily of course, much more powerful than ones material interests. Thus incumbency factor did not work in Gujarat election. The BJP had totally failed to govern but still could win by inciting hatred against Muslims and against the Congress as 'protector' of Muslims.

But, and it is a lesson for the moderates in the BJP to learn, there is hardly anything to celebrate the Gujarat victory. Soon the party will have to face hard realities. The hot heads will not allow it to govern and deliver. They are enamoured of their own extremism and would like to repeat it. They are blinded by their own emotions. As revolution eats its own children so does extremism and fanaticism.

The Congress also has to learn a lesson from what happened in Gujarat. It should, as pointed out above, abandon its policy of soft Hindutva and revive the spirit of secularism and togetherness of all communities. It should not allow Indian diversity to become victim of majoritarianism. It is dangerous omen for Indian pluralism. Secularism is the life-line of Indian polity. Nehruvian vision must be rediscovered by the Congress leadership.

The Congress should also realise the importance of secular alliances. It cannot govern India alone. Those days are over. It should take lead to form an alliance with all secular forces opposed to BJP's variety of communalism and politics of hate. There never was more urgency for such an alliance led by the Congress. India and people of India are above any political party. And India's diversity is above any single community be it in majority or minority.

The BJP and Gujarat Elections

Today everyone is watching developments in Gujarat with bated breath. The elections in that violence-ridden state are of great significance not only for the Gujarat but for whole of India. The communal carnage in that state had aroused world-wide condemnation. There is also a view, though difficult to substantiate or document, that Gujarat carnage was planned to win Gujarat Assembly elections, which were due in March 2003.

According to this view the BJP was loosing election after election – Panchayat, Zilla Parishad and Municipal. The Congress though very weak, disorganised and faction-ridden, was winning these elections by sheer default. This sent shivers down the BJP spine. The BJP was extremely worried and wanted to turn the electoral fortune in its favour. The only way the BJP knows is to somehow consolidate the Hindu votes to win elections and what an easy way to do that by provoking communal violence. Thus it began preparation for engineering communal violence. The spark was provided by the Godhra incident and carnage started in Gujarat in post-Godhra.

When Gujrat was burning there were rumours that elections will soon be held and if elections were held the BJP would win hands down and the Congress would be wiped out. It was suggested that the BJP might get 2/3rd majority. The rumours were not quite baseless. Narendra Modi dissolved the Assembly though it had comfortable majority and there was no crisis in the Party. He wanted to hold election before October when carnage was going on. The Gujarat state was, during those days, highly polarised and temptation to hold elections was too great for Modi to resist.

However, the Chief Election Commissioner J.N. Lyngdoh came in the way and after assessing the Gujarat situation found the intense sense of insecurity among the Muslims. He, under Section 174 of Indian Constitution, recommended that elections could not be held in Gujarat immediately. Hundreds of Muslims were in refugee camps living in inhuman conditions and were not in a position to return to their localities. The BJP tried to put up brave face and the NDA Government referred the matter to the Supreme Court through President of India for opinion but that did not help.

The EC announced election to be held now on December 10 after it was satisfied that now free and fair elections can be held. The elections in all the constituencies will be held on one single day so that the VHP people cannot go from one constituency to other and commit violence and intimidate voters or indulge in bogus voting to see BJP wins the election.

It is interesting to note that now situation seems to have greatly changed in Gujarat. It is extremely complex and fluid. The BJP, it is suggested by some observers, is more afraid of BJP than the Congress. BJP today is faction-ridden and Keshubhai Patel, the former Chief Minister ousted by Narendra Modi, can be a great stumbling block for him. He is not coming round to support Modi though the BJP is cajoling him and has made him chairman of election committee in Gujarat. It is feared by the followers of Narendra Modi that he may sway the Patel votes against Modi particularly in Saurashtra. Patels constitute some 16 per cent of voters in Gujarat. One has to wait and see how Keshubhai Patel behaves.

Now there is every reason for BJP to fear the Congress also. A secret survey conducted by the BJP shows that there are fifty-fifty per cent chances for both the parties. This is certainly a scary news for Narendra Modi who was dreaming of capturing two-third majority in the house and rule for another five years. It is no more a cake walk for Modi. And the situation is changing fast.

The past election results also show that even during hey days of the BJP it never got more than 44.81 per cent votes in Gujarat. It was in 1998 elections. The Congress had got 34.85 per cent votes in that election. The BJP got 117 seats while the Congress 53. It is ironical that in 1990 elections the BJP got 26.69 per cent votes and captured 67 seats while though the Congress got 30.74 per cent votes yet it could get only 33 seats. In 1995 the BJP got 42.51 per cent votes and took 121 seats and the Congress got 32.86 per cent votes and could take 45 seats.

Thus it will be seen that the Congress never fell more than 10 per cent behind the BJP even in the worst case. Now it seems the situation is even more challenging for the BJP today in Gujarat. The carnage now does not seem to be helping it much. Factionalism, the caste factor, misgovernance, various scandals, particularly the bank scandals and acute water shortage, all is going against it. Also, the communal carnage has caused tremendous loss of business, endless curfews, closure of business establishments, loss of jobs and loss of investments along with loss of prestige all that has brought tremendous suffering.

To compensate all this Narendra Modi is riding his *Gaurav Rath* and is talking of *Asmita of Gujarat* (identity of Gujarat) and pride of Gujarat. Naturally the opposition is raising the question *gaurav* (pride) of what? Of carnage? Of misgovernance? Of ruination of the Gujarat economy? The Modi is naturally miffed and talks of *asmita* and *gaurav* of 5 crore people of Gujarat. He projects himself as the champion of these 5 crore people of Gujarat. But he forgets that these five crores include 9 per cent Muslims and 1.5 per cent Christians who have suffered immensely at his hands. And still there is no end to their sufferings, particularly of Muslims. Still he has been using very harsh language against Muslims. His speech during his "*Gaurav Yatra*" in Godhra on

10th November was almost threatening. He blamed Muslims for the violence in Gujarat.

One can hardly be sure how effective Modi demagogy will be in Gujarat. It is, as pointed out, very fluid situation. Modi himself is certainly scared. He had won from the Rajkot constituency II last time with very narrow margin. Due probably to Keshubhai factor he is now wanting to change his constituency. He is not at all sure whether he would win from Rajkot. He tried to even pressurise his cabinet minister Harin Pandya to let him contest from his Elisbridge constituency in Ahmedabad. When Harin Pandya refused he was thrown out of cabinet. It is said that he may shift to Baroda. But nothing has yet been decided. His several cabinet ministers are also searching for safe constituencies.

The Election Commission is playing important role in organising Gujarat elections. It knows that Modi can resort to any method to win elections. The Commission wants to see that elections are not influenced, as far as possible, by Modi's communal outbursts. It has planned a series of measures. Since after the *Gaurav Yatra* the VHP has planned its own yatra, the EC has sought a report of the VHP yatra from the State Government.

The VHP considers itself a law unto itself. It claims that since it is not a political party it cannot come under the ambit of EC. The Sangh Parivar, as everyone knows, has several faces, the RSS, the VHP, the Bajrang Dal etc. What the BJP cannot say openly due to such constrains the RSS, the VHP or Bajrang Dal say publicly and try to influence voters in favour of BJP. The Earlier ECs never bothered about all this and did not notice what the VHP was saying during election campaigns in parallel meetings.

This CEC Shri Lyngdoh, however, does not desire to ignore the VHP outbursts as they are likely to deeply influence election results in the polarised Gujarat society today. The communal violence has also not ceased so far. Small and not so small incidents are taking place probably to keep the communal feelings alive. The CEC Lyngdoh, therefore, seems to be determined not to allow the VHP parallel campaign under the garb of not being a political party.

Everyone knows that the VHP nominates its own candidates who then fight election as the BJP candidate. In the present elections in Gujarat also the VHP, according to news paper reports, is demanding at least 25 seats for its own members. In the dissolved assembly too several VHP members were elected as BJP candidates. Harin Pandya and Zadaphia, both cabinet ministers, were the VHP nominees.

Lyngdoh is again on a visit to Gujarat to assess the ground situation himself. He, during his recent Gujarat tour, described the Gujarat situation as 'nasty' and when he was asked what he meant by 'nasty' situation, he said "provocative speeches are being made. In some relief camps, water supply has been disconnected for days. What else can be called nasty." Thus, Lyngdoh is well aware of the situation and he may not allow Modi and his followers to inflame communal passions during the election campaign. This is what the VHP wants to do during its planned Yatra. Fortunately, Mr. Lyngdoh has declared to ban the VHP yatra which otherwise would have resulted in building up communal tensions and might have even resulted in communal violence.

The security of minority voters also has to be guaranteed if they are encouraged to vote. Many Muslims may not venture out to vote and this also can influence the election results. Minority vote will undoubtedly play a crucial role. There are lot of Muslims in towns like Rajkot, Dhoraji, Morbi, Maliya and Wakaner. It is necessary to provide extra security for these Muslims.

It is unfortunate that in secular India with bewildering religious, linguistic and cultural diversity, communal card is sought to be played with such impunity to win elections. It is BJP politics, which has produced Narendra Modi. The BJP also came to power by dividing Hindus and Muslims on the temple-masjid controversy. Perhaps even the Britishers had not used divide and rule policy so blatantly as our own people. But one can draw satisfaction from the fact that people will not, and have not, always obliged such politicians. Let us hope in Gujarat too, they do not.

7
Legal Framework

Judiciary and Communal Violence

Communal riots have been taking place in this country since early sixties when the first major riot took place in Jabalpur in Madhya Pradesh in 1961. Since then hundreds of riots took place in India and innumerable people were killed. Hardly few people have been punished for killing and murdering in the riots. There are several reasons for this.

Those killed are generally poorest of the poor and those survive them hardly wield any clout. The police, also, therefore, show total indifference in investigation and filing charge sheets. The police has been communalised and distorts the case right at the stage of filing FIRs. In most of the cases investigation is closed after sometime saying further investigation not possible. Greater the communalisation of the police more of such closed cases. In Mumbai riots of 1992-93 too several cases were closed.

In many cases the police itself is the culprit in aiding and abetting the crime. In the Gujarat carnage of 2002 the police was openly helping the frenzied crowds and providing them protection. In many cases ministers were allegedly leading these crowds and so the police had all the reasons to either help the crowd or look the other way when murdering, looting and burning went on. How can then police investigate against itself. The only alternative for it is to close the cases.

And when it does investigate, it is half-way house and charge sheets are filed in a way the accused may be discharged. The police even manipulate the case diaries. The Madon Commission appointed to inquire into the Bhivandi-Jalgaon riots of 1970 strongly reprimanded the police authorities for forging daily diaries and manipulating its contents. Thus with such half hearted investigations and biased role of the police the culprits can hardly be expected to be punished. They are more often than not, discharged by the courts. Thus there are very few instances of accused in communal riots being punished.

The judiciary at lower levels is not much different. It is also often biased. It grants bail to members of one community while refusing the same to the members of another community. Also, as it happened in Best Bakery case in Baroda, it hardly takes careful and critical view of the case and tends to discharge the accused. And it is not for the first time in Gujarat. Gujarat has witnessed several riots in the past and judiciary has hardly behaved differently. In that state even the high court does not have record to be very proud of.

Since 1960 riots of Ahmedabad Gujarat has very dubious record in this respect. The then Jana Sangh and then the BJP have systematically made efforts to communalise the society, the police, the administration and the judiciary. It is as a result of all this that the Gujarat is proudly referred by the Sangh Parivar as the 'laboratory of Hindutva'. In no other states one would find boards in village after village that "Panwad in Hindu Rashtra welcomes you". Is it against the Constitution? Who cares any way. It is after all laboratory of the Hindutva.

It is, therefore only higher judiciary, especially at the Supreme Court level that provides relief to the victims of the communal violence. The Supreme Court rightly ordered the Modern Bakery case to be tried outside Gujarat. In that state where all the organs of the state and civil society too has been communalised how can one hope for justice within the state? The state prosecutors are often members of VHP and more than prosecution lawyers they act as defence lawyers.

It was in the light of all this that the Supreme Court maintained "Justice should not only be done but be seen to be done". Keeping in view the peculiar circumstances ... the ample evidence demonstrating subversion of justice ... system with no conducive atmosphere still prevailing, we di... the re-trial shall be done by a Court under the jurisdiction of Bombay HC.

It is total lack of confidence in the judicial system in Gujarat. The BJP, which talks of 'good-governance' has to do serious introspection. What kind of governance it is providing in a state, which is governed solely by BJP? What will happen to the judiciary in the country if ever the BJP comes to the power at the Centre. In M.P. and Rajasthan where it has come to power of its own saffronisation is going on apace and one shudders to think what will happen to judiciary there in times to come.

The Supreme Court has come to the rescue of the victims of communal carnage in Gujarat. It is the higher judiciary, which provides hope to the helpless victims. But for the Supreme Court the victims would have had to reconcile itself with gross injustices in the land of Hindutva. The victims of communal carnage in Gujarat felt unsafe at every stage. The witnesses were threatened and the state administration took no step to protect them. The prosecutors provided by the state, as pointed out earlier, were VHP members. There was no other way for witnesses like Zahira Sheikh but to turn hostile.

The Judge concerned of the fast track court also did not make efforts to find out why the witness had turned hostile. He simply discharged the accused on that basis. It was gross abortion of justice. Even the High Court was no different. The Supreme Court took serious notice of role of the High Court in Gujarat. "The High Court", the Supreme Court observed, "made unwarranted reference to personalities and their legitimate moves before competent courts, despite knowing it could not deal with such matters. Decency, decorum and judicial discipline should never be made casualties by adopting such intemperate attitudes of judicial obstinacy."

This admonition by the highest court in the land should be enough for any sensitive judge of the Gujarat High Court but one wonders if it would have intended effect on the Gujarat judiciary. The Supreme Court in its remarks even reminded the

...ple of "modern day Nerus". It is very apt reference to Nero ...hough it is not clear who the highest court has referred to as Nero. Nero was one who sent several Christians to death and was condemned to death by the Roman senate in 68 A.D. The Supreme Court judges observed in their judgement "The modern day Neros were looking elsewhere when Best Bakery and innocent children and helpless women were being burnt and were probably deliberating how the perpetrators of the crime can be saved or protected." Even more forthrightly the learned judges of the Supreme Court observed, "Law and justice become flies in the hands of these wanton boys. When fences start to swallow the crops, no scope will be left for survival of law and order or truth and justice. Public order as well as public interest become martyrs and monuments."

The court referring to acquittal of the accused observed, such acquittals were "unmerited, based on tainted evidence, tailored investigation, unprincipled prosecution and perfunctory trial and evidence; and threatened or terrorised witnesses", The Court also observed that if these findings were accepted that would amount to "travesty of truth and a fraud on the legal process." In these few sentences the learned judges have described very succinctly the situation in Gujarat.

Such strong remarks from the highest court in the land warranted immediate resignation of the Chief Minister but in the rule book of the 'good governance of the BJP no such action was necessary as all this was done deliberately to teach Muslims a lesson'. It is ironical that the same party is asking for the Muslim votes in the Lok Sabha elections taking place in the country and some opportunistic Muslims have rushed to the rescue of the beleaguered party. However it is a different story we are not concerned with here.

India is a biggest democracy in the world and we all are justly proud of the same. However, the politicians hungry for power have robbed our democracy of all its worth and used communal and casteist discourse for easy way to power. It is judiciary at higher echelons, which comes to the rescue of helpless victims of the executive organ. Thanks to the founding fathers of our Constitution that they thought of independence of judiciary and our judiciary at higher levels has been remarkably independent and this has given hope to the helpless victims of the executive organ.

The politicians with secular ideology also proved not very different and encouraged casteism and communalism for clinging to power. Only those politicians who are committed to left ideology have shown sincere commitment to secularism and communal harmony in the country. It clearly shows that only those who care for the weaker sections of society can be expected to maintain communal harmony. But among non-left secular forces there have been very few who showed sincere commitment to secular values except as public rhetoric.

If there has been such failure on the part of secular forces what of the BJP with its professed ideology of Hindutva? Can it ever be expected to care for rights of minorities and their securities? Certainly it is asking for the impossible. One should not be taken in by their election rhetoric of secularism and rush to elect them. They swore by 'secularism' on Father of Nation's Samadhi and began to use stark communal discourse within a year thereof.

The Indian intelligentsia should reflect deeply on the observations of the Supreme Court in the Best Bakery case and make all possible efforts to restore secular values of our democracy. Our democracy has been hijacked by communal and casteist forces laying political games. It is for the intelligentsia to rescue it from their clutches.

Triple Divorce–Need for Change

Recently several cases of on the spot triple divorce have been reported in the press. In Bihar just because wife of a person did not vote for the candidate of his choice in the Lok Sabha election he pronounced triple divorce and threw out his wife. Again just a few days ago, a husband came drunk in Bhadrak, Orissa on 3rd June, and had a tiff with his wife and pronounced talaq thrice but in the morning he realised his mistake and wanted to take back his wife but leaders of the Muslim community separated them insisting that it is irrevocable divorce and they cannot live together as husband and wife. Besides this many cases just go unreported.

There is now report from Kerala that members of orthodox Sunni organisations have threatened to agitate if women are allowed to pray on Friday in the mosque. In the girls college in Manjeri students have been praying on Friday in the mosque on college premises. But the Samastha Kerala Sunni Students Federation (SKSSF) has launched a public agitation against women being allowed to pray on Friday in the mosque.

What such acts of triple divorce or agitations against women praying on Friday in the mosque convey to the world? Do women have secondary status in Islam? Is it sin to pray to Allah in mosque on Friday? What sort of Islam is this? How can Islam banish women from praying on Friday inside the mosque? For these orthodox Muslims customs and traditions are more important than the Qur'anic injunctions.

They do not know that Islam was the first religion in the world to empower women and giver them equal legal status. The Qur'an clearly pronounces equality of sexes see verses 2:228 and 33:35. Commenting on the verse 2:228 Maulana Azad in his *Tarjuman al-Qur'an* says that it is revolutionary declaration of equality of sexes 1300 years ago. But the Muslim society under the influence of feudal social ethos never realised this revolutionary potential of Qur'anic teachings.

However, these old institutions developed under different social ethos cannot work today. The women are making fast strides in different fields of life. The extent of education and consciousness of their rights is far more widespread today than ever before. Even in conservative Saudi society the women are no more prepared to accept their traditional role. Only last week, i.e., beginning 12th June 2004 seventy Saudi Arabian scholars and intellectuals participated in the first day of third national dialogue forum in Madina to address the rights of women in particular prompt and full delivery of justice to women.

The overall theme of this three-day forum is women's rights and duties and their relation to education. Many women scholars read out papers in this forum to discuss ways to eliminate religious extremism in the Saudi Kingdom. In Madina the organisers hope to create an environment conducive for Saudi intellectuals and scholars to discuss the position of women in Saudi society and to find out the best ways to develop their status in line with Islamic teachings.

This clearly shows there is great deal of ferment among women even in the Saudi society. Women cannot be treated in the old ways any more. In India also Muslim women have become more conscious about their Islamic rights and are demanding changes in the Personal Law in keeping with the Qur'anic teachings. As pointed out the Islamic laws in relation to women are most modern in their approach but Muslim societies have preferred traditional interpretations by Imams in pre-modern feudal society to the clearly worded Qur'anic injunctions.

Talaq is a highly sensitive issue as it can break years of marital relations between husband and wife. Thus the Holy Qur'an is also very cautious in matters of divorce. Firstly, it has adopted most modern approach to this sensitive issue. It requires arbitration before any breach of relations. The Qur'an says, "And if you fear a breach between the two, appoint an arbiter from his people and an arbiter from her people. If they both desire agreement, Allah will effect harmony between them." (4:35)

Thus through arbitration the breach should be prevented and attempt should be made to bring them together again as Allah desires harmony. Despite such clear Qur'anic injunction we approve of triple divorce in one sitting and destroy marital life in one breath. How such an act be Islamic? It is greatest injustice, specially with women. Again justice (*'ad'*) is so central to Qur'anic teaching. And to throw ones wife but by pronouncing three words of *talaq* is most unjust act. There are three four key words in Qur'an – *'adl, ihsan, rahmah and hikmah* i.e. justice, benevolence, compassion and wisdom) and triple talaq is against all these key words. Neither it is justice, nor it is benevolence (ihsan), nor is it compassion (rahmah) nor is it an act of wisdom (hikmah).

All Muslims are also not unanimous on this form of divorce. Ahle-Hadith, Hanbalis and Shi'ahs reject this form of talaq. Even Hanafi Muslim countries like Jordan have reformed this practice and enforced the Quranic injunction of arbitration. Arbitration can and does save many marriages. The Qur'an does not permit triple divorce at all. Three talaqs has to be spaced over a period of three months so that husband and wife get enough time for reconciliation through intervention of relatives and friends. Moreover talaq can be given only when wife is in a state of *tuhur*, i.e., purity after menstruation. If talaq is pronounced during the period of menstruation it will not be valid. The Prophet has ordered wife to be taken back if the talaq is pronounced during menstrual period. Triple divorce disregards all this completely.

Some Muslim women have devised a standard *nikahnama* (marriage contract) strictly within the Shari`ah framework and given to the Muslim personal law board a couple of years ago so that Muslim women do not face such situations. Since marriage in Islam is a contract such *nikahnama* is perfectly valid and was approved by a great '*alim* like Maulana Ashraf Thanavi. But the personal board is hesitating to implement it. If implemented, it can give lot of relief to Muslim women. This is very modest piece of reform (in fact it is really not any reform or change but only a modicum of relief to suffering women) but the personal board is hesitating in implementing even this.

All 'ulama agree that pronouncing triple talaq in one sitting is *bid'ah* (innovation) and that *bid'ah* is sin and yet this sinful practice is enforced in the name of divine law. In fact triple divorce indeed is great sin as it so unjust and oppressive for women. Every possible attempt should be made to eradicate this sinful practice from our society. The 'ulama who are guardians of Islamic law should play a leading role in this matter. I have had discussion with many 'ulama who privately agree that this form of divorce should be abolished but do not have courage to say so publicly.

The personal law board should at least launch an awareness movement educating Muslim men about desisting from this sinful form of divorce and resort to the Qur`anic form of divorce as clearly spelled out. I am not aware of any such awareness movement. The Muslim men are Islamically illiterate and do not even know that triple divorce is a sinful form of divorce and Holy Prophet has strongly disapproved of this form of divorce. If the members of personal law board do not have courage to abolish this form of divorcc thcy should at least have courage to launch an awareness movement among Muslim men and appeal to them not to resort to such form of divorce.

Maulana Ashraf Thanvi and others had taken a bold step in 1939 and drafted the Dissolution of Muslim Marriage Act, which gave great relief to suffering women. Can the members of Muslim personal law board not show such wisdom and draft a comprehensive law codifying the Muslim personal law on the lines of the 1939 Act. It will give great and much needed relief to Muslim women.

However, there is no such sign of codifying the Muslim personal law and suffering of Muslim women continues. If Maulana Ashraf Thanvi and others could take such bold step way back in 1939 why can't our 'ulama in 21st century take such step? This will be not only in keeping with the true spirit of Islam but will also go a long way in improving the image of Islam in India. It is due to such un-Qur'anic practices that image of Islam has suffered and the demand for Uniform Civil Code surfaces.

The Islamic law is most progressive and in fact should become a model law for all others if our orthodox 'ulama care to understand and implement it in its true spirit. Maulavi Mumtaz Ali Khan, Maulavi Chiragh Ali, Justice Ameer Ali and others pleaded for reforms in late 19th and early twentieth century but nothing has happened so far.

Now it is for Muslim women to acquaint themselves thoroughly with Islamic law and launch a movement for reform and change. Women in all Muslim countries have struggled for change and succeeded. Now, as referred to above, even women in the most conservative Saudi society have begun to assert themselves. It is therefore, high time that Muslim women in democratic society like that of India struggle for reform within the Qur'anic frame-work and win their rights guaranteed by the scripture.

That seems to be the only way left for them. Progressive and believing Muslim men should also come forward and support such movement for reform.

After Abolition of Talaq

The Muslim Personal Law Board (MPLB) has taken bold decision to review practice of triple talaq at one go in its next meeting in July in Kanpur. The Board undoubtedly deserves congratulations from all those who are committed to women's rights and had been campaigning for this essential reform. Hundreds of Muslim women have suffered because of this pre-Islamic practice which, came back into Hanafi and Shafi`I Islamic law for reasons not to be gone into here.

It is unfortunate that the Sunni Barelvi ulama have threatened to launch an agitation if MPLB approves of abolition of triple divorce. They maintain that though it is *bid'ah* (i.e. sinful form of divorce) nevertheless once pronounced thrice it is valid. They have stated nothing new. It was because of this view by the Hanafis that triple divorce was practiced so long in India though it was abolished in most of the Muslim countries. The Barelvi threat should not deter the members of MPLB from abolition of triple talaq though the Board would like to evolve a consensus on the matter. It would be better if the MPLB persuades the Barelvis to agree.

It would be better if such consensus is worked out as Barelvis are in majority and if they do not agree the abolition of triple talaq by the Board may not be very effective. An overwhelming majority of Muslims in India follow the Barelvi School. It is also important to note that unless it takes the form of legislation it may not be effective if triple divorce is challenged in the court of law.

Suppose despite the MPLB abolishing it if someone pronounces triple divorce it will remain valid in the court of law unless it is abolished by law. Thus what MPLB has to do is to prepare a draft and give it to the Government to enact it. And as we have pointed out in our last article (See *Secular Perspective* 16th to 30th June, 2004) such a precedent already exists and the Dissolution of Muslim Marriage Act was drafted by the ulama led by Maulana Ashraf Thanvi and others and enacted in 1939.

But if such an exercise is undertaken by the MPLB it has to be quite comprehensive. There is great need for codification of

Muslim Personal Law today. It should be done as early as possible. What is known as Muslim personal law today, it is interesting to note was known as either as Anglo-Mohammedan Law during the British period or simply as Mohammedan Law and was enacted by the British. But after independence the terminology changed and the Anglo-Mohammedan Law, in order to wipe out its colonial stamp, came to be re-named as Muslim Personal Law. However, its contents did not change.

Thus mere change in its terminology was a political act, not a harbinger of social change as in other Muslim countries. To de-colonise its name is not enough, one must de-colonise it content wise as well. During the colonial period women were not supposed to play an active role in socio-political matters, at least among Muslims though there were exceptions like Bi Amma (Mother of Ali Brothers) and many other women who played important role in freedom struggle.

But now 56 years after independence much water has flown down the Ganges and Muslim women are also in the forefront of many social movements. They are far more conscious today than they were during the colonial period. It is after great deal of efforts that the MPLB has agreed to abolish triple divorce. Very important as this measure is, it is not enough. There is crying need for a comprehensive legislation to be drafted under the guidance of MPLB by the ulama and Muslim intellectuals and lawyers.

As I have often pointed out Islamic law is so progressive that it can become basis for a Uniform Civil Code. However, conservative Muslim society dragged the Qur'anic pronouncements to its own level and introduced, through human reasoning many measures, which curbed women's rights. Despite reforms in other Muslim countries women have not got full measure of equality, which the ulama theoretically concede. Iniquitous measures vary from country to country.

In Saudi Arabia, for example, women are not allowed to drive and they are jailed if they drive. In Kuwait until recently women were not allowed to vote and had to wage struggle for years before this right was conceded recently. There is debate raging in Saudi Arabia as to why women cannot drive while they can drive in other countries. Obviously issues like driving and voting were not in existence in early Islamic period. It is the ulama in Saudi Arabia and Kuwait who, using their own reasoning prohibited for women. And now women are waging struggle in these countries against these measures and ulama are opposing it saying it is 'sin' for women to drive or vote.

In many other Islamic countries like Indonesia, Malaysia, Pakistan and Iran women drive and vote without any religious constraint. Qur'an is the only unanimous divine source for Muslims and it remains most progressive in respect of women's rights. Ideally it grants equality between man and woman and should be the main source of legislation about women's rights.

The past interpretations of the Qur'an were constrained by socio-economic conditions and should not be binding on the present and future generations of Muslims. All great Islamic thinkers have repeatedly made this point and have prevents the central role of *ijtihad* (creative interpretation). It is only our social conservatism, not lack of theological sanction, which prevents our ulama from exercising it.

The attacks on Muslim identity by the Sangh Parivar also have been one of the reasons for resistance to any change. These attacks may continue and demand for Uniform Civil Code persist and find legitimacy if there is no initiative for change. Its attacks may even continue after such initiative. Our initiative for change is not motivated or restrained by these attacks. It should be based on the merit for change. Muslim women should not suffer and should get justice.

My plea with MPLB and concerned Muslim intellectuals is to initiate measures for drafting a comprehensive law duly codified which will embody the Qur'anic spirit. Triple divorce and unregulated polygamy has often been the cause of attacks on otherwise quite progressive Islamic personal law. Polygamy may not be abolished completely but strictly regulated as directed by the Qur'an. In fact both the verses on polygamy, i.e., 4:3 and 4:129 should be read together to understand the real Qur'anic intent. Even the first verse, i.e., 4:3 requires rigorous justice to all wives and ends by warning that 'if you cannot do equal justice then marry only one'.

The second verse, i.e., 4:129 makes it clear that equal justice is humanly impossible and do not leave the first wife in suspension. With such warnings polygamy should not be practiced unregulated. All other Muslim countries except Saudi Arabia and Kuwait have introduced strict measures to regulate it. Thus a draft law should introduce such regulatory measures and specify circumstances in which one could take second wife as has been done in Pakistan. Those circumstances could be when the first wife is terminally ill, or medically proved to be infertile or barren and that too with the permission of the first wife and the court of law.

Today, though by no means polygamy is widely prevalent among Muslims (it is much more among Tribals, Dalits and upper caste Hindus), still one finds cases of desertion of first wife and marrying another without giving justice to the first wife. This should not happen and this is strictly prohibited by the Qur'an. The Qur'an permitted polygamy to help women in distress like widows and orphans, not to do injustice to them. It is the duty of the ulama to educate Muslims in this respect.

Thus there is crying need for a new draft law which the MPLB can draft with the help of Muslim lawyers and intellectuals incorporating all these changes and ask the government to enact it. If it is properly drafted I am sure, it will become a model law for others to follow as in Islamic law women enjoy all the rights which modern laws have given to women like widow remarriage, compulsory arbitration before divorce, inheritance, right to property, right to earn and so on. And all these rights are unconditional and a wife also has right to lay down conditions at the time of marriage.

As such a law may take time since it is not easy to develop a consensus due to sectarian differences, the Board in the meanwhile should launch an awareness campaign against misuse of polygamy etc. it should also see to it that the amount of *mahr* paid is substantially high (part of which can be deferred) to discourage easy resort to *talaq*. The Qur'an itself encourages high amount of *mahr*. And *mahr* is woman's own untrammelled right. In case of divorce it can provide her with a measure of economic security. It is regrettable that in some Muslim communities *mahr* is only nominal and as low as Rs. 41 or Rs. 51.

In all these matters MPLB can play an important role as it has come to be acknowledged an authoritative body and in a sense representative too. Though it is understandable that it cannot rush into things, it can certainly cautiously proceed further leading the way. If the women suffer after all half the umma suffers and Qur'an does not admit injustice in any case.

Comprehensive Law on Communal Riots

The United Progressive Alliance (UPA) Government has promised, in its Common Minimum Programme that a law will be enacted to prevent communal riots but what is stated therein seems post-riot measures like special courts to punish the guilty, to pay uniform compensation to the victims etc. However, it is silent on the preventive measures which are more important than the follow up measures. Needless to say the comprehensive law should lay emphasis on preventive measures so that communal violence can be prevented in this country.

The most important players in any communal violence are politicians. No communal riot can take place without the direct or indirect role of politicians, much less Gujarat like carnage. I have been investigating communal riots since last four decades and I have yet to see any communal riot in which politicians have not played direct or indirect role. There are very few riots in which politicians have played even indirect role; in most cases they play direct role. Only politicians of the left are an exception to this game.

Thus it should be said with all emphasis here that without tackling political problem one can hardly check communal violence in this country. The most obvious role among politicians is that of communal politicians, i.e., Jan Sangh-BJP-Shiv Sena. These communal parties are not only motivated by their communal and fascistic ideologies by also by immediate political gains to be made in terms of increasing their vote base. The whole Ram Janambhoomi movement was motivated by their desire to widen their vote base among low caste and backward caste Hindus besides upper caste Hindus to multiply their seats in Parliament and they greatly succeeded in that project. To achieve this objective Mr. Advani took out *Rathyatra* from Somnath to Ayodhya which, of course, he could not complete.

It was this movement coupled with *rathyatra*, which polarised the Hindus and Muslims as never before in history. The BJP politicians like Uma Bharti and Sadhvi Rithambara were making highly provocative speeches against Muslims publicly. Bal Thackaray and other Shiv Sena politicians too were not far behind. In fact they were outdoing each other. If the Narasimha Rao Government had taken strong action against such provocative speeches and arrested concerned BJP opticians whatever their stature, Babri Masjid would not have been demolished and so much blood would not have been shed in riots which followed the demolition.

Thus first of all political will is needed to tackle communal violence. The law is there but it is never implemented sincerely. If section 153, 153(A), 295 and 505 of the Indian Penal Code which deal with promotion of religious animosity are used against any one making such provocative speeches, the whole trouble can be nipped in the bud. It is hardly ever done. Even elections are fought on such provocative campaigns. Modi's speeches during Gujarat elections of December 2002 were patently communal and he won two-third majority from precisely those areas where anti-Muslim violence broke out after the Godhra incident of February 27, 2002.

It is also strange that the parties which take oath for secularism at the time of registration of their parties with the Election Commission and also swear by the Constitution adopt 'Hindutva' as their parties programme? How Hindutva or Islamitva can be reconciled with the Constitutional secularism? The two are quite contradictory. An observation by a Supreme Court judge that Hindutva is a way of life cannot certainly reconcile it with secular spirit of our Constitution. Hindutva is a political doctrine of a Hindu communal party. It can under no circumstances be equated with secularism.

It is fine if a politician is intensely religious (either Hindu, or Muslim or Christian). It certainly does not conflict with our concept of secularism. But it is one thing to be intensely religious and quite different to spouse political Hindutva based on hatred of minorities. Our electoral laws also need to be stringently looked into to uphold our secularism and to consolidate it. The Hindutva forces are eroding secular values and replacing it with hatred and conflict. Any law against communal violence has to keep this political dimension in view. The UPA Government would need strong political will to achieve this. It should ask the Election Commission to keep strict vigilance on communal campaign and disqualify candidates using communal or sectarian appeal.

It is only politicians who prepare atmosphere for communal violence through provocative speeches and newspaper articles. The second stage is to spread rumour through a well planned manner and third stage is to start violence using some spark here and there. Any law has to tackle the problem at all these stages. We have already dealt with the question of provocation. Spreading rumour is done very stealthily and is not easy to deal with. It needs help from the people and an alert administration can take effective steps through people's committees to squash such rumours.

Thirdly, the sparking incident, unlike Godhra in case of Gujarat, are usually insignificant like teasing a girl of the other community, or quarrel between two groups belonging to two different communities, or someone knocking down a pedestrian etc. and in a surcharged atmosphere this is enough to start major conflagration. And if the police is also communalised, which is often the case, it can turn into a disaster. The Biharsharif riots of 1981 started with a brawl between a Muslim and a Yadav on the question of payment and turned into a major disaster thanks to the role of RSS and the police under its influence.

In communal violence after politicians another important factor is police. If police wants it can curb communal violence in no time. There are two conditions: (1) the police should be strictly professional and handle communal disturbances strictly as law and order situation and (2) it should be allowed to function without political interference as long as they do their job professionally.

The role of police has been increasingly politicised and communalised as I have been observing since the Jabalpur riots of 1961. In many riots lower level officers lead the mobs and take part in looting, burning and killing. Bhagalpur riots of 1989 and Gujarat riots of 2002 are flagrant examples of direct police participation with of course, honourable exceptions. The police is also becoming part of communal polarisation. Also, with communal parties coming to power they tend to oblige their political bosses by adding and abetting their communal misdeeds. In case of situations like Gujarat honest officers were punished by being immediately transferred.

The shocking thing is that all those police officers who were indicted by the judicial inquiry commissions were never penalised; instead they were rewarded by promotions. There were innumerable examples. Mr. Ram Dev Tyagi, who fired on Sulaiman Bakery people and killed innocent boys during January 1993 riots in Mumbai was severely indicted by the Justice Srikrishna Commission. Hardly any action was taken against him. Instead he was promoted as Commissioner of Police during the Shiv Sena-BJP rule in Maharashtra in 1995. Mr. P.C. Pande, Police Commissioner Ahmedabad during Gujarat carnage of 2002 was promoted and sent to CBI.

Any law to prevent communal violence has to tackle police problem and see that it behaves strictly professionally, as pointed out above. The Left Government in West Bengal can become a better model in this respect. It is well known that a communally sensitive state like West Bengal until seventies became a totally riot-free model state after the Left Front Government took over. There are two reasons for this: (1) it does not mix religion with politics and does not indulge in any form of communal rhetoric and (2) it has warned the police force that any lack of action to stop communal violence within 24 hours will attract strong action. The result is for anyone to see in West Bengal.

Bihar was also communal hotbed for long but since Laloo Prasad Yadav came to power the communal scenario changed. Bihar is also now almost riot-free state. Not that communal forces are lying low but do not succeed in engineering communal violence as the state machinery is ever vigilant. It should not, therefore, be difficult to have riot-free India under UPA though few states like Gujarat, Rajasthan and M.P. are presently ruled by the BJP. But UPA Government can send right signal to all communal mischief makers. No tempering with secular values and communal rhetoric will be tolerated.

And in case communal violence does break out the guilty, which should include politicians as much as ordinary citizens, provoking or taking law in their own hands and the police officers failing to control within a specified time period, should all be punished according to law through fast track courts specially set up for the purpose. If necessary, there should be a separate autonomous police commission to professionalise the police force and to make it independent of political interference.

Of course the law should see to it that the victims of communal violence get speedy justice and are uniformly compensated. Today it all depends on the chief minister concerned to announce the quantum of compensation. For every person killed at least Rs. 5 lakhs should be given by way of compensation and if a bread earner is killed, a job should be ensured to a member of the family. Often those killed happen to be poor.

I would again like to emphasise that the law should deal more stringently with pre-violence than post-violence situation. Prevention will prove far more effective.

Drafting the Law to Prevent Communal Violence

The Gujarat carnage had shaken the country very badly and it was felt that there should be a separate law to prevent recurrence of such carnage resulting in the death of hundreds of innocent people and bring shame to our country in the comity of nations. The UPA Government also promised such a law in its Common Minimum Programme but it is hardly its priority. It is no more talking about it nor is it preparing any draft for discussion.

Some NGOs like the Centre for Study of Society and Secularism and Communalism Combat took initiative to prepare such a draft and circulate it for discussion among other NGOs and other concerned people. Surprisingly Mr. Ajit Singh of U.P. also took initiative and drafted a bill to this effect and a discussion was held in Lucknow. We will throw some light on these drafts here. It is felt that such law must come into effect as early as possible so that future recurrence of communal violence may be stopped.

Before we proceed with the draft law it is also important to point out that some police and IAS officers who were invited to participate in the discussion on the draft bill pointed out that there was no need for such special law as present laws are sufficient to take care of any such situation. Problem is that these laws are not honestly implemented. The need, therefore, is to implement these laws effectively and punish the culprits who create disturbances in the society.

This is also a valid point of view. The laws are not implemented and not only this the guardian of law themselves violate the law, i.e., the police. The provisions of IPC Section 153 (A), if enforced honestly can prevent the provocateurs from delivering provocative speeches resulting in outbreak of violence. How far the police is responsible for this state of affairs? It would be of course unfair to blame the police alone though the police should also share part of the blame.

In fact the complicity of the politicians is no less responsible. If the state government is determined to prevent violence no communal riot can occur and if it does, it can be checked within no time. The best examples of this are states of West Bengal and Bihar. In West Bengal no major communal riot has taken place for last 27 years since the Left Government is in power. The West Bengal Government has issued strict instructions to the police not to allow any communal riot to take place and in the event of any riot taking place the police officers of the area will be held responsible and punished. It has worked very well. Similarly since Lalu Yadav took over in Bihar no riots have occurred though Bihar was highly sensitive state. The last major riot in Bihar took place in Sitamarhi in 1993. Mr. Yadav controlled it effectively.

But in most of other states the governments have no will to control communal riot as it is part of their political culture. Some chief ministers have even encouraged communal violence for their own selfish political gains. A chief minister in Maharashtra in early eighties even made a political deal with the Shiv Sena

Supremo to unleash communal violence for his personal political gain and Bhivandi-Bombay witnessed major outbreak of communal violence in 1984. Hundreds were killed and properties worth crores of rupees were completely destroyed.

Thus much depends on political will. In Gujarat carnage it is well known that Mr. Narendra Modi not only looked the other way when communal carnage was taking place but even allowed his cabinet ministers to lead marauding and pillaging mobs. This clearly shows that Narendra Modi was encouraging the violence. The violence went on unchecked for months. The police openly sided with rioters and marauders.

If the existing law is violated with such impunity what the new law will achieve? This question of course cannot be dismissed lightly. But still there is some point in drafting the new law. This will be a Central enactment. In fact law and order is a state subject. Normally Centre does not interfere with law and order matter in the states. But when state fails to ensure law and order the Indian Constitution makes a provision in the form of Articles 355 and 356 to intervene.

The proposed law will be a Central enactment and if a state government totally fails to check widespread communal violence the provisions of this law will apply and the Centre will intervene to check the violence. But if in the state and Centre same party governments are there the Central government may be reluctant to take action. When Gujarat carnage took place BJP was in power both in state as well as in the Centre and when in Mumbai widespread communal violence broke out after demolition of Babri Masjid in 1992 the Congress happened to be in power both in Maharashtra as well as in the Centre and hence no action was taken in both cases by the Centre.

But due to regionalisation of political power and possibility of only alliances of parties ruling at the Centre such probabilities of same party government both at the centre and in the state is becoming less and less. And even if it does happen and such a law against sectarian violence does exist one can file a case under this law in the Supreme Court. The Supreme Court has much better record for delivering justice to the aggrieved and hence it can be relied on enforcing provisions of such a law if state or Central governments fail in their duty.

Thus seen from whatever angle this law does have its validity. The Centre for Study of Society and Secularism took initiative to draft this law and requested Justice Daud to prepare a draft for discussion. A meeting of justices, eminent lawyers, retired and on duty police officers, writers and social activists were invited to discuss the draft. The draft provides both for pre-and post-violence situations.

The Bill was originally called the "Act to Prevent and Punish Genocide" but after discussion it was agreed to drop the word genocide and replace it with "sectarian violence". The statement of objects and reasons of the Bill says, among other things, "For more than 5 decades after getting independence this country had to contend with several genocides conveniently classified as communal riots, caste conflicts, and group differences. These carnages are a blot on the nation and seriously prevent its emergence as a strong, united and throbbing democracy. The origin of every group riot lies in something insignificant or obscure. It is the spark lit by the evildoers who have driven the targeted group into a corner by painting it as treacherous, lecherous, unreliable and unscrupulous. The yellow press, which unfortunately has a fairly large readership in this country, is not slow to embellish accounts received by it and knowingly publish accounts, which are untrue, or exaggerations of what has really transpired."

The Bill states that "With a view to prevent group-hatred and violence emanating there-from and in furtherance of the duty cast upon the Union Government under Article 355 of the Constitution of India, it is hereby enacted as follows" and then various sections of the Bill follows.

In Section 4 of the Act it is states "wherever within the territory of India, (a) speaks and or writes in any manner or publish matters tending to incite hatred or ill-will against any group or individual belonging to a group, resident of any State on account of their or his group identities; (b) aids or abates the physical, social or economic harm to any person or persons on the grounds of their affiliation to any such group; (c) advocates the perpetration or perpetuation of any injury to any group or individual belonging to that group as a constituent of that group, shall be punished with imprisonment of either descriptions for seven years and also with fine."

The section 5 of the Bill provides for registration, the investigation and the trial of offences falling under this Act shall be in accordance with the provisions of the Criminal Procedure Code, 1973. Under Section 6 of the Bill the Central Government shall have the power to issue directions to all authorities functioning in the land to do or refrain from doing that will trigger, aggravate or give rise to disharmony amongst groups of people in any part of the country. The authority so directed shall be bound to carry out the directions given.

The Act also provides for compulsory inquiry of all such acts of sectarian violence. Thus it says after every act of genocide irrespective of the number of those killed, wounded or maimed and the value of the property destroyed, the Central Government shall appoint a Commissioner to ascertain the perpetrators of the violence and destruction of the property, whether it be on individual or organisations, if the State Government has not done so. The report will have to be submitted in any case within 12 months of appointment of Commissioner and in section 8 the Central Government on the basis of the Commissioner's report shall compensate the bereaved families, the injured persons and those suffering financial damage as a consequence of the rioting, in full.

Thus this Bill will also take care of proper compensation as today it tends to be arbitrary. It will not depend on the whims of the chief minister. The section 10 of the Bill also provides for debarring the perpetrators, abettors and initiators of the violence from contesting or canvassing elections to any representative body for a period of 10 years. Today the perpetrators not only contest and win elections but also become ministers or chief ministers as it happened in Gujarat.

Thus enactment of such a bill will greatly help control communal violence and Gujarat like situation will not repeat. If the state government fails to act it will be the duty of the Central

Government to intervene and check violence and punish the culprits. It is for the UPA Government to enact such a law before communal violence again breaks out in any other State. The UPA government should fulfil its pledge to people of India on priority basis. Unfortunately so far it has not moved in the matter. It is for NGOs and activists for communal harmony to put pressure on the UPA Government to act as early as possible in this direction. This exercise by the Centre for Study of Society and Secularism is part of that campaign.

Uniform Civil Code or Legal Pluralism

Recently the Supreme Court while disposing of a case on Indian Succession Act, 1925 filed by a Catholic priest voiced its distress that the government has failed to enact Common Civil Code to end discrimination among various religious communities in the areas of marriage, succession and property, and said that such a code would help in removing the contradictions based on religious ideologies.

The Supreme Court also declared as unconstitutional Section 118 of the Indian Succession Act, 1925 which applied to Christians alone and not to any other communities and imposed restrictions on the community from bequeathing property for religious and charitable purposes by will.

It is not for the first time that the apex court has voiced its opinion for enactment of such a code. In other cases too it did so particularly while delivering judgement on the Shah Bano case which had perturbed the Muslims. However, in other cases the Supreme Court judges did not hold unanimous view for enactment of common civil code. Earlier Justice Shah had held that any imposition of such a common code would be against the provision of the Article 25 which guarantees "freedom of conscience and free profession, practice and propagation of religion".

The Muslims have also always maintained that imposition of common code will violate the spirit of Article 25. The Muslim personal law is part of the Shari'ah law and the Shari'ah law is integral part of Islam. According to them the two cannot be separated. How can then the Constitution allow freedom of religion and impose, at the same time, a law, which is contrary to ones religion?

There is some truth in the argument but not the whole truth. We will come to this little later. First it must be pointed out that imposition of common civil code is rather an elitist view, not a popular one. In fact only those who stand for gender equality irrespective of religious provision to the contrary, would accept such a code. But a vast majority of people from all religious communities, including the vast majority of Hindus, would reject it.

Even the members and supporters of the BJP would show hardly any enthusiasm for it. In fact the Hindu law is much more iniquitous for women than the Muslim law. Even after the reforms in the traditional Hindu law, and enactment of the Hindu Code Bill, which was vehemently opposed by the conservative Hindus and, therefor, had to be watered down, it is more iniquitous than the Shari'ah law. A Muslim woman can divide the ancestral property as her right to inheritance in immovable property is unconditional whereas there are problems in partitioning the ancestral property for a Hindu woman.

The BJP has unfortunately made common civil code a Hindutva agenda thus imparting it a Hindu communal colour. The BJP has adopted it as its agenda not because it loves gender equality but only because it is opposed by minorities, particularly Muslims. It was for this reason that all women's organisations dropped the demand for common code, as it became the Hindutva agenda. In a highly communally charged atmosphere no minority community would welcome such a measure.

Today with a deepening of democratic processes each caste and community is becoming more conscious of its identity and today our polity is mainly based on these identities. The politicians have been fighting elections mainly on the basis of caste and communities and thus have aggravated feeling of identities. In Rajasthan when Rupkanwar committed sati the Rajputs defended it as a matter of their identity. The Rajput youth stood with swords to defend the memorial created there.

Thus it is very difficult in such political atmosphere to think of enacting common civil code. The caste practices among Hindus are far more important than any law of the country. Each caste has its own customs and traditions, which supersede all laws of the country. In several parts of U.P. if any boy of lower caste marries girl of upper caste they are publicly beheaded. Such cases have often taken place between Jats and Jatavs of U.P.

The diversity of laws among Hindus is so bewildering in different regions and castes that to create a uniform law among them itself would be a great challenge. In Tamil Nadu and some other parts of south the most preferred form of marriage is between niece and maternal uncle while in U.P. marriages even within seven *gotras* are unthinkable. How can one reconcile such diverse practices within one uniform law?

The reality in India is much more complex than western societies, which have been totally secularised. The process of secularisation in India though not negligible is yet far more slow and tortuous. In many cases traditions and traditional practices are assuming greater importance than ever before. In many ways it seems we are regressing rather than progressing. And no law, however ideal, can become acceptable if it alienates people and ignores social realities. A law has to be socially rooted, in order to be acceptable. Thus sociological view is as necessary as legal view.

Democracy in a country like India with its pluralist tradition lasting over thousands of years cannot succeed without respecting pluralist ethos. It is interesting to note that the west has discovered pluralism recently – after Second World War and hence calls it post-modernist phenomenon. But India has known it even during medieval ages. We lived more in peace and harmony as we respected pluralism, different religions and different traditions.

The modernisation brought new problems and we began to imitate the west without understanding our own social realities. These problems are getting intractable as our society is not changing, especially when it comes to mass of people, as fast as upper class economic elite. This is much more so as far as Muslim masses are concerned. There is much greater degree of power and illiteracy among them compared to other communities. There is very weak middle class among them to advocate modernisation and change. It is precisely for this reason that priestly class which itself comes from poor strata has much greater hold over the community.

And yes we have to find solution to the problem of gender discrimination in the given laws in all communities. How to go about it? Common civil code is no solution. The solution can be found in legal pluralism. If we accept this way of looking things it will be easier to remove gender discrimination. But legal pluralism does not mean we retain traditional or religious laws as they are. We must make suitable changes and enact reforms to remove gender discrimination embedded in these laws.

As far as Muslim personal law is concerned there are two main problems oral or triple divorce and legality of polygamy. The Muslim personal law board must bring about these desired changes within Islamic framework. Triple divorce is not a Qur'anic injunction. And the Prophet has also strongly disapproved of this form of divorce. The Qur'an has, in fact, prescribed most modern way of divorce through arbitration (4:35). It is highly unfortunate that Muslims in India ignore such a clear Qur'anic injunction and practice form of divorce disapproved by the Holy Prophet. Moreover Hanbali, Maliki, Ahl-e-Hadith and Shi'ah Muslims do not accept the validity of triple divorce. Thus it should be abolished and replaced with the Qur'anic form of divorce or by Talaq-i-sunnah which are very fair to women. Triple divorce in one sitting is not practised in most of the Islamic countries. Even Pakistan and Bangladesh have changed their laws in this respect.

Similarly as far as polygamy is concerned the Qur'an has given permission for it in particular circumstances and most reluctantly and if the two verses on polygamy, i.e., 4:3 and 4:129 are read together it becomes impossible to practice polygamy. It is wrong to think that the Qur'an has permitted polygamy without any conditions. Its conditions are most rigorous and very difficult to fulfil and hence even in earlier Islamic period the Mu`tazila believed that it is as good as banned.

The Muslim women hardly suffer other disabilities, i.e., widow re-marriage, property rights, inheritance etc. and are much better off than other women. Thus Muslim Personal Law Board should take the Qur'anic spirit into consideration in reforming the personal laws and remove such disabilities as mentioned above. The personal law thus will not come under legal scrutiny again and again and would also uphold the real Islamic spirit. Many illustrious Islamic scholars of nineteenth century and early twentieth century like Maulavi Imtiaz Ali Khan, Maulvi Chiragh Ali and a legal luminary like Justice Amir Ali had advocated these changes within Islamic framework.

Thus legal pluralism will be much more in keeping with the democratic spirit than a common civil code and all right thinking people should work for these necessary reforms to do away with gender discrimination of traditional laws. Moreover no one has framed any common civil code so far, not even BJP which has been advocating it for political rather than reasons of gender justice. Very few men are prepared for gender equality in our society. Even if a common civil code is to be enacted one should frame one and publicise it for discussion by all concerned rather than simply talking of enforcing one. A social consensus will be highly necessary. Let us not simply politicise the issue.

Indian Muslims and Personal Law Board

These days Muslim Personal Law Board is in the news as never before. Reason? It has now multiplied into four and now Muslim women themselves have formed two personal law boards of their own. This is big news for media and many Muslims are worried about unity of Muslim *Ummah* in India. The Personal Law Board itself is maintaining that it is not split but that new boards have come into existence and no member of the existing Board has resigned and formed new board.

Some members of the existing Board have even alleged that 'some vested interests (mainly political) are behind formation of these boards'. Such stand is at best unfair accusation or at worst insulting to those who have formed these boards. It is not only Shiahs who have formed a separate board but also the Barelvis who are Sunni by sect. Also this is not the best way of sorting out grievances. Instead of hurling accusations the wise leaders should try to sort out differences or solve grievances.

As for unity of *Ummah* it has remained mere rhetoric for centuries. Despite one God, one Messenger and one Book

Muslims have remained divided along sectarian lines for last fourteen hundred years. All our Muhaddithun (i.e., those who narrate Prophet's sayings) have narrated a *hadith* from the Prophet (PBUH) that my *ummah* will be divided in 72 sects and that only one sect will be *naji* (i.e., on the right path). Of course the Qur'anic ideal is of one *ummah* but there is a condition attached: the *ummah* will remain united if it remains best of the people (*khayrah ummatin*). This qualification could not be fulfilled except perhaps by the first generation Muslims and once they ceased to be best of the people they were divided in several sects. Thus we find description of these sects in Baghdadi's book *Al-Farq bayn al-Firaq* (Difference between Sects).

Also, it is well known that even in Sunni Islam there are four different schools. Thus differences between Muslims have been there historically and we have lived with these differences. If one Personal Law Board has ceased to represent all Indian Muslims there should not be so much breast beating. Either our 'Ulama should show wisdom and bring about reconciliation in the best of spirits or if reconciliation is not possible we should learn to live with these differences.

The claim of Muslim Personal Law Board that it was sole representative of all Muslims in India does not bear any scrutiny. It did come into existence in 1972 in response to one Hamid Dalwai's repeated attacks on Shari'ah law and campaign for uniform civil code. The Government of India had never announced any intention of enacting uniform civil code. Let alone enacting it, it had not even indirectly hinted at such a possibility. Also, Hamid Dalwai had no backing from Muslims. He was backed by communal forces and even today these forces consider uniform civil code as their agenda.

All secular forces today have disowned uniform civil code as communal forces have adopted it. Even women's organisations no longer demand UCC as communal forces are demanding it. Thus today there is no threat of Shari'ah law being in any danger. But unfortunately if it is in danger it is from conservative 'Ulama of the MPLB. They have robbed the Shari'ah law of its dynamism and are perpetrating old formulations arrived at centuries ago. We would like to throw more light on this aspect.

However, first we would like to assert that MPLB does not represent opinion of all Muslims from day one. Let alone any voting it was not constituted even by any broad consensus among opinion makers among Muslims. Few 'Ulama and Muslim advocates and others got together and decided to constitute the board and later gave representation to other Muslims sect-wise. No opinion of prominent Muslims was sought about its representative character.

It is true that among Muslims in India there is no unanimity about application of Shari'ah law. Not only there are sectarian differences but also polarisation among them on the lines of progressives and conservatives. It is not easy to push through any decision unanimously among 150 million Muslims and differences are bound to arise. Thus MPLB should not claim in the first place that it is representative of cross section of Muslims in India. And the way it has functioned it has represented at best only ultra-conservative sections of Muslims.

Real protector of any thing is one, which also ensures its healthy growth. One cannot claim to be real protector of something when it begins to stagnate and cause injustices. MPLB has seriously failed in really protecting Shari'ah law by ensuring its healthy growth. It missed great opportunities repeatedly. It always showed its conservative face. The Shah Bano judgement is the best example. It was great opportunity for the Board members to give healthy lead to Indian Muslims by properly interpreting the Qur'anic verse 2:241 which says make provision for the divorcees in goodly manner.

However, the MPLB gave in to ambitious Muslim political leaders who were exploiting the Supreme Court Judgement for their own political ambitions without regard to interests of Muslims in general and Muslim women in particular. It should be remembered that the Qur'anic laws are very progressive and equitable and give women equal status with that of men. It was the first religion in the world which kept interests of divorcees also in view and required men to make provision for his divorced wife since she is usually in helpless situation when divorced. The Qur'an did not mention any period for such provision and left it to the requirements of time. It was opinion of the early jurists that provision be made at least for three months of *iddah* (waiting before she could remarry after divorce). This opinion could not have been binding as the Qur'anic injunction is.

However, the 'Ulama in MPLB simply protected the opinion of early Muslim jurists rather than true spirit of Qur'anic injunction, i.e., to protect the interests of divorcee and do justice to her. All non-Muslims in general and many Muslim women in particular thought that Islam is unjust to women's rights. The reality is quite contrary to this. Islam has shown greatest concern for women and their rights. The Qur'anic pronouncements in respect of women are far ahead of time.

If today Muslim women have formed their own board it is because of gross failure of MPLB to meet their demands, which are quite just and within Islamic framework. The triple divorce has been causing serious problems to Muslim women. It has nothing Islamic about it. The 'Ulama themselves maintain that it is sinful form of divorce (*talaq al-bid'ah*) and one fails to understand why sinful practice should be perpetrated in the name of Shari'ah. The Holy Prophet did not approve of it and Hazrat 'Umar enforced it in certain circumstances and those circumstances do not obtain at all. Is Prophet's (PBUH) opinion more sacred than that of Hazrat 'Umar? And those circumstances also do not obtain under which it was temporarily enforced. It is mere orthodoxy and refusal to change and nothing else. All Muslim countries also have abolished this unjust form of divorce. But our 'Ulama refuse to take notice of these developments.

A standard *nikahnama* was prepared after long deliberations by several Muslim groups and given to MPLB to approve of it. But the Board sat tight on it and dithered time and again and postponed its implementation. And even when it announced its approval it was its watered down version, which hardly benefits Muslim women. Should it then surprise them if Muslim women, tired of Board's inaction in the matter announced formation of their own Board. However, what is sad is that Muslim women have formed two boards. They should come together and form one board together and include women having proper knowledge of Qur'an and Shari'ah and with ability to creatively interpret the Qur'anic and Shari'ah injunctions to bring about reform and change and to make Shari'ah law more just for women in today's circumstances.

In Islam women have every right not only to recite the Qur'an but also to interpret it. *Ijtihad* (creative interpretation) is every Muslim's religious right given-proper knowledge and understanding of the text and causes of its revelation. As scholars of Islam know every verse in the Qur'an was revealed in response to some questions in the minds of believers or in response to some major events why then Muslims should not understand the Qur'anic verses in response to their own situation?

All major modern thinkers of Islam have maintained that *ijtihad* represents the dynamic principle of Islam and that every generation of Muslims have right to re-think Shari'ah issues in the light of their own experience and wisdom of their own time. However, since power is wielded in Muslim societies by conservatives such thinkers were either persecuted or totally ignored. Even great thinkers like Muhammad Abduh of Egypt met with the same fate.

It is high time for the Indian 'Ulama, particularly those associated with MPLB to shed bit of their conservatism and ensure healthy growth of Shari'ah law in secular India. In fact, given proper spirit and commitment, Islamic law can become model for UCC. Qur'anic law is most modern in its approach to women's rights. Its very spirit was killed by social conservatism and stagnation. Even Sir Syed and Iqbal, though proponent of change, did not assert themselves in view of social conservatism of Indian 'Ulama. Sir Syed requested Maulavi Mumtaz Ali Khan not to publish his *Huquq al-Niswan* (Rights of Women) in view of such conservatism. But the Maulavi did and it is a model book even today. The Maulavi was great scholar of Islam in his own right.

If MPLB does not learn any lesson from these developments, it will have itself to be blamed. Instead of blaming vested interests it should seriously reflect on its own policies and help infuse dynamic spirit in the Shari'ah law. Least it can do is to codify Muslim personal law with the help of progressive lawyers. They should take initiative which Maulana Ashraf Thanvi took in codifying certain aspects of Muslim law in 1939 and got Dissolution of Muslim Marriage Act.

Index

M

V

W

Y

Z